In the Blood

On Mothers, Daughters and Addiction

Arabella Byrne and Julia Hamilton

ONE PLACE. MANY STORIES

HQ
An imprint of HarperCollins*Publishers* Ltd
1 London Bridge Street
London SE1 9GF

www.harpercollins.co.uk

HarperCollins*Publishers*
Macken House, 39/40 Mayor Street Upper,
Dublin 1, Ireland, D01 C9W8

This edition 2024

2

First published in Great Britain by
HQ, an imprint of HarperCollins*Publishers* Ltd 2024

HB ISBN: 978-0-00-864843-5

MIX
Paper | Supporting
responsible forestry
FSC
www.fsc.org
FSC™ C007454

This book contains FSC™ certified paper and other controlled
sources to ensure responsible forest management.

For more information visit: www.harpercollins.co.uk/green

This book is set in 10.9/15.5 pt. Minion Pro by Type-it AS, Norway

Printed and Bound in the UK using 100% Renewable Electricity at
CPI Group (UK) Ltd, Croydon, CR0 4YY

For my mother, Julia.
For my daughter, Arabella.

"Sebastian drinks too much."

"I suppose we both do."

"With you it does not matter. I have watched you together.
With Sebastian it is different. He will be a drunkard if someone
does not come to stop him. I have known so many. Alex
was nearly a drunkard when he met me; it is in the blood.
I see it in the way Sebastian drinks. It is not your way."

EVELYN WAUGH, *Brideshead Revisited.*

Contents

Prologue

Omertà

Omertà/ noun. /əʊmɛːˈtaː/ a conspiracy of silence.

Omertà. A word you don't hear very often. A word that commands silence by its very declamation, its harsh consonants ringing off its opening vowel as a warning: don't speak, don't say a word. As a term it originated in Sicily, used by the Mafia to indicate a code of silence in the face of questioning by authorities. Its connotations are tightly wound up in family and the complex nature of intergenerational silence. Like any word, it looks different in different contexts. In the case of crime, it holds the dark threat of silence, of gags and bondage. But it can also gesture towards loyalty and solidarity in the face of threat, a bond between its initiates that binds and protects.

Alcoholics breed alcoholics. Alcohol flows across families like water over a landscape. Sometimes it moves in torrents, sometimes in floods, sometimes in trickles. It always shapes the ground it covers indelibly. In some families, alcohol washes over the generational landscape in a great typhoon, wiping out all in its path. In others, it spreads like damp, leaving a deadly and silent watermark, slowly destroying everything it touches.

And yet, despite the scale of destruction caused by the flood of generational alcoholism, its victims are still subject to the code of omertà. This code operates in mysterious ways in British culture. Die of alcoholism and every medical detail except the condition of alcohol dependence is listed on the death certificate. Suffer from alcoholism and both victim and bystander will go to any lengths to cover up the cause of anguish. Recover from alcoholism and you must keep it a secret lest you are ostracised and ridiculed by the drinking majority. Speak about alcoholism as the child of alcoholic parents and you are accused of washing your family's dirty laundry in public, of betraying your own flesh and blood, no matter how shot through that blood is with alcohol.

In the Blood is the story of how a mother and daughter ended up in the rooms of Alcoholics Anonymous, nine months apart over fourteen years ago. In some ways it is a predictable story: two addicts destroyed and drank and ransacked until they could drink no more. Then they got better. Addiction stories are, after all, the same the world over: from the depths of addiction to the mountaintops of recovery, the details of the addict are expunged. What makes this story different is the fact of its genealogical symmetry: a mother and a daughter journeying across the addictive arc at the same time before surrendering. Such surrender sparked a curious investigative urge; the need to trace the disease back through family lines, to locate the illness within the shared DNA. But to investigate you must break silence. Betray the family. Betray yourself.

In the Blood is the sound of the howling cry of illness and betrayal across generations, and what you do with that sound when you hear it.

PART ONE – DAUGHTER

Chapter One

Mother Love

Arabella

This cathexis between mother and daughter – essential, distorted, misused – is the great unwritten story [...] The materials are here for the deepest mutuality and the most painful estrangement.

OF WOMAN BORN, ADRIENNE RICH

A memory. It is a grey day in February and my mother has just got married for the third time. I am sixteen years old. I wasn't there for the other two marriages, but I have already seen my father marry someone else when I was five, so I pretend I know what I am doing. I smile, and people say how lovely it is for my mother to have me there. The bride is wearing a pink Max Mara suit and spiky pink shoes to match, like a rose with the thorns still on; I am dressed in a maroon skirt and a black top, the colours of grief.

At the reception, everyone keeps telling her how lovely she looks, but to me, she looks desperate; I can see it written all over her face and I know why: she doesn't know if her new husband will turn up or not. He has been missing since the ceremony and attempts to trace him have failed; I think she might have called his phone over fifty times until in the end it was simply turned off; *please leave a message after the tone.* In response to this disappearance, my mother has already had quite a lot to drink. We both have. Eventually, the groom walks in as if nothing has happened and everything that came before is hushed up and tidied away.

At the reception in the groom's sister's house in the countryside, other things go unnoticed in plain sight. My grandmother sits in a chair like a waxwork, her expression one of generational confusion and righteous anger. She has already been to two other weddings where her daughter has been the bride, so it is quite possible that she disapproves of this one. Her son – my mother's brother – stands on the other side of the room talking to someone, but my grandmother has not spoken to him for twenty years, so she looks straight through him. Most people have been briefed on this situation and know to keep her away from him. My grandfather, from whom my grandmother has been divorced for many years, is not here either as my mother has not spoken to him for twenty years. Silence covers the family like driven snow, destroying the composition of what lies beneath.

Luckily for everyone involved, a large amount of drink is on offer. Unlike the marriage itself, this detail has been well thought out. Cases of champagne stand in the kitchen and people cut through them like butter. The mood of the assembled crowd changes gear as the afternoon wears on; out of the corner of my eye I see my grandmother laughing with someone, her face animated. For my part, I feel the familiar untethering from myself that happens after a period of drinking: I am elsewhere, floating above the situation, entirely detached. I am no one's daughter and I drift amongst the crowd freely. The next day, I am covered in bruises from this drifting, which people tell me was mostly into the furniture. In other parts of the room people lean into each other on the sofas in what look like long and confessional conversations, their voices lowered. *Married after six months*, I think I hear them whisper, or *No, he has no children of his own*, or *Yes, I think Julia will sell her flat*. At one point, I stumble upon a conversation of two smokers outside who don't know exactly who I am, and I pretend to be an impartial observer to the day, nodding my head dispassionately when they talk about the groom. Dimly, I realise that I am spying on my own life.

After lunch, my uncle gets to his feet to make a toast. 'It took her three tries to find him . . . ' he announces to roars of laughter, 'but she did in the end!' The bride and groom look on and smile and glasses are filled again. In the photograph of this moment that I find amongst my mother's possessions some years after they have divorced, my mother and her third husband don't look like a married couple. They look like two people laughing at someone's joke the way you might at a party, their body language articulating some fatal separation between them, even then. Out of the corner of the frame I spot my grandmother, risen awkwardly to her feet to toast the bride and groom. There are two women in the picture, but it is to my grandmother that the eye is drawn, her face expressing some ineffable truth about that day, some sadness that I think my mother certainly felt but anaesthetised.

I sit on the bed to steady myself, girding myself against the change in emotional altitude that happens when you descend into the past. What is it, I wonder, that my grandmother is trying to say here? *This is a bad idea, Julia?* No, that would be out of character, and besides, I don't think she ever really thought that, I think she liked Mum being married; she was of the generation that approved of men. *Are you OK?* But that doesn't feel right either as I don't think she ever confronted Mum about her drinking and, apocryphally, never pressed Mum on her inner life beyond certain platitudes. The best that I can parse is that she knew something was very wrong with the whole arrangement, but not exactly what, her face a kind of silent scream. But to call her a Cassandra would be incorrect since Cassandra believed her prophecies and it doesn't seem like my grandmother could voice hers. An air of foreboding stalks the image like dark clouds gathering across the sky.

When I was at graduate school in the States, I read a lot of Susan Sontag in a self-conscious way on campus, making sure people could see the spine of my book. I loved her hair with its badger stripe and the cigarettes she smoked in all the photographs taken of her at her desk. I felt a connection to her through her time at Oxford and Paris and in her native America, a place where she was just as much a cultural tourist as I. I loved the morbid subjects she wrote about: death, illness, mourning. But it was her writing on photography that allowed me to access some part of myself that I had hitherto not understood. All my life, I had carried around the same tatty photographs of my childhood in an envelope, their status undignified by frames or an album. There were pictures of my parents before they divorced, pictures of me as a baby in my mother's arms, pictures of my mother's boyfriends. Sometimes, I jammed the photographs into books and would find them years later, little paper ghosts that frightened me.

'Photography becomes a rite of family life,' Sontag wrote. But she went further than that: 'people robbed of their past seem to make the most fervent picture takers'. This link between photography and the disappearing iceberg of what was the family, or the connection between photography and loss, stood out glaringly to me. The photos I carried around were a way of reconstructing a sense of family that I had never had, but they were also a peculiarly seductive form of denial around that same family, a way, Sontag explained, of 'encouraging whatever is going on to keep happening'.

The germ of this memoir was a photograph. In it, my mother and I are sitting next to each other at a table in a restaurant in France. Five years old, I am wearing my mother's sunglasses and holding a wine glass to my lips, directly aping her expression and mannerisms. My mother looks on, with an expression somewhere between amusement and bemusement, her expression tangled up in the net of motherhood where pride and frustration become indistinct. When I was a child, and my mother was still drinking, the picture was interpreted as funny, its symmetry so perfect as to look staged. *Like mother, like daughter,* people would cry when they saw it framed in my mother's house. Somehow, after my mother had sold that house and moved into another house with her new husband, that photograph wound up amongst my possessions. At university, when it started to be whispered that I had a problem with drinking, I pinned it up defensively in my university room, proof of some dark pact between my mother and me, proof that my nameless affliction stretched back further than myself.

When my mother and I both began attending Alcoholics Anonymous, the picture changed again. Our joint admission that we both suffered from the disease of alcoholism gives the

picture the feel of a crime scene: exhibit A, the wicked mother
encouraging her small child to behave in dangerously adult ways
with terrifying consequences. It is a candid portrait, too, of the
ways in which alcoholic adults can appear frighteningly childlike
to children themselves. That's one way of looking at it; she gave
me the darkness that ravaged my early adolescent and adult life.

But, as Sontag knew all too well, the commerce between
a photograph and the truth is shady, mercurial. So is addiction.
Did I catch addiction from my parents like some airborne virus,
or was it a part of who I was from birth? Alcoholics Anonymous
uses the language of invasion: *your disease is outside the meeting
waiting for you* or *your disease is always waiting for you, even after
decades of sobriety.* This is a seductive vision, the triumph of the
authentic self over an invader that seeks only to destroy. And yet,
for those who can also lay claim to several other family members
being addicts, the relationship between the self and the intruder
becomes more complicated, messier. Your parents give you life,
but what happens to that equation when intermingled with that
vital blood is the very thing that might endanger you the most.

You can look at the photo in another way too, in a way that has
nothing to do with addiction and everything to do with mothers
and daughters – the 'great unwritten story' that Adrienne Rich
started thinking about in the 1970s. Because there is something
in my pose that captures the way all daughters learn or imitate
a vision of femininity from their mothers, the first women they
have any real knowledge of. I'm doing just that in the photo,
mimicking my mother's body language and draping myself with
her accessories – wine glass, sunglasses – in the hope that, by
imitating her, some essential fact about womanhood might rub

off on me. In my mother's gaze, I detect the anxiety that this kind of mimicry brings to any mother, the awful realisation that your child might just be *too* like you.

When I became a mother myself, the picture changed once more. I think I understand, now, the pain of similarity and the flush of panic when the mirror is turned back on yourself. It is there when my daughter explodes with frustration at some object or skill she cannot master or when she is inconsolably sad and resists all comfort. Then I see the picture anew. This time I am on the right, in my mother's pose, watching my daughter imitate me, and my expression is just the same.

But let me start with my mother. It begins with her. Her name is Julia. Funny how when I hear her say her name in a meeting, 'My name's Julia and I'm an alcoholic,' I have no idea who that person is. To me she is Mum, Ma, my mother. When I was growing up, she was 'your mother', referred to in accusatory tones by my father or stepfather. *You're so like your mother*, people used to say when I was behaving badly, a remark I never took fully as an insult. But there's something in this split between Julia the person and my mother, Julia, that feels important and seems to capture the way I see her.

I can show you another photo. It sits on my bedside table. In it, my mother stands heavily pregnant with me in the sea on a Greek island. It is a curious picture not least because it is very blurred (as perhaps, all photographs from the era are) but also because it is taken at a great distance away from her, her silhouette alone on the deserted beach. The person who took the picture must have looked on at her from what seems like a considerable height, while in the near distance of the frame a rocky outcrop juts out of the beach, barely concealing the paraphernalia of discarded swimming things. I have looked at this picture all my life; as a child it hung on my bedroom wall and in early adulthood, I keep it among my things. At university, I looked at it a great deal; partly in disbelief, partly in longing. It seemed impossible that I could have been in the picture all along, something hiding in plain sight. As a child, the photo symbolised a perfect harmony between me and my mother, my biologically identical body growing inside hers in a chamber of fluid, just as she stands in the limpid waters of the Greek sea. As a woman, all I can see is how lonely my mother looks, marooned far from the mysterious companions whose clothes litter the beach, her position precarious, beyond dangerous rocks, observed – but not held – from afar.

Born in Scotland in 1956, my mother arrived at the low point of the family fortunes. Where there had once stood a grand house and possessions, nothing now remained: pictures sold, valuables auctioned, debts in abundance. The survivors assembled them-selves around the great crater of what had been and peered into it endlessly, contemplating their loss.

On his deathbed, my grandfather proved that he had never really left the crater, saying when asked for his address that he lived at Wishaw House, Lanarkshire, even though it had been torn down years before. In the planning of this book, my mother and I spoke – and argued – a great deal about how we should talk about her family. Could we mention the fact of their birth, their aristocratic title and former standing? *No*, I argued over and over. *No one would care, it would ring hollow in the times we live in.* 'It's where I'm from,' she would shrug; and besides, she went on, 'It's not like it ever made me very happy.' Gradually, I saw that it would be impossible to write about her without making any reference to the atmosphere of erosion and shame in which she grew up, an atmosphere from which I think she is still recovering.

From girlhood, she filled this central loss with words. Hiding away from her mother in the bleak Scottish farmhouse where they lived until her parents divorced, she read everything she could lay her hands on. To this day, I ask her before I start to read anything, certain that she will have read it; her natural habitat is littered with books, magazines, newsprint, and now online material, which she reads ceaselessly. Denied the chance to go to university where she would have excelled, she married a poet when she was nineteen. Byron, I think they called him.

By the time she had run away from that marriage and into the arms of my father, she was determined not just to read but to write. My father, a businessman with a sharp acumen and even sharper wit, ran his own insurance broking business. To my eye, they were hopelessly mismatched: he with his love of fast cars, ski resorts and casinos in Monaco, she bookish and resolutely bohemian in her tastes, far from the sort of wife he can have had in mind. But she toed the line by having me and then began to write in earnest, publishing six novels by the time I was in my teens and standing next to her at that third wedding.

Later, when alcohol had wrapped itself like poison ivy around her thinking life, she stopped writing altogether. To her enormous sadness, she even stopped reading. *How bad was it, really?* People ask that a lot about alcoholics, partly because they want to be shocked, and partly because they want their own drinking to be minimised and enabled. *Christ, I never did that*, they say, letting out an audible sigh of relief. But when people ask me about Mum,

I don't immediately think of her collapsed on the stairs or hysterical with drink – although all of that and more did happen – I think of her lying in bed during the day in her third husband's house not being able to read, her blue wine glass on her bedside table. *That's how bad it got*; I want to be able to say. But I don't because I suspect it's not what people want to hear.

On the day we scattered my grandmother's ashes over the fields bordering the road she had so loved to drive down near her house in Scotland, my mother and I were both sober. It was an uncharacteristically warm and bright day in south-west Scotland and we both squinted as we fiddled endlessly with the catch on the container of her ashes until they flew out suddenly, some across the breeze and some back towards our faces.

No one ever tells you how absurd some parts of formal grieving are: the remains of your grandmother caught in your ponytail, or the way your father's coffin slides down towards the flames like something on a supermarket conveyer belt. Sandwiched somewhere between the ridiculous and the sublime, we drove back to the hotel along the coastal road and stopped to sit on a craggy outcrop of rock by the sea, not dissimilar to the Greek landscape in which Mum had stood pregnant with me.

Mum was very quiet as we sat on the rock and looked out on a landscape that she had been looking at her whole life, a landscape she had tried so hard to escape. When I think about that day, which I do from time to time when I am driving, I think about how we never stop looking out towards our mothers, in life and in death. I think about how the maternal landscape that we first look upon is so adored and so reviled and, in the end, so necessary. 'She didn't like the sea much, you know,' Mum said, half laughing. 'It reminded her too much of the bay in Sydney, too reminiscent of her own mother.' We laughed.

The question of mothers and daughters has never stopped feeling urgent to me, partly because I now have two daughters myself, but also because I have long felt that there is some umbilical link with my own mother that has never quite been severed. Maybe, as the philosopher Jacqueline Rose would have it, it's amazing that 'emerging from the first morass of being, we ever buy into the illusion that we are self-sufficient, radically distinguishable individuals to begin with'. I think of the photo of my mother on the beach in Greece and the day we scattered my grandmother's ashes and consider that I've never truly left that state. Our parallel journeys of addiction ask us, as mother and daughter, to be separate individuals capable of self-containment. I wonder if we'll ever manage it.

Julia

Mother Love

It was Christmas Day, 2011, and the first Christmas I had spent with my father for a quarter of a century. We had had a long falling-out, which had suddenly dissolved. I was sober by this time, and somehow my father and I had reached the same conclusion at the same time: we should bury the hatchet. I felt like I was reclaiming a part of my family, so Mum's death seemed astonishingly pointed. Even in dementia, did she somehow know that I was spending Christmas with the enemy? I felt she was punishing me by just dying like that, without warning – turning her back on me in protest, as she had done so often in life. She was a great one for cutting off her nose to spite her face, and dying on Christmas Day was just another example of this tendency, if a rather extreme one.

No one at the nursing home she was in called to tell me she was dying. They just rang the next morning, Boxing Day, to inform me she was dead. Gone. Dead as Diocletian. The shock of it. I was in London at my brother's flat when I got the call. I left at once and drove home to Oxford, stopping at a petrol station on the A40 to weep hysterically at the wheel of my car. Underneath all this was something shameful, however: a massive sense of relief. At long last, I was free, or so I thought. But the dead live with you; the relationship doesn't end with death. In very many ways, it just begins a new chapter, as I was to discover.

Mum, Ma, Muv. Never Mummy. Ann, without an 'e'. Elizabeth Ann. An angelic small child in the tropical green of a garden in Warrawee, a suburb on the Upper North Shore of Sydney, New South Wales, wearing a white lawn dress, white socks, button shoes, pure Mabel Lucie Attwell. No sign in her sweet face of the darkness that would come to cloud her adult life. We search the faces of children for shadows, for a sign, a portent, but infancy is utterly compelling. It covers everything like snowdrops on a bank.

From the very beginning, I was afraid of her, aware that she was an autocratic monarch without having the words for what I knew. I was her hostage, her vassal, without power. My first conscious memory of her was when I reached out to touch the needle of the gramophone, which sat on a table under a window in the drawing room, and she shouted at me. At that moment, I came out of the prehistory of infancy into consciousness. She was angry. I was in trouble. The record was Jeremiah Clarke's 'Trumpet Voluntary', its glassy tones shattering around my head in a thousand pieces. I was entranced by the purity of sound, the icy beauty of the notes.

She was changeable. Her mood was my weather, invading my innermost spaces like a cloud of wasps. I was aware of the darkness in her before I could name it, and knew instinctively that I didn't want to attract its attention. I had to watch my step. I became an expert in those moods, like some indentured figure at an ancient court, shod in poulaines, coloured hose and a cone-shaped hat, expertly reading the runes, divining the changes of pressure in the emotional isobars surrounding her, and adapting myself accordingly. As a result, I became an accomplished chameleon, shapeshifting like someone in a fairy tale into the required disguise; hyper, hyper vigilant. If I didn't look round me all the time, I was vulnerable to attack. No wonder drink when it came was such a relief. It allowed me to relax and stop watching myself, stop monitoring my every move. Now I think about it, perhaps it had the same effect on her.

As I grew older, I got to know the best times to petition her for whatever it was I wanted, and these occasions always involved alcohol. The early-evening drink was the best moment: with a fag in one hand and a glass of whisky in the other, my mother was a different, much nicer person: amused by me, her creation, as she saw it – a benevolent dictator, Ann the Wise, Ann the Fun. With other people present, in particular, she was the 'good' mother, eager to show off her little helper. People never stopped telling me how like her I was to look at, which, as I grew older, I took as an insult. I knew what went on behind the facade and I didn't want to be like her in any way.

I loved it when there were parties, people in the house, the rumble of voices from the dining room. That distant, convivial sound meant safety; her all-seeing gaze was diverted elsewhere. After dinner, when the guests had gone back to the drawing room, I would descend from my bedroom to the warm, deserted dining room with its smoking candles and abandoned glasses with wine still in them, nibbling cheese, swiping chocolates, finishing off the dregs in the glasses. Parties were good. Drink was quite clearly good; a game-changer, a kind of alchemy that transformed my tense and rather dangerous mother into an easier, nicer person than the workaday version. And it changed me, too. There was a definite connection in my mind between drink and feeling safe, or a little safer, anyway.

Those mouthfuls of wine from other people's glasses allowed me to fantasise about the idea of booze-land as a wonderful place, somewhere I wanted to be. Although I didn't know it I was buying into the great myth that alcohol makes everything better. This lie, this giant untruth, rapidly twined itself around my childish but extremely powerful imagination; by the time I was fourteen or fifteen, I could practically feel its dark vegetable presence in my brain, altering the way I thought about drink. But I was alone in this, I could tell. My schoolfellows were able to take it or leave it. I was already stolen away by booze but something – shame, I suppose – made me keep quiet about it. There's a sinister little saying in AA, which goes like this: a man takes a drink, a drink takes a drink, a drink takes a man (or woman); I was taken so young I didn't even know it. In the rooms of AA people sometimes share how their alcoholism grew from their twenties onwards, or middle-age, even, or during the pandemic without a formal structure to their lives; they talk about crossing a line. I crossed a line very early but it wasn't just a line, it was a river as wide as the Ganges and there was no way back across such a vast and terrifying expanse. I was trapped on the other side very, very young, still just a child in many ways.

Looking back to the time before I was nine or ten, I was very aware of my mother's rigid grip on the household, from children to dogs to her exceedingly unmanageable husband, who couldn't seem to deal with anything, particularly anything money-related.

The weekly ritual of him giving her the housekeeping was agony to watch. My father fumbling and forgetful and, it must be said, reluctant, too, set them both on a collision course, which invariably ended in a scene. My own battle with my mother's controlling tendencies was almost entirely focused on the biscuit tin on top of the fridge, which to a four-year-old seemed like the north face of the Eiger. There were tempting things in jars in the larder, too, also under my mother's embargo: glacé cherries, for instance, water biscuits, olives, capers, bought from Stevenson's grocery in Castle Douglas, but the fact that they were on display didn't mean they were for the taking. I'd get in there sometimes and stuff mouthfuls of glacé cherries, my mouth sticky with sugar, sickening and delicious, but my mother always knew if I'd been helping myself: 'The rats have been in the larder,' she would say, and I would pretend not to know what she was talking about. But, *rats*? I'd seen a rat in the cow byre that seemed as big as a hare and I was terrified. I was also intimately acquainted with the wickedness of Beatrix Potter's Samuel Whiskers, so rats, as a description, was offensive.

Her roll-top desk was locked and a large part of my persona as a child was as a kind of private eye. What was she hiding? I'd wait for that moment of rare carelessness when she'd left it unlocked to have a rummage. I never found anything particularly important but doing this gave me a guilty feeling of being a thief, of burgling my mother's life, of knowing things about her that she didn't know I knew. She was controlling me and I was trying by these means to control her, too, I suppose. But she was definitely hiding something, I could sense it. Now, I think she was in love with the boyfriend she had left behind in Australia and that, as an essentially urban girl, the life she had landed in with a man she couldn't get on with in the middle of nowhere in south-west Scotland in the 1950s was a depressing shock. She had a baby quickly, too, which must have been another shock. My brother was born on my parents' first wedding anniversary, and my mother was trapped.

Her Australian childhood was a visible thread in the house. There was a map of Australia in the kitchen with its pictures of all the dangerous animals that were simply *everywhere* on that continent. *How did anyone survive?* I wondered, gazing at the tiger snakes, funnel-web spiders, saltwater crocodiles, box jellyfish and great white sharks that littered the landscape and seas of God's Own Country, as my mother sarcastically referred to it. Mum told me a story of having a tarantula in her bedroom and I'd lie in bed at night and think about that: a spider *the size of a soup bowl* in your room. How could she live with that? Then there was the story of how she always jumped the middle of the last three verandah steps in Warrawee, once missing the brown snake (the common death adder) that lay on that middle step impersonating a piece of wood.

'What happened to it?' I asked.

'Grandpa killed it,' she said. I tried to imagine Grandpa with his wooden leg (he'd lost his leg in the Great War) engaging in a battle to the death with the rearing snake and failed.

There were books from her Australian childhood, too – the Billabong series – which I inhaled as soon as I was old enough, along with various other books about the flora and fauna of Australia; there were happy stories of her girlhood at her father's farm on the borders of New South Wales and Queensland, where she could ride for days in the bush – I kept her riding boots for years and years – but the Australian part of her remained a mystery to me, as if the happier and more carefree person who had grown up there was someone else, not the mother I knew. That Ann, the wasp-waisted Australian version who, freed by the war, had been in the Royal Australian Navy and smoked Capstans, was a good rider and tennis player. This sporting version of my mother loved playing golf and adored going to the races. She liked naval drinking games, like Cardinal Puff. She had boyfriends whom she occasionally referred to, one of whom had surged up at her pretending to be a shark while she was out swimming in Bondi. I can't help but suspect he was the man she wished she'd married, but alas, he left her and married someone else.

By the time I knew my mother, she didn't do any of those sporting things, apart from gardening in a kind of fury, wrenching weeds and sighing in despair at things that wouldn't grow as she wanted them to. She had the face of a muse with her strong brows and straight nose but I think now that somewhere in the transition from Australia to Britain after the war, she lost herself. The circumstances of her life crowded in upon her; she must have felt she had to get married to save face and to avoid ending up as Granny's unmarried daughter and companion, so she married my father – a second cousin – as a way out, a marriage that led her into another labyrinth, one she didn't expect and that nothing could have prepared her for.

Married life for my mother began in the middle of nowhere in a house that didn't even have electricity to start with. My father, who had grown up between a castle in Aberdeenshire and the family seat at Wishaw House in Lanarkshire, suddenly had nothing. All the family money had vanished once his father had inherited the title. Where had it gone? No one seemed to know or, if they did, they weren't telling me. Dad had just enough money to buy a hill farm in Galloway, so while he counted sheep my urban mother had to grapple with domestic life, a new baby – all that washing – and an Aga that kept going out whenever the wind veered. I once stayed in a house in Majorca with no electricity and no running water – very *Jean de Florette* – but what it really means is that you spend all day doing thankless domestic tasks just to cover the basics of cooking and washing. No wonder by the time I was born she seemed to be permanently discontented and quite often simply furious for no apparent reason.

Was she an alcoholic? God knows, but what I do know is that she used substances to numb uncomfortable feelings, just as every addict does: the evening whisky changed her mood for the better, although drinking, like everything else in her life, was highly controlled. She could stop when necessary, but it was an effort – I could almost see her heaving and shoving at that rusted 'off' switch after a couple of stiff whiskies. It was clearly agony, but she managed it most of the time. Only at the end of her life with dementia did the gloves well and truly come off with alcohol. She stopped eating but took to the bottle instead. None of this was ever discussed, of course. The code of omertà was well and truly in place.

As a child, I was somehow aware of the fact that Mum took pills. I thought they were sleeping pills, but in reality, I have no idea what it was that she was taking. Those were the dark days of benzos being handed out by your local doctor without a thought – *Valium, anyone*? If she were alive today, I think she would have been diagnosed with quite bad depression and treated accordingly, but in Mum's world, a drink would solve it. I can almost see her nodding emphatically as I write these words. With her iron control, she made herself wait until a socially acceptable time, but the allure of a drink glimmered in the air any time after midday, bringing with it the enrapturing promise to alleviate all of life's ills. No wonder I was in love with alcohol myself. I had witnessed first-hand the miracles it could work.

The enormous silver drinks tray with its exotically labelled bottles gleamed invitingly in a dark corner of the drawing room. There were decanters on that tray, too, with silver labels round their necks telling you what they contained, alongside the much smaller bottles of bitters, placed next to the serried ranks of old glasses of various unorthodox sizes; glasses that had been endlessly handled by previous generations and somehow bore the imprint of all that vanished conversation and laughter, rendering that place a bit of a high altar in my mind. There was an allure, a romance, about that tray which wasn't really a tray at all but a magic carpet to a different land or a door into a happier room where everyone liked you and you hadn't done anything wrong. When no one was looking, I'd pull out a stopper and sniff the enthralling amber depths of the sherry with its transporting power – a free pass to somewhere else, somewhere not here. I never wanted to be where I was (or, indeed, who I was), and even when I was a child, drink was definitely on the list as a means of reaching those unknown regions – anywhere would do as long as it wasn't here and now. In that place, my mother was always the six o'clock version of herself: fun, chipper, ready to hear what I had to say and to approve of it.

The bond, such as it was, between mother and daughter, wore very thin indeed when I was sent away to boarding school. (Australian Granny was paying my school fees). I arrived in the January term, for some reason, a whole three months behind the rest of my year, who had already made friends or who had known one another from their prep schools in London or Norfolk. Timing seemed to be something neither of my parents ever understood, and as I grew up, I realised that what they did have in common was an almost complete lack of comprehension about how the world worked. Dad was baffled by it and ignored it by dwelling in Valhalla with his books on the Norse gods or tootling about inside the Border Ballads, and Mum's compass was out of whack mainly because of her total and utter inability to put herself in anyone else's shoes. I couldn't copy either of them or use them as templates; as trig points they were useless. I'd have to learn how to navigate adult life by listening and imitating other people and by reading books about it. In AA people often talk of not having 'the handbook' for how to live life. I felt like that, too.

Between the ages of twelve and twenty-three, when I had Arabella, I hardly saw my mother at all. She had fallen out with my father so badly that they never spoke to one another again, so that decade when I had known them as a couple vanished into the distance, overlain by adolescence and confusion and then, suddenly and wonderfully (to begin with), booze. I was like a Labrador puppy around it; once I'd started, I couldn't stop and I'd go on to the bitter end, wherever that was. No 'off' button. Even as a teenager, I was drinking to blackout. I remember being told off by some disdainful grandee at a Highland dance because I was drunkenly hamming up whichever reel it was, but all this rebelliousness was a pose, enabled by alcohol. The truth was I felt like an outsider. I didn't belong amongst all these staggeringly entitled people. I was a poor relation, a drunken one, acting out my sense of alienation. This feeling of not belonging even if you appear to is one of the defining marks of an alcoholic. I may have been posh, but I was chippy, just like my mother, in fact – a realisation that only dawns on me as I write these words. I had a gigantic but unacknowledged feeling of resentment towards all these blithely rich, marvellously landed, entitled toffs in their castles and palazzos. *We had one of those once*, I wanted to say, but who would listen? Who would care?

I remember one particularly painful scene with my mother when I was about sixteen. It was the school holidays and my brother was hosting a party with a school-friend somewhere in Essex. It was quite a wild party and I met a boy who liked me. At once, I was in love, or what I thought love was. Without understanding what I was doing, I was using the idea of this boy as a way of trying to fix myself, to make me feel better and look better to my peers. I don't remember exactly what happened on the night of the party – kissing, I suppose – but I was excited to have got off with someone at last, one of my elder brother's friends, to boot. I felt this lent me some much-needed status.

The next night, our last, the party was well and truly over. The boy had gone home and I was left with my mother in the twin-bedded guest room. Something had happened to her too during the course of that party – she had fallen out with her co-host. I didn't want to hear her story and she must have picked up on my unwillingness: suddenly, she was shrieking and ranting about my father and how awful he was, how he had left her with all the problems, including, I was to understand, me. She was raving. Everything she said made me feel sick and trapped; I'll never forget that feeling of being ripped apart by her words. All I wanted to do was get away from her.

Not long afterwards, she decided to go back to Australia. Did I want to go with her? *No*, I said, *I want to stay here.* The romance with the boy was still going on by letter but when it inevitably folded, it took with it my feeling of excitement and of being buoyed up by someone else. I was overrun by a feeling of utter despair and darkness that terrified me. I felt abandoned. I was wounded, *stricken*, I think would be a better description.

As a result of all this pressure, I had a breakdown at school, which went mostly unremarked. My housemistress called me in and I told her what was going on at home, which she seemed vaguely aware of. She was kind but I wasn't offered any outside help or even the opportunity of another talk with her. No one had heard of mental health in those days. I couldn't sleep and cried all the time. Eventually, I made a recovery of sorts, stumbled to my feet, dusted myself down, but the only way I could function was to pretend I was all right. I had to banish that broken girl inside me because she was causing me so much pain. Drink helped to keep her away from me. I swiftly developed a new muscle: denial. But the net result was that my emotional growth was stunted. I was afraid of everything, and I stayed that way for years.

Fast forward to my mother's death on Christmas Day 2011. She was dead, but she wasn't by any means gone. Our difficult relationship remained unresolved. At the time, I felt crucified by guilt that I hadn't been there with her as she died. In her last years,

I had neglected her emotionally. I had done what had to be done with regards to her care – talked to the doctors and housing officers and all the apparatchiks involved in the care system – but I had not engaged with the underbelly of her emotional life. In effect, I had abandoned her, just as she had abandoned me as a teenager.

Chapter Two

Need

Arabella

We think back through our mothers if we are women.

A ROOM OF ONE'S OWN, VIRGINIA WOOLF

We weren't allowed to eat between mealtimes at my grandmother's house. Three meals a day: breakfast, lunch and supper. What you didn't eat at one sitting was brought forth onto your plate at the next. Cold broccoli for breakfast, accompanied by a lecture. The long shadow of the Second World War tilting itself, at the furthest stretch, into my childhood and onto my plate. Rationing, shortage, need and want. *Finish what's on your plate or have it for breakfast.*

Mostly, I did so out of fear. But there were times when I couldn't, when the food felt too much, when even one mouthful more seemed impossible. Times when food ceased to be simply food and turned into something else. The irony, of course, was that I spent the long afternoons daydreaming about food, fantasising about what I could steal and smuggle up to my bedroom like high explosive. Anything would do: glacé cherries stolen from a plastic pot that was difficult and noisy to open, the catch making a sound that I was sure would wake my grandmother up while she had her afternoon rest; sausages eaten standing in front of the open fridge late at night, its light casting a strange penumbra around the kitchen; ginger biscuits coated in chocolate stolen in the morning after she had gone upstairs, their aftertaste bitter in the mouth.

I was a child, so I didn't ask myself – couldn't ask myself – the real questions about what this hunger meant. Now, it is perfectly obvious to me that the endless hunger signified a form of emotional starvation that could only be sated with a feeling of artificial fullness: eat so many biscuits and sausages and crisps until all that is left is for you to lie there and look up at the ceiling and not think.

I don't ever remember my grandmother liking the food she produced, let alone eating it. Always, before the first mouthful, the apology: *it's not quite right* or *so and so's is better*. I can still see her now, bent over the electric ring cooker in her little yellow kitchen, her brow furrowed as if she were conducting major surgery in a saucepan. Sauces, soufflés, cakes that had to rise in special ways; meat braised, not fried; vegetables held prisoner in aspic. There was no simple assuaging of hunger, no straightforward way of answering the body's need. Food was performative, its transformation from brute ingredients into something beautiful but complicated emblematic of the transformation that I think she felt eluded her in her own life. What would have happened if you had cooked her, I wonder? Would she have risen, obediently, or turned limp at the touch of a spoon? If you stirred her, would there still have been lumps?

The story of my grandmother's life is best told through the

story of taste. Or at least that is how I feel she narrated it to me. Born in Australia in 1924, she evoked the land of her birth, to me, her granddaughter, not through pictures but through taste. The Chinese food she ate in Sydney as a girl, the strange flavours rising up in the mouth in bizarre and unexpected ways, doused with a mysterious black liquid called soy. It seemed hard to imagine her eating that. She spoke of other, sharp foods. The red chillies smeared onto her lips by the elder children at her school as a punishment. For what? We never got that far with the story, but my lips burnt for her in any case.

Food was love, too. She told me about the servant who made bread-and-butterr pudding in the shape of a globe, the creation wheeled forth into the dining room for all to admire; here was something totally finished and safe, its edges melted into one another until you forgot that what covered the edible structure had once been squares of bread. That should have been metaphor enough for the power food held to alter reality altogether. When she told me this story as a child, all I could think of was the round pudding as the world, its terrain brown and golden and perfect, there for consumption but only with the right implement.

When I was a child, food must have been produced at regular intervals throughout the day. No child could stand any other regimen; rebellion would have soon broken out. During the long summer holidays that I spent at my grandmother's house in a remote village in south-west Scotland, food *was* the day. Breakfast, lunch and supper all served up at the same time each day, each sitting as vital as oxygen itself for our survival, physical or otherwise. In part, this was a generational belief in the childhood need for strict routine and habit-forming in all areas. It's all there in the rhyme I know I learnt under my grandmother's tutelage: *Patience is a virtue, virtue is a grace, Grace is a little girl who never washed her face.* Wash your face, be meticulously clean at all times, stay accountable for your own shit, literal and emotional. Such a simple, naive belief in dirt and its ability to be wiped cleanly away is something I still cling to in my own house; some expression of fear that finds its loudest voice in bouts of manic cleaning that my husband finds bewildering. Of the emotional dirt that I must have had visibly smeared around my face as a child, my grandmother said very little.

What might she have said, I wonder? *Do you know where your father is? Do you know why your mother has left you here?* Or even, the most obvious question of all in the face of frequent tears and tantrums: *Are you all right?* I don't remember her asking me explicit questions about my happiness and I don't think I would have known what to say if she had; we cleaved to silence far more, her back to me in the kitchen as she stirred something at the cooker, my habit of getting into her bed in the early morning and lying, reciprocally, with my back to her and counting the handles on her dressing table.

Instead, she fed me. Providing nourishment in the way she understood, in the way that was *right.* Some of these memories are the happiest of my life, rare meetings of need and satisfaction. Macaroni cheese before bedtime, chocolate digestive cake cooled in the fridge with a Smartie wedged upon each slice, scallops cooked in a white sauce, beef olives slow cooked all day in the tiny oven. Love – melting, cooling, congealing, frying, baking, roasting, boiling, toasting – love.

Food is also a good prism through which to understand my

mother. Let me tell you about some of the things she used to eat and probably still does: Ryvita and cottage cheese, any kind of cooked meat straight from the packet, celery, boiled eggs by the dozen, large hunks of Cheddar torn straight from the block. Once, even, the burnt tops of matchsticks or dog biscuits as a child in Scotland left to her own devices. As I write this list, I can feel the hunger radiating off the page; food torn and gobbled, ripped and sawn off. Hunger had become so divorced from its civil counter-part as to be a hindrance, something you attend to standing in front of the fridge late at night.

The care which her own mother had taken with food was long gone. Her relationship to food was part of a rebellion against the silent tyranny of her mother's highly controlled universe of performative food, what she called the 'laboratory' of the kitchen. Through food, my grandmother created a currency in which we all dealt but only she controlled. Occasionally, as a child, the cur-rency would change; coins and notes that had been in circulation suddenly became devalued. *I won't make that any more*, she would say with irritation to us unknowing ingrates sitting around the table. Exasperated, Mum said that it had always been the same, that my grandmother had controlled her and her brother in the same way. *Just make anything, Mum, it really doesn't matter*, my mother would plead with her. But you don't spend a lifetime dealing and trading only to lose interest in old age. *No*, she said. She would make food in the proper way, from scratch. In her house, at her table, she set the base rate.

In the summer holidays, my mother would make the long drive north to Scotland from London to deposit me there for a month or so. She would return to London to write or go away with her artist boyfriend to France. If this sounds rebarbative and neglectful, it wasn't. I was happy to be in my grandmother's house. From my bedroom window I could see the sea and, further into the distance, a castle upon which I used to project elaborate fantasies of abandon and recapture. Still to this day, when I lie awake at night, I imagine myself back in that bedroom with the sea and the castle beyond and some childhood somnolence washes over me and I fall back to sleep easily.

For my mother, the room cannot soothe in the same way. *I feel like I'm in the museum of my bloody life*, she would say as I asked her about the photographs of her hung on the walls, or, mysteriously, the large boxes of Victorian coins that she had collected as a child, perhaps in response to her own mother's transactional universe of shame and reward. *Where were you here, Mum? Do you remember?* to which the answer was almost invariably, *Oh, in London somewhere, probably*, which is more of a shield than an answer, designed to put you off asking anything else. Because if the person in the photo doesn't know, then what hope does the spectator have? Better, perhaps, to stick to the sea and the castle for which there were endless scenarios without need of reference.

There was one subject, though, upon which my mother would elaborate and even answer questions. It didn't hang on a wall, and it wasn't a photograph, but rather, the story of her life. It is a story for which I can conjure remarkably vivid images, more vivid than some photographs. It goes something like this: as a young girl growing up in a forbidding farm on the Scottish borders, my mother was at the mercy of my grandmother's terrifying moods. So terrifying were these bouts of rage that, apocryphally, my uncle was said to have been tipped out of the car and left on a country lane in the dark as punishment for some unremembered crime, accompanied by the screams and pleas of my mother to go back and get him. Her wrath, my mother always said, extended far beyond these incidents. Permanently in a bad mood, my mother learnt never to ask things of her and largely kept out of her way. As her marriage to my grandfather collapsed under the weight of impending bankruptcy and infidelity, my mother acted as the go-between for her parents, taking pity on my grandfather, whom she idolised. Eventually, my mother was sent away to boarding school where she was desperately unhappy. During this time, my grandmother returned to Australia, the land of her birth, while my grandfather married a cruel woman who bullied my mother. Doubly betrayed by both her tormentor and her hero, my mother turned to drink. Soon after, she turned to men and then, catastrophically, to both.

I know this story. It is familiar and foreign all at once. It is the story of my mother's life and the messy business of need in its most abject state. Parts of it are not dissimilar to my own. Even before I was familiar with its complete arc, crumbs of it fell onto my plate, always at the kitchen table, the symbol of our mutual discontent. Bitter arguments between my mother and grandmother would erupt, the result of so much unfinished business, proof of the dangerously unsteady pillars upon which our family rested. Sometimes these were conducted over the phone, and I would hear the sound of the receiver being slammed down long after I should have been asleep. Other times, they would take place in person. The worst of all took place when I wasn't there, my ringside seat unfairly denied to me after being their primary spectator for so long. I don't know what happened – recollections vary – but upon my return, a great frost covered their relations. Periodically, I would overhear my mother talking about it in furious tones; no thaw seemed likely. Months passed without any contact at all. Long after, when other arguments had papier mâchéd themselves over this one, I learnt that it had started as a disagreement over food served at a lunch. I understood perfectly and at once what had happened.

In her final years, my grandmother forgot all about food. She forgot about a lot of things. Her house, perennially immaculate, became disordered, full of uneaten food – always scampi in a basket ordered from the local pub across the street – which she ordered out of habit and then neglected to eat. When my mother enquired of the cost, the landlord told her that the bill had run into thousands. Having reigned for so long over her domestic kingdom, she abdicated suddenly and dramatically, leaving no plans for her succession. An intervention was sought, and she moved to a nursing home nearby. *It overlooked the sea*, they said. *It will be just like home*, they said.

It was nothing like home. Her distress, when she was lucid enough to recollect her surroundings, was visible. Living in America by this time, I only visited her there once. It was a freezing, grey day of the kind only Scotland can deliver in early summer. Rain lashed the windscreen as we drove through the village towards the Georgian house on the sea, Mum clutching the steering wheel, her expression inscrutable. Inside, in the day room where the inmates sat, a large sign read 'Today is Tuesday' with a slot to change the day of the week accordingly. A television blared noisily at the side of the room, but no one watched it; an old woman with knitting in her lap stared into the middle distance.

'Does she come down here ever?' Mum asked but I knew that the answer was a flat no. 'No, never. She hasn't left her room for over a year,' the manager replied with some element of contempt – or blame? – in her voice, her red painted nails like claws reaching up to smooth a hair back into her platinum-blonde bun. Up and up we went across hallways painted a pale shade of antiseptic green with assistance handles on all sides, past rooms with doors open from which more inmates stared blankly back at us and radios droned to deaf or sleeping ears. Finally, at the end of a corridor we reached her room. From the landing window you could, it was true, see the sea.

She was asleep when we walked in, sitting up straight in bed with her head slumped to one side on her chest. Her hair, which she had kept meticulously permed and coiffed throughout her life, hung about her shoulders like a grey veil, an elderly bride lurking behind it. 'Ann, Ann, wake up, your family are here,' the manager cooed, her broad Scots accent ringing out across the room. The word 'family' hung in the air like cigarette smoke; I had long ago stopped thinking of us in tribal or familial terms. We were a line of women linked by dark blood, mutual anger now our defining characteristic. Slowly, she lifted her head up, the grey curtain of hair matted on one side of her face, like a child's after a long sleep. She looked at us blankly, her expression shut like a door. Then she did something totally unexpected. She smiled broadly and reached her arms out towards me, agitating for me to come close, the bedclothes falling to reveal her naked legs. I froze. 'Julia, is that you, darling girl? How was your drive?' she said as I moved towards her, overpowered by the stench of the incontinence pad. 'I was just about to peel the potatoes,' she said loudly.

As I think about that day, I think about recognition. I think
about what it means to recognize someone and how little that
has to do with seeing clearly. I think about how my grandmother
looked at my mother and I and saw something familiar in a different person, in the *wrong* person. I think about how our sense
of need – of brute nourishment – doesn't always map neatly onto
the people or things we want it to. I think, rather sadly, about the
potatoes lying on the kitchen counter that she would never peel,
their skins browning and curling as she lay in that bed.

Somewhere, in amongst the potatoes and the bedclothes of that
day, I also think of my grandmother as a happy person. She was
a happy child once. Ann of Warrawee, New South Wales, smiling
in the Australian sunshine. Ann of Warrawee watching the bread-
and-butter pudding being wheeled into the dining room as she
looked up adoringly at her father. In the white fug of dementia,
maybe she had found her way back to that person, forgetting the
stories that had fed her resentments until all she was left with was
a wholehearted participation in the present, the simple need to
remember to peel the potatoes for supper.

Julia

Need

'You used to be such a nice little girl,' my mother said to me once. This reference to another me, a better me, was disturbing, as it was intended to be. It was a threat disguised as a reproach, a perfect example of passive aggression, although nobody in our world knew what on earth that was in those distant days.

Somehow or other, without even noticing, I'd fallen out of Eden and come to as a fallen person, aged four. A person who had once been 'nice' – still a little girl, mind – but one who was not giving satisfaction, who was not being pleasing enough. Aged *four*! When my brother had turned four a couple of years before, he had asked my mother the question: 'Can girls be four?' The answer was yes, my mother said, refraining from adding that they had to be sugar and spice and all things nice. Transactional love in all its glory.

It was absolutely vital to me to please, because my mother was a dark and capricious kind of goddess who might just donate you to a stranger if she felt like it, or drive off and leave you on a moorland road in the middle of nowhere as darkness fell, as she'd once done to my brother when he misbehaved in the car.

She was, I remember, utterly unmoved by my terror and tears at what might become of him. He did get home, somehow – I can't remember the detail – but I never forgot her stony coldness, her suddenly visible and terrifying streak of utter ruthlessness.

All children need approval, but they also need to understand that if they don't get things right for whatever reason, they'll still be loved. I didn't have that assurance – it wasn't explicitly stated, of course, but children intuit such things – and I knew that if I wasn't 'good', I, too, would be left on the equivalent of that moorland road. Constantly questioning your safety is no way to live, but I learnt it at my mother's knee.

Enter the mask-wearing people-pleaser, accompanied by an insistent feeling that I had to watch my back all the time. I observed my mother forensically as she weeded maniacally on her kneeling mat, bottom in the air, violently wrenching at the things that shouldn't be there, or crashed saucepans in the kitchen cooking yet another meal for '*your* father', as if it was somehow my fault that he needed feeding. Why was she like that? I hadn't a clue but I thought that if I watched closely enough I could understand what she was really thinking. I was trying to read her mind. No one knows what another person is really thinking but this tendency to think I can read other people's minds began in childhood. It's exhausting and pointless but I still do it when I'm tired.

Playing bridge distracted her; she was obsessed: Goren's *Bridge in a Nutshell* sat on her bedside table in its place of honour. I thought bridge was a good thing because it brought people into the house and my mother was always nicer when there were people around. Bridge – which incidentally I've never learnt to play – paused the continuous assessment of my behaviour, but even as a child I was aware that I was two separate people: the real me, the part that had gone underground, and the mother-pleasing version, the official version, if you like.

My major problem was that my mother was so difficult to predict. Which mood would she be in when I came home from school? Which mother would I get? The nice, kind version, or the one who was already offended by *something*, though I didn't know what? Being 'good', therefore, meant I had to be a contortionist, shaping myself to the prevailing winds of her volatile weather system. All this created within me an unarticulated need to shore up the rickety joists and piles of my own inner world.

I suppose I was looking for fullness; for completion – a sense of being attached to something safe. All this unacknowledged tension and anxiety around my mother literally altered my brain as it was developing, I learnt later. No wonder alcohol seemed such a wonderful solution – it stilled the fear, numbed it, clobbered it, in fact, at least until the next morning. As a teenager, I used alcohol as a way of escaping from that broken, frightened part of myself. Booze became a sort of jet ski that I could drive at high speed out of my everyday life into another climate, a different sea, a different continent, if you like, thousands of miles away from where I had come from. I was, in the beginning, entranced by its possibilities, the way it made me feel whole, a part of things, all right, sorted. In everyday life as a teenager, before alcohol, my default setting was a kind of anxious unease. With booze, it was as if I'd logged on to Wi-Fi: I suddenly got it. Everything was OK. I was OK.

You can make yourself feel safe and anchored as a child if it's mirrored to you, but with hindsight, it's abundantly clear that my mother didn't know how to do it either. Her own mysterious inner world was clearly a dark and perilous place. Her jitteriness, her mood swings, her cruelty to her children and to her husband made this perfectly obvious, even though I couldn't have put it into words.

I was a classic case of insecure attachment, a space walker without a rope holding me fast to the mother ship. That hateful, dizzying feeling of being a lost little girl would follow me around for years, tugging pathetically at my sleeve until a long time after I got sober, when I finally had to find the courage to pay proper attention to the bewildered, unanchored part of myself that I'd turned my back on. But, even now, I can still forget. My mother abandoned me as a child and I did exactly the same thing, not only to that lost part of myself, but also to my own child. It's classic generational trauma. We were an old family with a lot of quarterings but if there was a psychological equivalent of this practice, ours would have shown over and over again down the generations on both sides: abandonment and alcoholism, entwined together like a pair of serpents, a heraldic image, of sorts.

Around the age of eight or nine, I began to steal. I didn't know why, I just felt a compulsion to take things – other children's toys, the money from the saucer at Miss Little's dancing class in Kirkcudbright. Now, I think that money and *things* seemed, perhaps unsurprisingly, to be a metaphor for that elusive feeling of fullness, a sense of being in the game, a part of something, not this person always on the margins who could never have enough and who was angry about it.

My world seemed profoundly unfair to me. I had very limited pocket money. My peer group at the village school had more than I did. I vividly remember standing in the queue in the sweetie shop in Twynholm run by Mrs Paterson, a sort of Mrs Tiggy-Winkle figure, who measured out sherbet fountains and love hearts and other assorted tooth-rotting goodies from behind a hatch, rationalising in my head the fact that my friends would soon eat their way through their stash and then we would be the same, even if I didn't have as much at the beginning. It was my way of coping, but it was distorted thinking, all the same. Everyone else always seemed to have more than I did: more pocket money, nicer parents, a happier home life, more toys. I was always the last, the lost, the left-behind one. When I got to AA, I discovered to my astonishment that almost every alcoholic says exactly the same thing. Who knew?

My father had the habit of flinging his change onto the top of the chest of drawers in the room where he dressed, which was off the bedroom he still shared with my mother. I helped myself to that change – he was so vague he didn't notice – and availed myself of some proper bounty from Mrs Paterson. I laid out my haul on a table in my bedroom and was promptly busted by my mother. 'Where did you get the money for all that?' she demanded, making a swift calculation of the cost of the assembled loot.

Pocket money was then cut off, but of course the need remained, dangling in space like an uncut thread or an unmoored umbilicus. Needs were not to be acknowledged, discussed or met in any way. It did not occur to my mother to ask me why I felt the need to steal money to buy sweets. She was a narcissist, and other people's feelings or motivations were only of interest to her if they affected her directly. She was also emotionally a Victorian: surfaces were everything and what lay beneath was a mystery. It's no great surprise to me that psychoanalysis was founded towards the end of the Victorian century, or that the Great War happened when it did. There is a definite link between that epic violence and those unexploded, unexplored feelings crowded and crushed under the surface of things.

I then started to collect coins. *Coins!* I mean, how much more explicit could I get? Another potent symbol for what I didn't have. Victorian pennies were still in circulation then and I conceived a passion for them, particularly the bronze 'bun' pennies, where the young Victoria wore a laurel wreath with her hair in a simple bun tied with a ribbon. There was something about this charming girlish image of the old queen that stirred me, a token from a vanished past that I could connect with, another way of escaping the painful present. I remember the thrill of discovery in a handful of change, the head rush it gave me to find one. My mother, for some bizarre reason, sanctioned all this (it was history, I suppose, and she definitely approved of Queen Victoria) and allowed me to have a magazine called *Coin Monthly*. I think she thought this coin-collecting mania was a sign that I might become a titan of something later on. God knows we needed to become titans of something, so hopeless was the family money situation. A Scottish brewery had even taken our name, but nobody ever did anything about it. It was just one of those things. *Money doesn't grow on trees* was a favourite, bleak little saying of hers. I hated her referring to money because it was one of the signs that the weather was changing for the worse.

Money, or the lack of it, was a major problem in our household, and invariably led to rows with my father, who was pathologically vague on the subject. When my brother went to Eton (paid for, as far as I know, by the selling of more pictures and silver) my father accompanied him to Coutts Bank in the High Street to open an account for him as a sign of his impending adulthood. At some point, the bank manager enquired how much money he would like to deposit in the account and my father looked dumbfounded. Banks were for taking money out of, surely, not putting anything in? Eventually, after rummaging in his jacket pocket, he pulled out a limp five-pound note. According to my brother, the bank manager hastily leant across the table, grabbed the note and shoved it into a drawer. It could be a scene from an Evelyn Waugh novel.

My father had been born into a great estate: two huge houses and a vast acreage in Scotland. But death duties and other family complications, combined with my grandfather's shattering incompetence (he was an active alcoholic), meant that the whole lot was almost literally pissed away. By the time it was my father's turn, there was precious little left. Thus, when Dad ran short of cash, he sold things: paintings that were old friends suddenly went missing, leaving frame-shaped rectangles on the wall where they had once hung. There was just a general sense of lack amongst us – both inner and outer – lack and unease. The blank spaces on the wall seemed a rather apt symbol for it.

That sense of unease, of a volcano preparing to erupt, became palpable when my parents stopped sharing a bedroom. I was eleven. Dad moved into the bedroom next door to me, and I would drift in there frequently when he was out and tidy up a bit. The room was always in chaos: piles of books on every available surface, a pipe jammed in an ashtray – yes, people still smoked in bed in the good old days – clothes in limp piles on the floor. I felt sorry for him in his new-fangled equivalent of bachelor hell. He was a child in so many ways, totally unable to look after himself, though he had been in the army (which might, possibly, have taught him something about tidiness) in a barracks in Northern Ireland when the war was called off, having never made it to any front. Army life somehow failed to give him a sense of responsibility for himself; even the most basic things like clothes and shoes were somehow unmanageable. He never knew what to wear and had once been spotted in London wearing a tweed suit and a bowler hat, or so I was told. Sartorial errors didn't get much bigger than that in the London of the fifties and sixties, or the kind of old-school London he inhabited, anyway, which definitely wasn't of the nascent Mary Quant variety. He was, in fact, one of the greatest filth packets on the planet and it drove my mother mad. He left a trail of domestic chaos behind him as he ambled through the house in a blizzard of crumbs, jam, and ash. For a control freak such as my mother, there could not have been a worse choice of husband.

I remember with a pang the sorrow when his regiment was cancelled, its long history occluded by some bureaucratic reshuffling of the army. It was always about loss in our household. Everything that had once been wonderful had been lost and, as a result, we were lost, too. In the intensely hierarchical county life of my childhood, we were regarded with pity. I knew it and I hated it. We were the poor relations. At the end of his long life, Dad admitted to me that he had been 'a lost child'. I had first witnessed evidence of that, without knowing it, at the age of eleven, but the biggest blood loss so to speak was the psychic drain brought about by the loss of his beloved family home. He never recovered.

I had discovered in my forensic rummagings in my father's desk drawers (unlocked and open to the world, unlike my mother's) a series of letters from my parents to one another, written before they were married, in which, in a rather guarded way, they discussed their future prospects as a married couple. Both seemed a little uncertain but their shared family background (they were cousins) – those quarterings – was clearly the deciding factor. The trouble is that the shared family background contained whole riverscapes of alcoholism, disappearing fathers (especially on my father's side – his great-grandfather had gone to look for the source of the River Niger and never returned: 'Lost with the canoe party' was the official version – my father's take was slightly different: he couldn't bear his wife and settled on the banks of the great river with a local woman and had lots of blue-eyed Black children) and disconnected, distant mothers (on my mother's side, surprise, surprise). On the surface, an arranged marriage seemed like a good idea, except that it wasn't a good idea at all, as it turned out.

I guess Dad drove her mad from the beginning. He was totally undomesticated: a dedicated pipe smoker, he would thrust whichever pipe it was into the ashtray in his grey A35 van when he came to collect me from school. I remember the way the lit ash would pour out from that ashtray like lava, burning holes in the red plastic scrotum that enclosed the gear stick. My mother would never let him near her car, which had the see-through plastic covers left on long after it was brand new to protect it from us and, presumably, him. She was probably right; he was a terrible driver with very little road sense. I remember he would always accelerate if he saw a red light, instead of slowing down like a normal driver. Later, in the brief period when he was on his own after he and my mother finally parted, the cottage he was living in not far away caught fire, either from the offending pipe or a black-pudding holocaust in a frying pan that got out of control. He was indeed Little Boy Lost.

I can still feel the emotional pain I felt for him in his bleak little cottage. It was so strange to see him uprooted out of the familiar detail of family life – even our deeply dysfunctional family life – and living elsewhere, as if I was suddenly aware of him in a new and poignant way, not only as my father but also as a lonely, unhappy man who had lost pretty much everything. The ship was well and truly breaking up by this time, 'breaking deep', they call it, when the damage occurs below the water line and the ship takes water. That's what happened to the *Titanic*. We were breaking deep and deeply broken. My darkest fears were about to be realised.

As the adult child of an alcoholic father, I now think my father had learnt early on how to compartmentalise his life in order to survive. Just as his own father had lived many quite different lives – soldier, writer (he published several books with John Murray, then still *the* publisher of exotic travels since Byron's time), poet, Arabist, Galloway pig-farmer, drunk – my father, too, was now about to embark on a new life all of his own, in which the feelings of his existing children were no longer of any real interest to him. I needed him so badly as a teenager, having enjoyed the warmth of his love and attention as a child, but he turned his back on me. This was a terrible blow I had not foreseen. I don't blame him, or, at least, not any more. He was only doing what had been done to him, as I would do, too, to my own child.

There are family trees – shake an alcoholic's family tree and quite a few would probably drop from the branches – but trees with their height and foliage don't reveal what lies hidden among the leaves; we need another image for families now so much more is known about genetics and inherited patterns of behaviour, a family algorithm perhaps, a form of notation given to each member of a family as a rite of passage at a certain age – puberty perhaps – alerting them as to what their genetic baggage might contain. I've spent so much of my life trying to figure out what was wrong with me. In the end it was electrifyingly simple: I'm an alcoholic.

Chapter Three

Trouble

Arabella

In the wood, the trees are tall and silvery, their branches reaching up endlessly into the sky. It is inky dark in the canopy beneath and I can hardly see where I am going but I am not scared. My father is nearby, his cigarette smoke wafting towards me through the leaves; unmistakably him. I like it when he smokes because it means he is in a good mood, the red and gold box of Dunhill opening with a click. If he is in a good mood, he will call me by my nickname, and I know everything is all right. If he is in a bad mood, he will stare into the middle distance and drink from his wine glass and call me Arabella. No one should approach him then.

There is another person with us in the woods because my father and I are never alone, however much I want us to be. To my left, a tall, thin blonde woman is watching me walk across the trunk of one of the fallen silvery trees. I almost lose my balance several times and the blonde woman watches me encouragingly, moving a little closer each time. When I get to the end of the log, she lifts me off slowly and deposits me on the ground before calling for my father to come and get me. In her arms, there is the smell of cigarette smoke and some other, bitter adult smell that I can't identify. My father is still some way behind, and I want him to come and pick me up. I think I want him to take me away from this other woman.

When I am five, my father remarries. I don't remember meeting her for the first time and I have no memory of their wedding, although I was there as their bridesmaid. The photos show me standing in a yellow frilly dress on the lawn of the house she and my father already lived in before they were married. I am smiling in some of them but there is one in which I am hovering to the side of the frame, standing apart from the group. My head is hung low and I appear to be looking down at the ballet shoes on my feet. There is something in my pose that makes me think I must be cross, some arrangement of my shoulders that looks like I am shrugging. The other people in the photograph – including my father – look forward and smile on. Later, this photograph will be printed and framed as a photo of their wedding day. You can't see me unless you look quite hard and, after a while, I stop looking for myself in it. Two weeks after my father has died, I find this photograph in a desk drawer in his office and wonder why it was put away. Did he not want to look at it any more?

The woman in the woods and the woman in the wedding photograph are the same person: my stepmother. She is, my father tells me many times, an explorer. 'What's an explorer?' I don't understand what this means. 'She travels to far-off places on her own, sometimes on a horse, sometimes in a microlight,' my father says, taking one hand off the steering wheel to light a cigarette with the car lighter. 'She's very brave; lots of people have heard of her,' he adds. Because I am only five, I don't know what a microlight is;

I imagine it to be a miniature version of a cigarette lighter but I'm too scared to ask how this will take you to far-off places.

Once, when I am at their house, he makes me watch a video of her being interviewed by Terry Wogan. In the video she has long blonde hair and is wearing a pink blouse with huge shoulder pads. Through the grainy screen I can see her fixing her eyes and concentrating as Wogan asks her what it was like to live with a tribe in Papua New Guinea on her own for two years. I can't hear her answer but that is probably because my father is talking over the video, telling me to concentrate on what she is saying, turning the volume up. When I watch the video again, at my father's behest, I hear her say that the tribesmen of Papua New Guinea made her an honorary man. I don't understand what this means either and ask my father. He ignores my question and gives me newspaper clippings detailing his famous wife's adventures to give to my mother. My mother throws them straight in the bin and then I throw my yoghurt pot in the bin after her and watch the strawberry yoghurt drip down a picture of her tribal tattoo.

Having a stepmother is a bit like walking along a log in a darkening forest. The pitfalls are huge. Let me tell you about some of them. Make too many demands of the newly remarried parent in the presence of the stepparent and you risk humiliating them, your needs threatening a pact you were never supposed to be a part of. Make any mention of the now-banished parent – with whom you probably still live – and you risk upsetting the stepparent for whom comparisons are odious. Mention the (now-distant) past in which your mother and father lived in some form of matrimonial harmony, and you sleepwalk into yet another unfortunate comparison between the then and the now. For a child, this level of self-censorship and disavowal is hugely damaging, not to say catastrophic.

For the stepparent and stepchild relationship to function, the stepchild must do a combination of things. First, the stepchild must renounce the past and adapt quickly to the new material and emotional reality. Second, the stepchild must, for the most part, remain mute. As a symbol, she may be carried over into the new reality, but only upon condition of her silence. As an accessory to the parent's new reality she is – if largely taciturn – an advantage even, showcasing a capacity for love and nurture, but this can backfire should she speak out of turn, or at all. Third, the stepchild must treat the stepparent with a new and strange kind of affection bordering on deference; this affection is not the same as filial love for which the stepparent has no need but is rather an artificial form of respect that frees the parent from guilt at their decision.

As a child, I fall off the log often. I give many explanations for my inability to keep quiet: the bed I am made to sleep in is scratchy; I am hungry and not fed enough; I am frightened of the dark; I do not like the cigarette smoke in the car; I am bored. Very often, I commit the worst crime of all: I scream and cry out for my mother. Bathed in the flattering light of homesickness, my mother is now a goddess, the only person who can make anything right. At this, my father becomes furious, his face so knotted with anger when he turns to look back at me in the car that I scream even more.

As an adolescent, I do away with the log altogether and exist in a permanent state of fallen grace. I am sullen and don't want to go and spend the weekend in their house because it is boring and my father has a glassy look in his eyes and no one asks him why. But before I discover that I can steal his alcohol, I work out that I can steal money from his dressing table. This illicit transaction makes me feel better about the peculiar state of loving exchange between us, though of course I don't understand it in that way at the time. I just feel safe when the pound coins are in my pocket, my fingers silently touching their edges. At first, I steal coins but very quickly I become bold and start to steal notes, twenties mostly. My fingers reach in and take one, then two, my heart racing as I hear voices downstairs and footsteps approaching. It is a high – the first of many – and I feel exhilarated afterwards. Soon, I find better ways of achieving this feeling. I swig wine from his bottle in the fridge and then I tell my stepmother that I am worried about my father and his drinking. I am trouble.

Looking back, it strikes me how little my stepmother had to do with these behaviours that seem more to do with the relationship between my father and me. Was my unhappiness her fault? I don't think so, but she stands accused anyway. No other relationship is quite like this: the stepmother travels across the biological borders of the family and holds a mirror up to both parents. Like the mirror in *Snow White*, it warps the reflection even as it brings it into sharper focus. Since I can't remember a period in which my parents and I lived together, my formative reflection of them both is the one my stepmother held up. In it, my father stands emasculated, scared of the Amazonian woman he makes me watch on television and who now occupies the other side of his bed. The fact that he calls her 'Tiger' confirms that what I see in the mirror is true: she is an animal of prey.

The reflection of my mother in this mirror is more confusing. She is safety and comfort, so different from the forbidding, angular frame of my stepmother, known to many as the 'stick insect'. She is my White Knight, arriving to rescue me on Sunday nights when I am allowed to go home, my eyes ringed with tiredness. She is refuge. But she is also, as my father and stepmother tell me, trouble. She is trouble because she writes novels, and novels are clearly dangerous because they make things up. Worse still, novels don't make any money, they say. She is trouble because she lives with an artist who also doesn't make any money and lives in a studio where the lavatory is outside, and the bath is in the bedroom with a big stick for stirring the laundry. No good will come of the novels or the artist or her mad family, they say together in unison, and other people, like the Tiger's sister who is often in their house, agree, and then they all laugh.

Which reflection makes more sense to me? I don't know, because it is a circus mirror and it changes all the time. I compare my mother and my stepmother constantly but since my stepmother has no children, the comparison is moot. Like two entirely different species, the mother and childless woman stand apart. In practical matters, the difference is screamingly obvious. My stepmother does not know what to cook for a child nor how to plan for it. Bedtimes are done away with and the coat hanger of routine that children thrive on is non-existent. My father, who could have helped her if he had wanted to, makes no effort to do so, and she flounders.

When I am a child, I realise that there are advantages to having a childless woman for a stepmother because there is a part of that woman that is more playful and untainted by the slog of childrearing. In this regard, my stepmother is on my side and I think I love her. She makes obstacle courses for me to run through, complete with tunnels and slides. An able horsewoman, she finds a pony and teaches me to ride bareback across the field behind the house. She decides to rear a litter of puppies and I spend all day in their pen, picking them up and arranging them one on top of the other. She will do long and complicated jigsaw puzzles with me on the floor in front of the fire. In these moments, I am happy. In these moments I don't stop to ask myself why I am playing with a woman who is not my mother or why my father is rarely there with us. I don't stop to ask myself why my mother and father have each built a reality that has nothing to do with each other. It seems perfectly normal to me.

Quickly, I become adept at playing one woman off another. My mother enjoys hearing the instances of my stepmother's domestic failures and I delight in telling them, happy to please. When I want to please my stepmother, I tell her about my mother and her chaotic life and this delights her, too. For a while, I am playing the game and winning. I feel as if I have wrested the mirror into my hands and I am able to show each woman what she wants to see. Much later, I will see that there are no winners in this game, only losers. To cope, in childhood, is to quickly adapt, to shapeshift to fit the new reality, to play the game even if it feels wrong. As an operating method in adulthood, it has, in some circumstances, served me well. But it has also kept me in wildly dysfunctional situations long after I should have left. I find it hard to distinguish between normal and abnormal; very often, I can't see the difference. I am trouble.

When I am writing this book, I look the Tiger up on the internet. Although she was a part of my life for twenty-five years, I hold no material mementoes of her: no photographs, no letters, no postcards, nothing. I have not thought about her for a very long time, almost ten years. After my father died, she simply fell out of my life, and it occurs to me that this vanishing act is peculiar to stepparents. What other figure in the family constellation could just fall out of your life in that way, the ties that held even loosely simply dissolving into nothing?

I type her name into Google and am surprised by how many results are returned; maybe she was famous after all. Interviews, reviews of her books, details of her charitable foundation all stare back at me. I find it hard to connect the woman I knew to this online avatar, this explorer of note, this Fellow of the Royal Geographical Society, this 'humanitarian' with whom my father built an entirely separate life and next to whom he died. I am reluctant to click on the links and think of closing the search window altogether. It is too much, especially so close to the tenth anniversary of my father's death. I have stumbled into the pornography of grief, seeking out what will harm me and what is inappropriate. I think of calling my mother to tell her what I am doing, because when we talk about our respective stepmothers, the gap between mother and daughter closes and we are neither mothers nor daughters, but survivors.

One search result stands out: an appearance on *Desert Island Discs* with Sue Lawley. My attention piques and I realise I am drawn to this like my father was; pulled in by her fame, seduced by the idea of her notoriety. I dimly remember being made to listen to the episode as a child. I check the date, 1994; I was no longer a young child by that point. I would have been eleven, old enough to remember having listened to it. In my head, I hear the conversation I would have had with my father about it. 'Tiger was on the radio; you should ask her about it,' he says in a tone of voice that lets me know that none of this is optional. She is on the radio and I must listen and act reverent: it is a validation of his choices. Next, I hear my mother's voice on the subject, its tone heavy with irritation. 'Have they given that woman more airtime? Again?' I can't hear my own voice, only theirs. Both responses displease me. My father for his obsequiousness, my mother for directing her displeasure at the Tiger and not my father. I press play to drown these conversations out of my head.

Her voice fills the room, and I am five, six, seven all over again. I have heard the stories she is telling the presenter well, but they sound strangely disembodied coming out of my computer in the house I live in as an adult, as a wife and a mother. I wonder how much of herself she understood through them as I hear the cadence of her voice speaking in the sing-song way that people do when they have told the same anecdote many times before. She grew up in the African bush, she explains, and exploring was her destiny: her grandmother travelled across China in the late nineteenth century; she is descended from a line of fearless women. She travelled across Africa on a horse, she says, losing herself in the wilderness, so much so that her mother, unperturbed, did not hear from her for months on end. She drove across some other desert expanse in a Land Rover with three other people and fell out with two of them. She rafted across rapids and nearly died but mysteriously didn't. She travelled across such treacherous terrain to a remote outpost in Papua New Guinea that she earnt an honorary manhood from the tribesmen. A witchdoctor gave her a potion for bronchitis. As part of an initiation ceremony in Papua New Guinea, a tattoo in the shape of a crocodile was emblazoned upon her arm. At this, I wince; I know that tattoo, I remember my father proudly showing me her arm as a child.

'Was it painful?' Sue Lawley asks.

'The theory of initiation is that it's meant to be painful; you go through pain and fear and come out on the other side,' she answers, and I half wonder why I never asked her more about it, since it sounds remarkably like childhood. I look down and realise that I am clutching the top of my arm in the same way I must have done when she told me that.

The interview goes on and various pieces of music are played: 'In the Bleak Midwinter' for when she was travelling across the Sahara and wanted to think of something cool; 'One of These Days' by Pink Floyd; some other track by Genesis that I vaguely remember them playing in the car. I'm about to switch the recording off when she announces that her next song is 'Les Amants' by Charles Dumont and Édith Piaf; unmistakably, plainly, connected to my father. As Dumont's voice booms around the room – *c'est sur qu'ils pleuront* – I feel an enormous rush of unidentified emotion that I think lies somewhere between embarrassment, pride and protectiveness; I didn't know my father was even mentioned, I had always thought the exploring and the marriage were the exact antidote to one another. 'When I'm on this desert island. I don't want to forget that I've got a husband who I adore, because he's a very special person,' she says. I throw my head back and I think of how proud my father must have been to be mentioned on the 'Beeb' by his adventurer wife and I feel a sharp pang of contrition for having caused so much trouble; I imagine how much of a nuisance I must have been to them. I want to erase myself from it all, to rub myself out, to start the recording without me in it.

Instead, I shut the computer and consign her voice to the deep shipwreck of the past.

Anger and sadness, happiness and regret, trouble and calm. How do you hold these things in both hands? *Grant me the serenity to accept the things I cannot change*, I murmur to myself as I walk downstairs. I look at the clock: two hours before I need to be somewhere; if I hurry, I can make the meeting. I'll be in trouble if I don't.

Julia

Trouble

When I was about twelve or thirteen, I began to sense a deeper, more seismic change in the family weather system, registering unsettling tectonic tremors from deep beneath the crust of my domestic world. The balance of power was shifting and I could feel it. My mother's rule as an absolute monarch was coming to an end. The endgame for dictators is never good: release from tyranny is always accompanied by chaos and the ever-present likelihood that something worse will take its place. And this is exactly what happened. My father, whose way of coping with his difficult wife had been to immerse himself in books (a habit I inherited from him) when he wasn't out on the farm talking to his animals – all of whom had names (fatal in the farming business) – had moved out of their shared bedroom. He had also taken to going to London whenever he could. Eventually, in the not-too-distant future, he would jump ship altogether into the arms of a waiting siren, who turned out to be even more dangerous than the one he had left behind. I didn't believe such a thing was possible, but Dad managed it somehow.

My way of coping with this series of alarming changes was not to eat. Not eating made me feel powerful to start with because it unseated my mother who prided herself on her cooking. I was casting around for ways to control and numb my feelings as my parents' marriage collapsed into the abyss. As a child I had run through my father's study and the ceiling had fallen in just as I closed the door behind me, coating all the books in a kind of gluey plaster dust, some of which was still there years later. The emotional equivalent was happening now on an almost daily basis as the war between my parents intensified.

Here I am aged fourteen, at the barrier at Victoria Station, just back from a school skiing trip to Saas-Fee. Dad is supposed to be meeting me. I've spent the night in a couchette and have had very little sleep. I know I look dishevelled and not my best. I'm trying not to think about the boy who said to me the night before, 'You look better in the dark.' I feel lost and rather crushed, with a dash of fear thrown into the mix. Where is Dad? No sign of him.

My school-friends, met by loving and attentive parents, scatter. I am alone. I have the phone number of my best friend's parents written on a piece of paper, just in case. Just in case I have nowhere to stay tonight. I can still remember that number today: Noble (602) 3157. My best friend lives in a huge rambling apartment in a magisterial block of flats opposite the Kensington Odeon Cinema and next door to the Commonwealth Institute. I want to live there too with them and for her wonderful parents (who are still happily married) to adopt me, although I don't say this. They know me well. They have carpeted bathrooms and go on holiday to ski resorts in the winter and hot white places in the summer. There's an ease and a happiness in their household. My friend's mother is an attentive listener. I can tell her things I would never tell my mother about my feelings. I feel soothed when I talk to her. Weirdly, we share the same surname but appear to be no relation.

I assume Dad is at the House of Lords, which is where he's taken to hanging out in these strange, post-split no-man's land days between being with Mum and being a separate, self-determining entity; in other words a single man. All that is about to take on a new significance, as I will shortly realise.

I take a cab to the Palace of Westminster, and even in my shabby, somewhat sleepless state I pass the inspection of the kindly lackeys at the desk: 'Eldest unmarried daughter, sign here, please, my dear . . .' and set off, mulling over my newly discovered label as 'eldest unmarried daughter'. I am the only unmarried daughter, as far as I know. On up the great, red-carpeted stairs, through various antechambers, feeling more and more Lilliputian, pausing to admire the huge painting of the trial of Strafford, past the library (no women allowed) where I glimpse a selection of ancient peers enjoying a post-prandial nap, to find Dad in the bar. He rises from the table where he is sitting with a group of friends when he sees me in the doorway, giving a half-hearted wave. Seated in the chair next to him is a bare-armed woman with the kind of bullet-proof, honey-coloured helmet hair-do favoured by Raine Spencer and the gossip columnist of *Harpers & Queen*, the fearsome 'Jennifer' of 'Jennifer's Diary', a friend of hers, as it happens. She is wearing a poison-green silk sheath dress (by Worth, she later tells me) that accentuates her slimness. At the same time, however, it attempts to hide the oddness of her shape: broad-shouldered with slender arms and elegant, spillikin legs like Osbert Lancaster's famous role model, Maudie Littlehampton, for she is also curiously barrel-shaped around her middle, without any waist at all, which makes her resemble a triangle standing on its tip.

When I first see her, she is seated, her tiny, twig-like legs crossed at the knee, crocodile stiletto dangling off one rather large, bony foot – a crocodile, she will later tell me, that she'd shot herself. I feel immediate solidarity with the croc. I am, as a potential stepdaughter, firmly in her cross-hairs. There is a matching bag, too, apparently, but I can't remember if it was in evidence that fateful afternoon. What is immediately obvious, however, is that this is a woman who will let nothing get in the way of what she wants. And what she wants is Dad.

He's her latest trophy. His scalp might as well be hanging from her non-existent waist. Blimey, is all I can think. I've never met anyone like Rosemary before. A woman who shoots crocodiles and has their skin transformed into a pair of shoes and a bag. A sense of the unseen hands of a thousand nameless lackeys passes briefly through my mind; the faceless ones who have to deal with the beast from corpse to bag. Rosemary is one of those people who gives off the vibe of having a lot of flunkeys around to do her dirty work: private jets, private islands, staff, including, probably, a taxidermist, to help with preserving all the dead animals she has shot over the years.

In retrospect, there was an unhealthy sense of menace about this woman, slightly muted perhaps for the purposes of polite society but unmistakably present. I clocked it at once, without quite knowing what it was. The fact that she was skilled with a gun was a warning sign. She was lethal.

Why, in God's name, had my Little Boy Lost Dad hooked up with a woman like this? Later, I was told by my father's London landlady – the wonderfully named Vi Fearnley-Whittingstall (who only took peers and wing commanders as lodgers) – that they had met at a party somewhere, probably a rather raffish one, given by one of my father's newly discovered gang of friends in the House of Lords. Mrs FW did not approve of Rosemary and told me so. I was both baffled and rattled by this confidence. What in hell's name was I supposed to do with it?

After his difficult time with my mother, it was obvious to me, I suppose, that Dad was enjoying a new-found sense of freedom and fun. It was 1970, after all, sex, drugs, rock 'n' roll, even for dads. Drink would have played its part, too. Rosemary was an active alcoholic, and her behaviour influenced my father's. He drank hugely when he was with her, much more than he ever had with Mum. But still, in retrospect, it was *un coup de foudre, un décharge électrique*, although I didn't know what that was then, and we all know what happens when the *décharge électrique* wears off.

Formerly married to a Scottish multi-millionaire baronet, Rosemary had lived the kind of jet-set life I never even knew existed – well, I sort of did but didn't think it applied to anyone I would ever know: an island in the Bahamas; a huge shooting estate on another very different kind of island in the Hebrides, not to mention a social life on New York's Upper East Side when she was in town – her ex bore an uncanny resemblance to Clark Gable, apparently, and was always getting the best tables as a result – endless shooting trips in exotic places, hence the poor old croc; a couturier in Paris, nannies, butlers, game-keepers, lackeys hither and yon, all devoted to doing Rosemary's will – or, at least, that was the impression I got. Her life, it seemed, was so complex on so many fronts that she needed a vast team of people dedicated to helping her get everything the way she wanted it, down to the last detail. Except that somehow, mysteriously, everything kept going wrong and had been doing so for quite a long time. People simply would not do her bidding.

She was by this time in her mid-forties and in crisis, although she would never have acknowledged it. I look back at her now almost with a sense of pity – *almost*. At the time, I found her grotesque and implacable in her rightness. She was deliberately cruel. Her attitude to life and to other people was based on the assumption so often spoken of in the rooms of AA of being 'special and different'.

Very quickly, I would discover quite how wrong her life had already gone, in spite of the massive privilege she had enjoyed from birth onwards, as the daughter of a Tory MP and, subsequently, as the wife of a very rich baronet and mother to five children. She was always embroiled in conflict in one area of her life or another. When I met her, the fracas was centred on her ex-lover. During the interminable years of her marriage to my father, the endless on-going drama attached itself to different people: her ex-husband, her ex-lover, my mother, her own putative pregnancy by my father (which, thankfully, came to nothing), a lawyer who was first an ally, then a crook, on and on *ad nauseam*.

Almost every sentence she uttered had the coda 'Am I right?' attached to it. Any half-baked amateur Freudian would realise that was a huge neon sign flashing 'trouble'. But I had no defence against her as a teenager. I was a sitting duck, not to mention a rather overweight one, in her opinion. I now recognise that this behaviour is a central plank of the alcoholic lifestyle. Her life was unmanageable, out of control, a total mess, and fighting with people was as necessary to her as the whisky she drank from mid-morning until dusk and beyond. As a raging alcoholic, the endless, on-going chaos was a means of distracting her from her real problem: herself.

After Rosemary's marriage to the multi-millionaire baronet was over, she went off-piste and shacked up with what the popular press later loved to describe as a 'gamekeeper' (a former commando sergeant whom she'd met at a fashionable West London shooting range) at yet another shooting estate in Inverness-shire, where, living as his wife and taking his name, she became pregnant and had a daughter by him. Predictably, the relationship soured – he was a drinker, too, according to reports (alcohol, *again*) – and, one Sunday morning in 1967, fuelled by rage at discovering the shooting lodge was in Rosemary's name only, he cracked, and went on the rampage, firing several shots into the study of the house where her former ladyship was lurking, along with two others.

I mean, wow! It *was* quite a story. When I recounted it to other people, they would say the same: *Wow!* I told it to lend myself some lustre, some interest, to try to extract some value out of what had happened for my own benefit. But I always felt flat afterwards. Really, it was just a sad, shabby tale of a pair of boozers who had had a spectacular bust-up, one of whom had thought that taking a pot-shot or two at her ladyship was a way of keeping her in check. It was, after all, a language she was fluent in.

The gamekeeper-who-wasn't-really-a-gamekeeper was sentenced to nine years in jail for this drunken shindig and, of course, the press went nuts: the scandal, with its Lady Chatterley-esque overtones, had all the juicy ingredients of a terrific tabloid toff-fest. This middle-aged woman over whom such inglorious battles had raged was now to be my future stepmother. When I mentioned her name, people rolled their eyes. I mean, she was hardly Helen of Troy, although I suspect she thought she might be. The ancient Greeks must have rolled their eyes about Helen of Troy, too, and all the trouble she brought.

When I first met her, she was obsessed with the idea that the ex-lover commando gamekeeper was plotting to kill her from inside his jail. The fact that he sent my mother a Christmas card from jail by mistake, getting his ladyships in a muddle (much to my mother's outrage), suggests the reality was rather more pedestrian. Jail was probably a relief after living with Rosemary.

The child of the union had to be adopted by my father to keep her safe, according to Rosemary, in case the vengeful gamekeeper/ commando came after her, too. I watched as my father was sucked into this vortex of drama and conspiracy and remained there, waving his arms about futilely, endlessly firefighting absurd causes on the domestic front as well as the political one (encouraged by Rosemary), for the next twelve or so years. Each fed off the other: it made them feel important, I suppose, that they mattered.

Going back, however: at dinner in the House of Lords that first night, Dad told me, proudly, that he was going to marry Rosemary. *But you're still married to Mum*, I said, which he didn't like, so he ignored it. He was a goner, I could see that. Or could I? Is all this the wisdom of hindsight? It's difficult to know now, so many years later. What I did understand, however, was that the white heat of his attention was now focused on Rosemary. My mother referred to her, rather unoriginally, as '*that* woman'. Harrods continually muddled my mother's account with *that* woman's (they only had two people with that surname on their books, so one wonders what happened to people called Jones or Smith), charging Mum for lots of expensive underwear – silk bras, lace knickers – which, of course, enraged her as she bought her own steadfastly utilitarian pants at M&S in Dumfries. Not for my mother the careless vulgarity of the unthinking rich.

That was a watershed night. I kind of knew it at the time. Dad had left his old life and crossed over into a new and different one, and I would have to fit into this new world whether I wanted to or not. I had always felt on his side in his battle with my mother and had seen myself as his plucky comrade in arms, his trusted confidante. It was to me that he had said he felt like 'a pariah' in his own house and when I asked him what that meant, he told me he was an outcast. I still remember the sadness I felt for him when he explained this to me, and the feeling of rage towards my autocratic mother, but I also felt that we were comrades in arms and I liked that feeling and held it close to me for comfort.

Back at school, I received a letter from my mother, who had got wind of the meeting at the House of Lords, condemning my father's new wife-to-be, more or less implying that Rosemary was a harlot. I was shocked and upset at the vitriol in this letter (with my old expertise I knew that some of it was intended for me as a warning). I made the mistake of telling my father about the letter and, typically, instead of dealing with it himself, he told Rosemary, who told her lawyer. She was the kind of person who always had a lawyer on tap. The lawyer wrote to my mother threatening her with libel, although the letter in question to a *child* had been procured unjustly. Rosemary wouldn't have got very far with *that* but my mother, instead of stepping back or attacking Rosemary, attacked me instead. She called me a traitor and didn't speak to me for a year. I was sacked. I was also trapped between two crazy women, my mother and my stepmother. Alcohol started to creep into this painful void in my life. I felt comfortless, adrift, afraid, scorched by powerful feelings of fear and resentment, but mostly fear, which I couldn't deal with. Both my parents had abandoned me in different ways. My worst fears had come true. I remember crying a lot at school, being unable to sleep. My concentration suffered and so did my schoolwork. My aim of going to Oxford began to seem impossible.

Looking back, I realise I was having a breakdown. I kept Dubonnet in the Ribena bottle in my washing cubicle and had a nightly swig, or several, to take the edge off. I already saw booze as my friend, soothing and benevolent, powerful, entrancing. My story is a classic case of how alcoholism begins: its dark roots take hold in the empty space left by a lack of love; its manure is feelings of worthlessness and self-loathing, of being unlovable, of despair. In these conditions it thrives. I had inherited a genetic predisposition to use alcohol as a way of numbing emotional pain and this period of my life lit the fuse. I became, without being aware of it, fatally engulfed by the idea that drink was the answer to all my problems. This monstrous mental, physical and spiritual illness already had me in its clutches. I see alcoholism as being in the grip of something like King Kong. He holds you gently at first and you're unaware of what is happening – it feels like a safe, comfy place – and by the time you realise what's going on it's too late. It's a battle no single individual can ever win, as I learnt to my cost. And I should know. I tried for years to control my drinking and failed every single time. I had no 'off' button. Once I had that first drink I couldn't stop. Not a chance.

When I think about my relationship with my father I can see now that my desire was always to protect him, to forgive him, to think well of him. That was my instinct where he was concerned. But why? I talked about all this years later in therapy, and my male therapist said to me: 'But he didn't intervene with your mother when she was behaving badly towards you, even when they were together.' I brushed this aside – it didn't fit how I saw the facts – but now I realise it was true. He didn't intervene and he turned away from me when it suited him. My loyalty to him was always greater than his to me. Now, I was the outcast, the pariah: I fitted nowhere: not with my extremely troubled mother, nor with my alcoholic, poisonous stepmother who hated me and made sure I never had a moment alone with my father. But what was most hurtful, I suppose, was that my father appeared to have forgotten who I was. I became a stranger to him, a nuisance, someone to unburden himself of. I was a girl (still a second-class citizen in those days in my kind of family) and he off-loaded me to Rosemary to deal with.

My stepmother was critical of my appearance, and my father, unforgivably in retrospect, joined in. She sent me to some quack private doctor in Harley Street for drugs to make me thinner. My father approved. He was a lover of the thin. I was not thin. Or not thin enough. The fact was that I was no longer under his protection, no longer enjoying the immunity of a parent's uncritical love, which I thought I had had with him, if not with my mother. With this new woman, the archetypal wicked stepmother, I had no immunity at all. She was my version of Jane Eyre's Aunt Reed.

This was when I really took to drink. Earlier, I had tried not eating to control the way I felt, but alcohol was much easier. All the pieces were in place, and I turned into its dark embrace with a feeling of relief. I lost my virginity at about the same time with some nameless toff at a party in a house in Hampstead. I was being careless with myself and this recklessness with something precious was all part of a greater pattern.

As a bridesmaid at a London wedding, aged five, I had got drunk on the remains of what people left in their glasses at the reception. I remember draining glasses and throwing them over the terrace balcony into the Thames. I had to be removed by my mother who thought it was hilarious and taken back to the Basil Street Hotel to sleep it off. The reception was at the House of Lords, which, now I think about it, has turned out to be a slightly doomed place for me.

But the point of recounting this is that, with hindsight, the template was in place, genetically speaking. Alcohol was waiting for me to find it. What child goes on drinking dregs, after all? Most would spit out the disgusting stuff, but I didn't. I must have liked the feeling of being smashed. I remember my great-aunt bearing down on me – she bore a considerable resemblance to Queen Mary – and telling me off. I said something rude along the lines of 'Bugger orff, you old bag' – I can't remember exactly what, but she was horrified. I still remember the expression on her face and the gleeful sense of reckless power it gave me. This was my first time being truly drunk. A harbinger of things to come.

The unbearable feelings I had around the long and painful break-up of my parents' marriage (wrecked marriages go on sending up bubbles from the seabed for years after the actual break) was like a switch once thrown that turned on the genetic patterning. A whole hidden underground fire was lit within me that started to devour me from the inside. The obsession with alcohol was just beginning. Very, very quickly it seemed as necessary to me as breathing and, like breathing, it was unconscious. It was just the way things were. I was enmeshed.

In my early teens, I was acutely aware of the fact that Rosemary drank too much, much too much, but what did I know? Whenever I stayed with her and my father in her hideous house in Regent's Park where all the furnishings were shit-coloured, from the carpets to the bedspreads to the curtains and sofas, I remember how she would appear in the first-floor drawing room at about 11 a.m. – not that late, I suppose, for a woman of her class without a job. Her child was looked after by a nanny who must, I suppose, have taken her to school. To my knowledge, Rosemary never did any of that.

Eleven o'clock in the morning meant not coffee (which she must have had in bed to help with her hangover) but whisky; whisky, moreover, in a special, huge, fat cut-glass tumbler to gentrify it. The glass somehow made it OK. I can still remember her enormous gold charm bracelet clunking against that glass – her large and ugly hands must have been shaking – and the fuchsia stain of lipstick on the fag perched on the edge of the matching cut-glass ashtray the size of a curling stone.

I had no sense then that this was my direction of travel, no idea whatsoever about the perils of alcohol or that I had a genetic predisposition towards using it when I felt overwhelmed by my feelings; *what will become of* me. All I knew then was that I hated her but that, in order to survive, I must conceal it. Somehow, in spite of Rosemary's deeply dysfunctional relationship with alcohol, it seemed attractive. I needed *something* to help me, and that something was always going to be drink. It's amazing to me now that even at my boarding school in the late 1960s and early 1970s we had some form of sex education – a banana and a condom float into my mind – but nothing at all about drugs (this was the era of hippies, so they were in the news constantly) or, more importantly, the legal drug that is alcohol. I was already acutely aware of the benefits and totally ignorant of the perils. By the end of my drinking I was that curious creature who was a world-expert on boozing but who knew *nothing whatever* about alcoholism. I learnt in AA to my utter astonishment that alcoholism is a deadly mental illness, as well as a physical one, not to mention its capacity to completely crush your soul, but as a young girl I saw alcohol as a magic wand that would transform me into the someone else I had so wanted to be for so long. I didn't want to be me, I really, really didn't.

Chapter Four

Home

Arabella

I found a picture I drew of the house not so long ago when I was clearing out a drawer. It shocked me, and I immediately shut the drawer as if it contained something frightening. My brown childhood hand with its dirty fingernails reaching up out of the past and into the present, unbidden, just like that.

The picture is wonky and outsized, the roof reaching up fearfully high into the sky as narrow and sharp as a pin while the house itself appears unbelievably small, buckling under the weight of the top structure. There are windows but these are also small and dotted around the building in strange places: one just below the roof, another on the far-left-hand side near the edge. There is no door. Of all the obvious things about the picture, it is the fact of there being no door that strikes me most. No way in.

We moved there after my parents had divorced. How old was I? I always say four but something about this assertion feels wrong, as if I am making it up. Perhaps I was five. When my eldest daughter was five she seemed to pass over some threshold of consciousness where she is able to master the lived past and the near future.

I don't think I had mastered either when they divorced, or maybe that's because the present had crumbled beneath my feet, leaving everything else so structurally unsound as to be dangerous and boarded up.

Either way, I have no memories of my father ever living with us. No distant sound of his footsteps on the hall floor from a bedroom in which I should have been asleep. No sound of his key in the lock in the early evening. No sound of his voice. Now he's dead, I strain to remember his voice, but maybe I've been straining to remember his voice all my life, whether he was dead or alive.

I read once somewhere that children of alcoholics grieve for their parents long before they actually die of alcoholism; that life and grief are fatally intertwined in a way that is almost impossible to unravel in adulthood. Children of alcoholics are recognised now by charities and on the internet, famous people and politicians speak publicly of their own experiences of growing up in the shadows of addiction. The important work of blowing the doors off that particular house of shame has begun. But still, there's a voice that persists in my head: *pull yourself together, he never shed any tears for you*. Or, worse: *it was a long time ago now*; said in a voice that would tolerate no argument. Instead, for years, I just carried around a grief that bled messily into other parts of my life at unexpected and inconvenient times: sudden, hot tears in the middle of job interviews or a burning rage that I would direct towards stunned friends who backed away.

We lived in the house in the picture in the late 1980s after my parents had sold the family house in a nicer part of London, a part you wouldn't be ashamed to bring your friends home to. The new house was in a shabbier part of town, although not actually that far away. Because of this proximity between the old house and the new house, we passed the streets that belonged to the old life all the time, some unsayable sadness gripping me as we drove on, my fingers digging into the car seat until they hurt. It was a nice street, I suppose; early Victorian houses with balustrades, some repainted to give an idea of their former glory, some not, their frontage reeking of desolation. Ours was not. Which is not to say that Mum didn't make it nice inside; our things, a mixture of inherited and acquired, gave everywhere we lived the same unmistakable idea of home; a rootedness with the distant past, faces peering out from photographs and pictures, a past that was far more soothing than recent history, newly shattered by divorce. Children adapt quickly to new realities. Soon the new house was home, its arrangements similar, but not identical, to the other houses.

Lots of houses, but I'm still wandering around that one in my dreams, well over a quarter of a century since we were there. *We will not regret the past nor wish to shut the door on it.* That's a saying in AA, recited in a reading called the Promises, read aloud at the end of meetings. It's a kind of wish-fulfilment mandate that we read aloud until the promises come true. But there's something about the metaphor of doors in relation to the past that speaks to me most, perhaps because living in active addiction had all the feeling of living in a derelict house: some doors swung on their rusty hinges, some were boarded up with nails and others; perhaps the most dangerous of all were just doorways leading onto a gaping mass of nothing. The idea that I could leave a door to the past open, without automatically slamming it shut, was – and continues to be – revolutionary. Already as a child I rejected doors, literally drew them out, as per my picture, but could there be a compromise with the past whereby its door was open, invitingly?

It was in that house that I pushed through a door that was firmly shut to little hands. I must have pushed through the door of my bedroom to get there, the light shining on the landing to guide me down the stairs and onto the tiles of the hall floor, cool beneath my bare feet. Normally, there were other people in the house. To keep us from running out of money altogether, we had a succession of lodgers who lived in the spare room and Mum often had friends over in the evenings.

She had a boyfriend, too; an artist who didn't live with us but was often there after lights out, the smell of his cigars wafting up through the banisters. The fact of him being an artist felt important: here was someone who could shape reality on a canvas as Mum did on a page, a conjuror, a shapeshifter. Mostly, I liked it when other people were there because it diluted the strength of Mum's sadness. She was always happier in other people's company, her face brightening, her voice different; she found a home in other people more than she ever found a home in herself. On this particular night, though, she was not at home anywhere.

I have, like most people, very few memories of being five. I find this even more disconcerting than I used to now that I have children. What will she remember of the long afternoons we spend together? Will she remember the games we play on the way to the bath, the way we carefully balance the boats on the side of the bath with little toy mermaids and wait for them to capsize? I don't think so.

What I recall of being five is piecemeal: the pattern of a dressing gown I wore when I was allowed to come downstairs, the feel of the sofa underneath my bare legs when I was watching television, the sight of cigarette smoke weaving through the air in a sunlit room, the smell of a babysitter I disliked. These memories, which must have taken place in many different places, all seem to gather in my mind in that one house. Some crucial link between safety and home became fractured there but I'm still working out why.

She must have been drinking for a long time by the time I came downstairs. How do children sense the quantity of alcohol drunk by those around them? Not in metrics of bottles or glasses but in other, more instinctive, bodily measures: a flushed face or a shaky hand, the metallic tang of booze on the breath at bedtime, perhaps. But these are all physical signs that I'm not sure children are acutely attuned to. Love is as plain and vital as oxygen; does it matter that your mother has a flushed face if she is looking after you? No, children measure the line between safety and danger in far more subtle ways: a barked instruction or an impatient word. Or, more confusingly still, excessive declarations of love and promises, all to be forgotten the next day. How did I know, then, aged five, that she was drunk? I don't know that I did particularly, but I knew I shouldn't have been there, that I had crossed some vital line between innocence and knowing. She knew it, too.

She was standing at the kitchen sink, her back to me. Twenty-two years later, in a different kitchen, I would tell her that I was an alcoholic myself and she would still have her back to me.

I didn't see the knife in her hands, or maybe the cloak of memory has drawn itself tightly around me. Maybe this entire memory has become informed by the account of it that I heard given by Mum in an AA meeting years afterwards. It's hard to pin it down. But the arrangement of the kitchen itself remains vivid. There was a large table to the left on which the detritus of drinking was scattered: an ashtray stuffed with cigarette butts, a Habitat bottle opener, the kind you could get everywhere in the eighties that I never see now, and a green hardback diary open on a page with her handwriting visible. Although she wrote her novels on a giant Amstrad computer whose green cursor flashed menacingly from her study, it was in her diaries that she seemed to pour most of herself. I have never been able to read her handwriting with any kind of fluency, but throughout my childhood, these vital documents were left on tables, chairs, unmade beds, car seats, just about anywhere you cared to think, as if she dared someone to pick it up and read it.

That evening, she hadn't dared anyone except herself, hadn't bargained on anything other than total privacy. But the arrangement of the table, and the way the objects were scattered across it haphazardly, has stayed with me, I think because it struck some other chord to do with the very chaotic arrangement of Mum's internal life at that time; the business of her private life. Her home was where the bottle and the ashtray were, but these things were neither comfort nor intimacy to her. At best, they provided some relief, at worst, they propelled her towards the kitchen sink with a knife in her hand.

I don't remember the exchange that took place between us once she noticed I was there. Memory protects us from the blunt edges of the past, the pain filed behind some closed door in our heads that we never open. Until, of course, we do. She must have gone through the motions in a panic; led me upstairs with her heart racing, tucked me back into bed and returned, with some relief, to the kitchen. Maybe she looked at the knife, discarded on the chopping board, and felt a longing to finish what she had started.

She didn't kill herself that night and I went back to sleep.

***

When I was drinking, and for a long time in sobriety, I found it hard to feel at home anywhere. *I lost my home when I was sixteen*, I would say to people before explaining slowly and circuitously how my mother had remarried for the third time and sold our home to buy another with her new husband. How the things that had followed us around for years were suddenly in different surroundings in a house in which I was not entirely welcome. How I had nowhere to go at the weekends. How I stayed for weeks in friends' houses, until the chaos of my drinking booted me on to somewhere else. *I want to go home*, I would say to people when I was drunk, and the ones who hadn't heard the story would listen and nod sympathetically and the ones who had would roll their eyes and scowl behind my back.

It is not entirely coincidental, I think, that my alcoholic decade began with the loss of a home, although this is only a half-truth. I used to think that this fact, more than any other, was the Ariadne's thread to my life, that the labyrinth could only be navigated with this piece of information. But when I first started going to AA, I noticed with some annoyance that plenty of alcoholics say they don't feel at home anywhere. It's how most people open the narrative of their addiction, *I didn't fit in*, which is another way of saying you find no home in your work, in your relationships, or, most upsettingly, in yourself. Not feeling at home did not, as I thought, single me out or speak to any of the peculiarities of my childhood. It had the opposite effect: it assured my place among the other self-proclaimed homeless. Alcohol, conversely, feels like home: a familiar horizon, a known landscape, a warm room, a shared language, a rehearsed and repeated ritual. *Nowhere to call home?* Pour yourself a drink and make a home amongst the familiar fantasies of alcohol only for them to evaporate the next day and leave you out, again, on the street, your possessions scattered around you.

Of all the houses that we lived in, the house in the picture was not the most memorable. I can't find any photographs of it in the small collection I keep. But photographs and memory are caught in a strange, non-reciprocal dance. Why, for example, do I look at a photograph of my mother and me standing outside a London terraced house and immediately think we are in the house from the picture I drew? All the evidence points to the contrary: I am much older and wearing a different school uniform. Still, the association persists. In another photograph, Mum smiles back at the camera from her desk, a cigarette burning in an ashtray beside her elbow with a wine glass next to it, her expression faintly distracted. There is no giant Amstrad computer behind her, a relic she has told me she abandoned when we left St Elmo Road. It doesn't matter. Home, or some idea of it forged in that house, stalks all the photographs of my childhood. In the writing of this book, I ask her about St Elmo Road, trying to parse some crucial fact from her impressions. 'It had dry rot,' she reminds me. 'It wasn't a nice house really.' Dry rot: the silent decay of a building's timber leading to eventual collapse of the structure. Suddenly, the topsy-turvy picture by my child's hand makes more sense.

Once, in a meeting, I heard her talk about St Elmo Road. I don't think I knew she would be speaking to the assembled group, or I might not have come. After two or so years of sobriety, we tried to keep our meetings separate. She would go to hers and I would go to mine; it seemed to work better that way and our sponsors always advised it. To begin with, I missed her. I wanted to share the meeting in the way we had shared alcohol and so much else. Gradually, I got used to it.

That day, I had come back to Oxford unexpectedly in a fit of restlessness, unable to cope with myself in London. My depression, a shadow I could never quite shrug off, had returned; a sense of restlessness dogged me and left me sleepless, each morning the same wide-eyed agony as the last. At Paddington, I got on a train and hoped that the sight of the landscape rushing by would change my feelings. It didn't, and I reluctantly concluded that a meeting was the only place I had left to go.

She was laughing when I came in. She can always make people laugh, especially in meetings; she has the writer's knack of drawing people into her mental landscape with a light touch. It was a packed meeting and I pulled up a metal folding chair and skulked at the back, hoping not to be recognised. After playing her story for laughs – the bottle of vodka hidden in the frozen turkey and other anecdotes – her tone changed. She began talking about the Samaritans, about how she had called them one night after she had tried to kill herself when she had been drunk. I listened in the way an eavesdropper does to a conversation through a wall, with fascination and something bordering on regret, knowing I could never unhear the words.

'It was in the house we lived in right after my second divorce from the father of my child; there was something about the house that was never quite right. Something haunted, I suppose. The roof was falling down, the whole place was riddled with dry rot, a decay that ate into me at that time too, I suppose. My daughter, Arabella, she was four at the time – many of you know her actually, she's sober now in these rooms – she came downstairs in her nightie and caught me standing at the kitchen sink with a kitchen knife in my hands. I wanted to kill myself, I just couldn't take it any more. She stopped me, I guess. But I drank for many more years after that.'

From where I sat, I could begin to feel the mood of the meeting shift, some higher emotional gear had been engaged, and the room became quieter. I knew that she wouldn't have said those things if she had known I was there; I knew I had to leave. My unassuming presence in that room that night, tucked away at the back almost behind the tea tray, suddenly became too much. I ran out into the square by the church, fumbling through my bag desperately for a cigarette and a lighter, my breathing so exaggerated that I had to sit down on a bench. To look at me, you might have thought I looked like any young girl in a student town who had had too much to drink: eyes wide, faintly dishevelled, swept away by some emotional distress. In some ways, I did feel drunk. Drunk on the past, intoxicated by the mention of the house and that night there, all imbibed from my mother's voice. It can't have been a shock to hear her say those things; in adolescence I think I must have reconciled what she said about the Samaritans with that incident. Somewhere along the way, I must have joined the dots, however messily memory had presented them.

No, the shock of it was the mention of the house. I always thought that it was there that I had lost a sense of home, like a teddy bear left on a train or a bus. Pinning the feeling to one place gave me a sense of control; Ariadne weaving her thread through the labyrinth with the ravening minotaur close by. But it wasn't that at all. No, as I sat on that bench, I realised that home – a feeling, a place, a substance – was not lost so much as behind a closed door, if only I would push it open.

After a while, I got up and pushed through the closed door into the meeting.

Julia

Home

I never felt at home, not in myself, anyway. I felt familiarity with the place I lived in, but that's not the same thing by any means as being at home in yourself. When I was drinking I couldn't stand myself and the idea of being alone for more than a few hours filled me with an overwhelming sense of fear and emptiness. Home was a place I was scared to be alone in, so I drank. Drink was where I felt at home, or so I told myself, in spite of mounting evidence to the contrary.

One of the reasons I've been able to get sober and stay sober in AA is that, amongst alcoholics, these feelings – feelings of being afraid of yourself and others – are commonplace and discussed all the time. Alcoholics feel persecuted by their thoughts. Your worst fears, the things you are most ashamed and frightened of, are common currency when alcoholics get together. This radical honesty saved my life. Sharing my fears in meetings with other alcoholics reduced them in size, and I began to feel an actual sense of safety when I went to an AA meeting – that concept was so alien to me I didn't even know what it was to start with – so much so that within a matter of weeks, even the thought of a meeting I was going to go to in the evening gave me more pleasure than the thought of a drink. Because of this, I think, the physical craving to drink left me very quickly, which is extraordinary, really. For years I had automatically turned to alcohol to numb my fears and I was completely physically addicted, but being able to talk honestly about what was going on with me – whatever it was that day, instead of drinking to blackout – began to heal me very fast. Talking into a safe space in a circle of other alcoholics made me feel I belonged in a way nothing else came close to. I felt understood. I felt heard. I felt held.

I was getting the psychological relief I had sought through the bottle for so long and I quickly began to feel knitted into the fabric of AA, as if the fellowship somehow kept me afloat – a sense of being at home amongst my own tribe. I'd enter a room and be greeted and recognised and do the same in return. A warm, happy feeling would come over me. It was beautiful. I'd finally found my home, usually in some dismal church hall with a mug of instant coffee in my hand. Who knew? Sometimes I'd come to a meeting clutching the aforementioned cup of coffee instead of a glass of wine and be amazed all over again. *Look at me not drinking*. It was a miracle. I'd drunk alcoholically for more than three decades and now I was sober for a day and then another and another and another . . . I couldn't believe my luck. I'd find myself having completely unfamiliar feelings in meetings of actual *joy*: joy to be there, joy in laughing at myself, intense joy in hearing the stories of others, joy at being part of a gang. People in AA refer to this state in early sobriety as being on a 'pink cloud', which I was. But a shard of that pinkness pierced my heart and has remained with me for years now. I still feel it every time I go to a meeting.

AA meetings, my new home, usually ran for an hour. Sometimes there was a reading from *The Big Book*, AA's handbook, put together by its founders and published in 1939, or there would be what's known as a 'share' or a 'chair' – no one ever seems to know which it is – in which a member talks about their experience of alcoholism and how they got sober. I found myself identifying powerfully with the stories I heard. It didn't seem to matter who was talking and how different they were from me; I invariably connected with their words, and the more this happened, the more a part of it all I felt myself to be. I, the outsider, a part of something, at long last. I adored it.

Two large cream scrolls dominate every AA meeting room: The Twelve Steps and Twelve Traditions of Alcoholics Anonymous. I used to stare at them in early meetings trying to understand them. *We admitted we were powerless over alcohol, that our lives had become unmanageable.* It had never occurred to me that my life was 'unmanageable', although it so clearly was, nor had I believed that I was 'powerless' over alcohol. I couldn't resist it and I certainly couldn't stop, but describing this as being 'powerless' somehow allowed me to understand that acknowledging and accepting my powerlessness over alcohol made me powerful. To be honest, I still don't really understand how it works but what I did know was that I was being handed a new map of the world, devised by AA, and given the freedom of a new language with which to manage my illness. Willpower is not enough. I had massive willpower (what my ex-husband described as the Hamilton 'super will') but it never stopped me from drinking, not a chance.

Powerlessness and 'a power greater than myself' are very closely linked in AA. If you can humble yourself enough to admit that you're powerless, then that other power steps into the void. God, Higher Power, whatever you want to call it.

I had always believed in a Christian God, but my God was a punisher and a bit of a sadist: he took an inventory of my life ceaselessly, and the verdict was always the same: *no good*. My spirituality, such as it was, was unripe. It had withered on the vine, the seed fallen on stone. I was a hardened critic of myself and of other people, too. God was still the finger-wagging, all-seeing authority figure with eyes in the back of his head from my childhood, my mother in disguise.

I was so broken when I arrived in AA that I wisely didn't reject the idea of a different version of God to my own, which, given my experience, I might very easily have done. Instead, I waited. Gradually, very gradually, as my sobriety deepened, I began to discern another kind of God altogether, who moved mysteriously in the rooms amongst the instant coffee, the scrolls, and the ever-present laughter, and, sometimes, the tears; a God you could see and hear in what people said and how clear their eyes looked. I went back to church and began to hear the gospel in a completely different way, as if my ears had been opened by my experience in the rooms. Gradually, I began to understand that I really had found my place in the world at long last, entirely through my experience of AA; I was broken, true, but I realised for the first time in my life that I could also be healed. I had never had this experience before, ever. In church I'd felt an unworthy imposter. I had to come at my religion through AA to understand it, to feel it and to know its truth.

This feeling of not being at home was already rooted in me when I was very young. I was suspicious of my parents. *Were they really my parents?* I remember aged five watching my father feeding the dogs and asking him if I was adopted. I wasn't, as it turned out, but I felt extraneous, sort of grafted on to the family I found myself in, rather than the *I am the vine, ye are the branches* kind of family feeling I saw my contemporaries enjoying with their parents. I longed for that unspoken ease. Alcoholics feel like perpetual outsiders, even before they start drinking. I certainly did. Scratch an alcoholic and you'll find someone who feels like a misfit, at odds with themselves. Once, I heard someone describe this as feeling like you've been rolled naked in ground glass, which sums it up pretty well.

For the alcoholic, this inner dis-ease is instantly soothed by booze and the immense cloud of almost indescribable romance that accompanies it, the fantasist's friend. *Oh,* you think, *I see . . .* this is how *normal* people feel. The beam-me-up swiftness of the way alcohol works is what makes it so utterly compelling. Home, if only I had known it, you think, is here in the snugness of the bar with its other weird and wonderful denizens, the dog under the stool, the guy reading the newspaper by the fire with his pint, the proprietor washing glasses and chatting, or it's sitting outside at a particular, gratifyingly seedy café in a French town where the locals gossip amongst themselves, ignoring incomers but somehow, tacitly, managing to give the impression that they approve of our consumption; or it's that lunch in Tuscany somewhere on a long, hot afternoon under the vines with one indistinguishable carafe after another, so much less incriminating than bottles, so much easier to deny how much one has had. Boozers are a fraternity, easily recognisable to one another, never mind the language.

Very quickly, though, like the soul hunter it is, booze exacts its price by throwing an invisible but immensely strong mesh like an unseen net over your inner life: its presence irrevocably alters your view of the world, without your even being aware of it, because it has captured that most powerful of organs: the imagination.

When I began to drink heavily in my late teens as an antidote, amongst other things, to the chronic social unease I felt at parties and the habit I had of blushing purple in public, it was like logging in to the way the world *really* was, the way I imagined other people saw it or felt it. Suddenly, I got it. It was OK. More importantly, *I* was OK. I could cope.

My drinking didn't take years to build up – rather, like a Harrier jump jet, it was a vertical take-off, nought to three thousand feet in a split second. I loved it. But right from the beginning, booze did weird things to me: I threw up, had hill-cracking hangovers, almost instantly became addicted physically and mentally. I had that mental obsession with alcohol that is one of the hallmarks of alcoholism right from the word go. I couldn't go a day without a drink, even half a day was hard. As previously mentioned, there is a saying: 'A man takes a drink, a drink takes a drink, a drink takes a man.' I was 'taken' in that sense by the illness almost immediately, stolen away by it, like someone in a gruesome fairy tale and placed under a powerful spell. Alcoholism conceals its savagery until you're hooked, like the ogre it is.

Once upon a time, there was a certain, rather louche bar in a beautiful, ancient, frequently visited Provençal French town where I felt my most Julia-ish: a bohemian writer drinking in the summer sun, the leaves of the plane trees making pretty shadow patterns on the ancient walls opposite, the bored child ignored, the work assignment unbegun. I spent a lot of time in this place with my artist boyfriend. I allowed the romance of alcoholism to delude me into thinking I was at home, in my right place, exactly where I belonged.

Advertisers have long known all about the selling power of the romance of alcohol: booze ads are set in hot countries for a reason; the stunning backdrops – like that of my favourite French town – reinforce the message that booze is our special friend and that the right drink – whether it's Peroni or Grey Goose or Jameson's – will take us there: in that place, we will be our fantasy selves with better clothes and hair and relationships that work. All the shame and despair magically vanished away: the drunken rants, the midnight shopping bouts – what a friend describes as 'inter-night' shopping – the dents in the car, the vast crater in your bank account caused by all the collateral damage the drinking somehow always entails: extra nights in hotels, damage waivers on the hired car having to be paid for, taxis back to where you think you left your handbag. The list is endless and certainly never mentioned in the ads.

The truth is that, if you're an alcoholic, the spell wears off pretty fast and 'home' becomes just another sordid dive where you're making a fool of yourself. Booze makes us unsexy, broke, emotional vampires. Those long lunches end in a poisonous row before dinner where things are said that can never be unsaid; the charming pub becomes a place where you fall asleep in the loo with the graffiti on the door, smashed, trousers round your ankles, all dignity gone. The bohemian cafés in French towns turn into dystopian sojourns where the regulars whisper unflattering things in their quaint local dialect as you make your unstable way past their table under the large, framed photographs of the town as it once was to the disgustingly insanitary loo *again*. The fact that you can't fall asleep in there because it's a hole in the floor doesn't stop you trying.

We cling to the idea of drink as a passport to glamour, and to that elusive sense of home, in part because doing so gives us a terrific hit. A surge of dopamine accompanies the memory of place – dappled sunlight, tables in the ancient square – amounting to a powerful, supremely addictive flush of feeling; alcohol, above all, is a drug that selectively allows you to remember only the good things. When non-alcoholics ask, 'Why can't she just stop?' this is one of the reasons why. It's way, way beyond the reach of willpower, deeply entwined in the complex neurochemistry of that dark and mysterious country of the brain.

From an early age, almost as soon as I could marshal such thoughts coherently, I started to play with this feeling that 'somewhere else' was better, and I think this is what people mean when they say, 'I was born an alcoholic.' I had good reasons to seek an escape from my reality, it's true, but I suspect it was a genetic predisposition to try to escape myself before booze even came along that I had perhaps inherited from my alcoholic grand-father, or possibly my restless, depressive, perfectionist mother. Without knowing it, I was already prepping the neural pathways, deepening the already well-etched lines of the addictive template I had inherited.

I engaged in fantasy, creating my own secret inner world, feeding my voracious habit with books. I read until I could read no more. This helped my writing as an adult, no doubt about it, but it also gave me the means to ignore detail that I didn't like, particularly later on, when it came to men. It contributed not only to my alcoholism but to my love addiction, too. Fantasising was useful to me as a child because it gave me relief, but it turned toxic when it morphed into the powerful denial I had about the reality of my situation as an adult.

As a child, I had a shopping list: number one was different parents. I soon found the first lot just down the road. I was at primary school with one of their many children and I got myself invited to stay with them as often as possible. They lived in an enormous and (to my mind) romantically dilapidated house, certain parts of which had not been touched since Victoria was on the throne. With my friend, we roamed through these distant, forgotten rooms, blowing dust off pictures, opening trunks of clothes put away a hundred years before, laughing over the random objects we discovered. Fantasy central, in other words. When I read Lampedusa's description of Tancredi and Angelica at Donnafugata roaming the old forgotten parts of the enormous palace, I was powerfully reminded of those feelings first cultivated in childhood, that profound sense of finding yourself in some beautiful, undiscovered lost past, so infinitely preferable to my uneasy, fraught home life, where I had to spend a lot of time dodging my mother if I was in the house. Whatever I was doing was wrong, indoors that was. Outside was another matter.

Go out and play, she would say, so I would, ranging far and wide across the countryside on my bike. It never occurred to her to ask where I was going or what I was going to do, and it never crossed my mind to tell her.

Upon one memorable occasion, however, I was minding my own business on the road to the Forestry Commission houses where Mrs Kirk, our cleaning lady, lived, when my mother screeched up alongside me in her half-timbered shooting-brake ESW 376G, an older version of what's now called an estate car. I was astounded to see her.

'Why are you here?' I asked.

'Have you seen a white van?' she asked at an angle as she cranked the passenger window down.

'No,' I shook my head, 'no . . .'

'Get in,' she said, in that voice she used.

'What about my bike?'

'Leave it. Your father can come and get it later.'

This was her car and keeping it clean was a priority, much more than the fate of my bike.

'But what if someone steals it?'

'Just do as you're told,' she replied, predictably. Reasoning with children was not in my mother's lexicon.

Much later, I discovered that there was a man in a van on a mission to abduct little girls. This was Scotland. They caught him, I think, but that was the only time my mother ever came looking for me. I ran away once, but even then, it was my father who retrieved me, not my mother. *If she wants to run away, let her*, I suppose she must have thought. Quite different to the face-losing potential of my being accidentally abducted and murdered. That might get into the newspapers. I'll never forget the feeling of outrage it gave me to see her that day in what I regarded essentially as *my* space, a Mum-free zone, the open road. It was a harbinger of things to come: I was on my way somewhere else to become someone else, even on that seemingly innocent bike ride.

I never felt at home while at home, but it's only when I look back at my life that I realise how restless I've been, how often I've changed houses or flats in search of a cure for the great, aching empty space within without knowing that's what I was doing – what they refer to in AA as doing a 'geographical'. Moving jobs, houses or countries in search of a new me, a fresh start. I moved house, that was one aspect of it, but I also moved men.

Moving men is very hard work, just as hard as moving cities or countries. In fact, each man is more or less the equivalent of a whole new country with its own rules, demands, political system, and, last but not least, its economic system, usually pretty precarious amongst the kind of arty people I chose, reverting to type after Arabella's father. Going to a new male country meant earning a whole new set of rights: working hard to be loved, to show I was a good citizen of my new kingdom and practising being a nice person, all the time. It was a way of putting off the dreadful reckoning of what it really meant to be me. My lostness was subsumed in the firm boundaries of someone else's territory, or that was the idea. It never quite worked out like that, however.

These emotional voyages into new countries were, in fact, tediously symptomatic of the illness I was in the clutches of. I wanted someone to fix me, to make me all right, to still and soothe the terrible fear I had encountered as a girl, to keep it away from me. I wanted a safe space where I didn't have to watch my back the whole time. Somehow, I had got hold of the idea that I couldn't deal with this fear myself – it was too much for me; I couldn't look at it; it would turn me to stone; I would die. And the more I turned my back, the larger it got, something I only really learnt in therapy years later, when I had stopped lying to therapists.

After my second divorce in my early thirties, I went through a series of disastrous emotional journeys that nearly capsized me: the alcoholic war correspondent who 'had' to drink because of what he'd witnessed – during the short period I was with him, my consumption rose hugely and never went down again. The Italian film-maker so handsome and chiselled that my friend Felix referred to him sarcastically as 'Mount Rushmore in a blazer'. He was also a Grade-A narcissist, so bad that even I couldn't cling on, a type of personality I specialised in, having had to deal with my mother since birth. All this with a child in tow, an extra. I needed an anchor, a protector to stop me and my child from sinking altogether. Although I was a mother, I was still, in effect, a terrified child myself. The denial around my drinking was also a denial of the brutal truth of my situation; they were meshed together. I thought that mesh was my protective covering, but it was more of a poison shirt than a protection. I had zero understanding of all this, no language with which to understand my alcoholism, so I denied it. In society, as a whole, alcoholism is a dark and dirty secret. It is not understood or even discussed most of the time. There is no language for it, and if you suffer from something for which polite society has no words other than fed-up exhortations to just *stop*, for God's sake, you think you're a freak. I certainly did. *Just cut down*, they say, but no real alcoholic can do that. If only!

When Arabella was a small child, even before I split up with her father, we'd already moved three times. After the divorce,

I moved her again when she was four into a house in Shepherd's Bush. By then I was almost drowning. I had rung AA in my mid-twenties but done nothing. Denial was my middle name. I'd managed to completely and utterly convince myself that drink was my beloved friend, the one thing I really couldn't afford to lose, but I'd quite often black out fully clothed and wake up in what I called 'the threes': those darkest and most dangerous of the night hours when the world is ending and you're going down with it.

There's something rather slatternly about waking up with your boots on, especially when combined with a pounding head and a dry mouth. Fully clothed: well, maybe I simply dropped off while I was reading, but the boots? The boots were symptomatic of some-one who just cut out and happened to be lucky enough to fall onto the bed. I knew that, but I also denied it to myself. *If you had my life, you'd probably fall asleep fully clothed, too.* This is the refrain common to every alcoholic in active alcoholism, the symphony of self-pity, of blaming everyone else, of refusing to acknowledge the problem. I had no idea quite how indentured I was to drink, how entangled I was in the slave/master relationship, but I had previous when it came to being in the clutches of something bigger than me, a way of life I'd learnt at my mother's knee. Alcohol also came with my mother's imprimatur and it was so much nicer than my mother, at least to start with. Hindsight is a terrible thing sometimes.

After I was about twenty-two or three, all my houses looked exactly the same. If I were to go to Mars, I would furnish my spaceship in a similar way. This sameness of all my spaces disguised the fact that there had been so many of them. This was my recipe: take one really large painting and as many others as you could find, mix with a thousand books and jam them into any given room. Plonk an ancient gilt mirror over the fireplace, get a chair or two out of the nearest skip, accessorise with a few threadbare rugs and a dog on the sagging sofa, and there you had it: bohemian style writ large. Arabella still remembers with shame the time I brought a moth-eaten red velvet Victorian curtain with the hooks still in it to sit on at sports day. I couldn't see the problem. Well, I could, sort of, but I was precipitately downwardly mobile just as everyone else was financially in the ascendant in the eighties, caught up in a whole new wave of outsider-itis: divorced, single-mother, writer: lonely, broke, drunk.

At the house in St Elmo Road where I often came to fully booted and spurred, a darker urge appeared inside the net: suicide. I remember the evening vividly: I was having an affair with an artist who had gone away to France on a painting trip. In the group was his old girlfriend, also an artist. They were staying in the house of a third friend, another artist, American, who, Annigoni-style was surrounded by flocks of hangers-on, wannabees, girls who fancied him, plus the occasional grown-up child from a previous relationship. It was a working trip, I was told. No room for you, alas.

The old girlfriend, whom I'd met, was a drama queen, always creating situations where she needed to be rescued. I felt my lover shouldn't go if she was going to be there. But he paid no attention to what I wanted and went anyway. That evening, I felt spurned and hysterical with fear. Somehow, I was, without meaning to be, in my darkest place, the place I had gone to so much trouble to avoid.

All this took place in a world unrecognisable to today's lovers:
no mobile phones, a world of landlines and postcards, telegrams
in an emergency, practically Victorian in that respect. There was
a house phone at the artist-friend's place but whenever I managed
to get through the sound barrier, I got some doped-out sounding
hanger-on, who would say in that madly laconic American way,
'Sure, I'll get him to call you . . . ' He never called back other than
once to tell me not to call again. *It was embarrassing*, he said,
adding a further humiliation to the already bubbling cauldron of
despair and self-loathing.

I tore the number out of my phone book so I couldn't call it
again and sat down at the table. I was hardly able to breathe. I felt
as if I was suffocating and, to be honest, I would have gladly died
rather than keep encountering and re-encountering such pain. It
was the reckoning I had tried for so long to avoid: the knowledge
that I was unloved and unwanted and that nobody cared. It was all
true, after all, however much I tried to pretend it wasn't. I couldn't
live with such pain. I went into the kitchen and selected a knife.
I remember running its edge over my left wrist when I heard
a sound behind me. Arabella.

Someone did care, and, what's more, that someone was dependent on me. I turned around to face her, allowing the knife to
clatter into the sink behind me. I forget what happened next. I must
have gone upstairs with her and put her back to bed.

When I came downstairs again, it occurred to me suddenly
that I could call the Samaritans, so I did. I owe my life to the kind
man who talked me down off my desolate, high branch. Someone
rang me the next morning and asked if I would like to go into
Samaritans HQ and have a talk. I refused. It was an opportunity

lost, a chance to cut through the mesh and escape, but I wasn't ready. I pushed the deathly anxious girl-child back into the dark and carried on in my life, condemning myself to another fifteen years of alcoholic drinking and all it entailed.

The artist came back, and we went on for a while together, but I had already hardened my heart against him. Never again would I trust him. No home there. I began to plot my escape to a different emotional zone. I left him in the end, breaking his heart in the process, rather to his astonishment, and married someone else instead, after a whirlwind romance. A tailor-made script for the drunk I was: high drama, betrayal, love at last, happy ending. What could possibly go wrong? Almost everything, as it turned out.

Even by my standards, this was a catastrophe. To start with, though, it all looked so perfect, of course it did: I was a professional fantasist and so, to some extent, was he: he was a writer, he had a large and eccentric artistic family I really liked and, more importantly, felt I could hide amongst. We would have children (I was still just about young enough in my early forties) and live happily ever after.

After a year, during which I had two miscarriages (feeling terrible about drinking), he began to talk about a divorce. We'd only just got married, for God's sake. I couldn't admit defeat. I was also terrified about money and, yet again, what would become of me. We stumbled on. I drank more and more. That was the era when I kept the vodka in the hollowed-out ribcage of the turkey that hadn't got eaten the Christmas before. There were shot glasses everywhere in my office where I sat and pretended to work, as well as on my side of the bed on the bottom shelf of the bookcase. It was the endgame.

On New Year's Day 2009, one of the great clan of cousins came to lunch. An angel in disguise is a cliché but he was that angel. He wasn't drinking because he'd been sober in AA for twenty-plus years. I wasn't drinking because it was a new year, and I was going to stop drinking. I had had the same New Year's resolution for the last thirty-plus years.

He told me a little bit about AA, enough to make me want to know more. I was becoming more and more curious to find out how people (and by 'people', I mean alcoholics) could simply not drink. I could scarcely get to 10 a.m. before I started to drink. How was it done? There was clearly a way, because the cousin was a living example of it.

It took a few months for me to work out what I was going to do. AA seemed obvious after new year, but I'd been a couple of times before and thought, hilariously, in retrospect, that it wasn't for me. I wasn't alcoholic enough, I felt. In AA there are various metaphors for this state of mind: your house is burning down but you don't like the colour of the fireman's hose. That's my favourite. But during the months between January and May 2009 several other things happened that changed my way of thinking about my problem – one being that my GP sent me for a scan of my liver to see how much damage it had sustained. It was an ultrasound scan, the same machine used when you're pregnant to see how the baby is doing, but this time they were looking for damage, not new life. I was really shaken by this. I also had a revelation - a moment - when I realised the truth of my situation - I was a drunk and alcohol was running my life that shook me to my boots. I knew then that the game was up.

On 26 May 2009, I went to an AA meeting with a changed heart and attitude. I admitted, at long last, that I couldn't stop drinking and that I needed help to do it. At that moment in that meeting I arrived at the home that had been waiting for me all along.

PART TWO – ADDICT

Chapter One

Revelations

Arabella

I know I have a problem. It's been clear to me for some time, although I don't like to connect the dots. I think it's pretty clear to others, too, but again, I don't like to think too much about that either. I find the 'Are you an alcoholic?' questionnaires jammed into drawers and books all the time.

When I can bear to linger over them, I see that I have marked some of them with ticks and crosses like a good student. 'Does alcohol affect your professional life?' There's a tick and a cross next to this one. Maybe I filled it out when I was drunk? On the face of it, yes, alcohol does affect my professional life. That is how I have come to wind up living in my mother's house, aged twenty-six, after a breakdown that happened when I was fired from my job because of my drinking. Tick.

But like most alcoholics, I'm an expert at shapeshifting. Alongside my full-time job of drinking and being hungover from my mother's spare bedroom, I'm also doing a master's degree at Oxford. Nothing to see here, no damage, tick. Except, I know the truth: the master's is a smokescreen that keeps people off my back and allows me to drink in the way I need to. I don't *have* to be anywhere until way past noon most days and it gives me some time to think. Am I an alcoholic? Yes *and* no, cross *and* tick. People go on like this for years, a lifetime even.

Next question: has your drinking caused trouble at home? Again, this would be difficult to put a cross or a tick against. To look at me, you might say that I am at 'home' because of my drinking, because of all the things that happened when I was living in London and long before that. Privately, I know that I have put an enormous strain on my mother by coming back. But the truth is, this house, the one in which I am lying in bed in the middle of the day, is not my home. I left my home at seventeen when my mother remarried, or at least I thought I did. No, it is the house my mother shares with her third husband; really it is *his* house and we are simply squatting in it. Soon, the divorce will begin in earnest and then we will both have to leave. Other questions spring up like weeds. Is it my fault their marriage is failing? Is it because of my drinking? Or is it because of my mother's drinking? I don't know where I would put that in a questionnaire; I actually think you need a different questionnaire for that, a questionnaire that asks you about what happened to you in your childhood. I've been filling those out inconclusively for years.

How much does your mother drink? A therapist asked me that once and I said I didn't know. Another question I can't answer properly, another thing I can't put a tick against. She drank a lot when I was a child, yes, but she's a shapeshifter too. Women addicts are, generally. They have to be: don't drink while you're pregnant, don't drink until after you get the children to school and back every day, clean the sink (you can do that when you're drunk, luckily). No alcoholics here, there's no time. And yet. Six months ago, my mother wouldn't have wanted to talk about her drinking at all. Now all she does is talk about it. She's sober now, doesn't drink a drop, not even one, not ever. I don't understand how that works but I can't ask her. Every day, sometimes even twice a day, she disappears off to the 'meetings'. I don't know what they do there but from one day to the next she stopped drinking and the old her went up in a puff of smoke. She's disappeared before – into other marriages, her writing, intense friendship – but this is a disappearance like no other.

I throw my arm out towards the bedside table and try to find my phone. Generally, I don't like to look at it in the mornings in case it confirms my worst suspicions: concerned messages from friends or confused messages from people I have called by mistake. In other words, total blackout; pitch black, can't remember a thing. Much better not to look at it at all and deny everything later. This morning, though, it keeps buzzing away, insisting I pick it up. I look at the screen and see several messages from a friend on my course: 'Are you OK?' 'Did you make it home all right?' 'Call me'. I feel intensely annoyed by every single one of these messages. *Of course I'm not bloody OK*, I want to reply, but I don't because then she'll send me another volley of messages.

This friend is very different to my usual company. Firstly, she is American and secondly, she hardly drinks at all. I much prefer to hang around with people who drink like me; I court these people like lovers. When we are in the pub after lectures, she will nurse the same glass for the entire evening, taking small sips and insisting on there being something to eat with it. Two weeks ago, I mentioned to her that my mother was now 'in AA' and her face lit up in a strange and prescient way. 'That's wonderful,' she said, 'let me know when she gets her one-year chip.' I nodded and smiled back, although I had no idea what she was talking about, none whatsoever. I don't know why she wants to be friends with me. Perhaps she wants to save me, and good luck to her. I decide to leave her messages until later and sit up and look for a cigarette, although if I find one, I will be amazed. I have always run out of everything: alcohol, drugs, cigarettes, money.

Downstairs, I can hear my mother making coffee. Ever since she found the Fellowship nine months ago, she is always making coffee. Coffee in the mornings, coffee throughout the day, coffee with other people from the meetings, coffee at the meetings. Yesterday, I even heard her making coffee late at night; clearly, some replacement mechanism is at work, I think to myself smugly. *She needs Coffee Anonymous*, I think, and almost text a friend to say that before I remember that the whole situation is not that funny. My mother has a chronic, severe drink problem that has driven her to Alcoholics Anonymous, a place she said she would never go back to having stumbled in there three years ago only to start drinking again. I should be applauding her, not making crass jokes about caffeinated drinks.

Somehow, I find this very difficult. It isn't, I think, that I don't want her to be happy: God knows she deserves some happiness, particularly as her third marriage has just fallen apart as all the others have. But this jaunty, caffeinated happiness looks phony to me, as if she is just trying it on in a shop, a coy smile on her face, before giving it back to the assistant. I want to tell her to stop it, to put it away; I want to tell her that this unadorned good cheer is not who we are. *Not who we are.* But who are we, exactly? We are people for whom life is painful; we are people to whom life has been unfair. We have lost things and had things taken from us and more often than not, we have sabotaged things. Because of all of this we need to drink. The drinking and the painful life go together. You can't have a painful life and not drink; the dance needs two partners. Soon, she will realise this, and life will return to normal.

There are other reasons for my guardedness. Now that she has stopped drinking she is less pliable: for money certainly, but also for sympathy. When I am hungover, I can feel her gaze rest upon me in a way it never did before; some disapproval hangs in the air where before there was a pact, something that bordered on camaraderie. Now she sniffs the air when she comes into my room and looks at me with a mixture of pity and frustration. There is also, imperceptibly, a look of smugness that irritates me. She is, after all, now the world expert on drinking, or not drinking, or whatever it is she is doing now.

On this particular morning, I feel more hostile than usual to the set-up in the house: my mother, my stepfather, the impending divorce, my inability to get anything done. But there is a change afoot within me; some emotional tectonic plate has broken off from the others; I've been feeling it for a while now.

I cast my mind's eye over the previous evening: an event at the university, people in black tie, perhaps even some of the tutors. Like loose change in a pocket, I count out what I have left: a bottle of wine before I left the house while listening to loud music, walking through the cold, drinks at the bar, how small the drinks seem, can you go back to the bar before people notice, where can you smoke, sorry, yes another please, excuse me, I'm OK, yes, I'm fine, is that my glass, I'll pay, shit, my leg, really, I'm fine, leave me the fuck alone. And then, nothing. Total darkness. This is normal, or it's become normal. Presumably there was a time before this, but it has receded like the tide.

I light a cigarette end from an ashtray next to my bed and stare up at the ceiling. As I see it, I have two options. Either I carry on as I am, stuck like an insect in aspic in a state of semi-infantilisation and early-onset convalescence in my stepfather's house. Or I go somewhere else. But I've tried that before, and it turns out nobody will have me: I am what is known as *unreliable*. I also have no money to speak of, crucial to any escape plan.

Lately, I have been looking at the Alcoholics Anonymous booklets in my mother's office when she is not there. It strikes me as a form of reverse spying: instead of looking for clues about my mother, what I'm really looking for is a tip-off about myself. I found something the other day when she was out at a meeting, something that felt disarmingly true. So true, in fact, that I slammed the book shut and forgot to put it back in place like a clumsy robber. It was in what is called *The Big Book*, in one of the stories at the back, past what looks like the sanctimonious Bible bit:

> *It seemed that all they talked about at meetings was drinking, drinking, drinking. It made me thirsty. I wanted to talk about my many big problems; drinking seemed a small one [. . .] I am amazed at how many of my problems – most of which had nothing to do with my drinking, I believed – have become manageable or have simply disappeared since I quit drinking.*

The pretentious part of me wanted to find fault with the prose, to correct it somehow. But you can't correct a statement like that.

It is above amendment. I think about that paragraph a lot now; it's as if a rift has opened up within myself and all sorts of irksome hypotheticals have swung in. Would my depression be better if I stopped drinking? Would I be able to leave my stepfather's house and cope somewhere else? Would I be able to work again? Would, would, would.

What I *would* like to do is to go back to a time before my mother got sober and before I had started reading the books that she now lines her office with. I took one into my room the other day to look at the things she had underlined because I like to keep tabs on her as much as myself. I was amazed by the schoolgirl-like enthusiasm in the margins – 'yes!' or 'so true!' – on almost every page. It's been years since I underlined any book in that way and as I turned the pages, I started to feel some pang of jealousy, an old feeling of being left out.

Slowly, I begin to dress myself to go downstairs. This isn't hard as I'm wearing my usual grubby tracksuit bottoms. A large bruise shines yellow, grey and purple on my leg; from its position on my leg, I guess that it must have taken the impact from a fall – a bad one; I am always covered in bruises.

In the kitchen, my mother is sipping coffee at the sink, its acrid smell floating outwards. From the set of her shoulders, I can tell some dark exchange has just taken place between her and my stepfather. Upstairs, I can hear him talking to someone on the phone, probably his lawyer. These are, admittedly, hardly ideal conditions in which to make a devastating confession but I have no choice: life is in session, with or without my scripting.

'Mum, are you listening?' I croak, my voice flexing its usual smoker's baritone. 'I think I'm an alcoholic. I have a problem;

I have *your* problem. I can't stop when I start. I'm really scared,' I stammer, my voice cracking, my eyes filling with tears of self-pity and relief and something altogether darker: revenge.

The urge to find a cigarette is by now overwhelming. I almost think of pausing the conversation and going to buy some, but I realise this will undermine my delivery.

As she has her back towards me, I can't see how this has landed. From the way her shoulders are tensed, I foresee trouble.

'Oh, really?' she replies in a tired tone, slowly turning around so I can see the irritation pulsing across her face. 'But I don't think that's really the problem, though, is it?' she says, tersely.

'I am, I'm an alcoholic, I've been reading the books you leave lying around the place,' I say, by now sensing that I have lit upon the most electric and dangerous truth, one that she wants to extinguish as quickly as she possibly can.

'It can't have been that bad, darling. Things like this happen all the time when you're young. Why don't you have a coffee and then go back to bed and have a rest and see how you feel?' she says, all the while gathering her things as if making to leave, the coffee now long forgotten on the side. She is probably going to a meeting. Better make sure it's not the same one as me.

'You can't stop me, you know. I'm going to a meeting today no matter what. I've found out where one is and it says *everyone bloody welcome*,' I retort with a flourish before climbing the stairs and slamming the door to my room sending plaster flying from the ceiling.

All my life, I have sensed a likeness to my mother, a primal feeling of sameness. But what does it really mean to be the same? We don't look alike; in that regard, I am my father's daughter, same nose and brow, same colouring, same physique. Everybody says so. No, our sameness runs in a different tributary of the self, one that runs deeper than our looks. This morning, I am convinced that I have located the foundation stone of this likeness, the very thing that has bound us together. The fact that she seems to want to put me off doesn't deter me. If anything, I find it completely intoxicating.

Back in my room, I am breathless; I catch myself in the mirror and see that my cheeks are red, my eyes slightly manic. A silence has settled upon the house, even my stepfather has stopped talking on the phone. At last, I have commanded people's attention. I lie on the bed and search on my phone 'AA meeting, Oxford, today'. Within seconds, I have a plan: 12.30 p.m. St Giles' Church Hall.

I've walked past this church hall many times. You wouldn't notice it ordinarily: timbers, a blue door, a few signs pinned onto a noticeboard outside. On this day, I am like an astronaut, walking along lunar ground, each step a new discovery. I scan the notice board and see a circular sign with the AA logo that I recognise from my mother's books. A group of people stand outside smoking, warming their hands with cups of tea. There is an air of levity. Some are laughing while others smile when they see me. Do they know my mother? It seems hard to imagine her here; it is even harder to imagine *me* here. I join the others inside sitting around a trestle table and quickly scan the room and see I am the youngest person by some way.

Before long, a man in his forties sitting in the middle of the assembled group starts to talk. To my astonishment, he starts to talk, not about drinking, but about his childhood: his parents' divorce, his father's drinking, the lack of emotional sustenance.

'When I did eventually start drinking, it was like pouring petrol onto a naked flame,' he says calmly, 'I didn't stand a chance.' As I listen to his account, I feel unbearably full, to the point of losing control and shouting or crying hysterically. I think briefly of running out and feeling my legs move beneath me, taking me to anywhere but this room where the white heat of a stranger's truth is burning me.

I don't run away. I stay in the room. I listen as one person after another raises their hand to share back to the speaker. I am about as uncomfortable as it is possible to be. As the hour draws to a close, a person in the middle of the table asks if there are any newcomers to the group. I freeze; I say nothing; I imagine the gaze of the others upon me. When I look up, I see that no one is looking at me and that the meeting has moved on to other business; people start scrabbling in their bags for pound coins to put in a bag to pay for the tea. Suddenly, people get to their feet and stand, their heads bowed in reverence as they say a prayer. I don't know the words, but I murmur along in the way one does in a church, the chorus as much about the collective noise as it is about the words themselves.

As I walk back home across town, I think about mumbling the words – any words – to something you don't know, the way you might hum a song you only half recognise. I think about how one day I might know the words to that prayer and what it would mean to know those words. I think my mother knows the words. Maybe she can teach them to me.

Julia

Revelations

It's February 2010, Oxford. I'm living with my third husband and Arabella in a tall, thin Regency house in Oxford with a view of the London Road and, on the other side of it, South Parks, a great green space with a stand of trees at the top of its gentle rise. If my living arrangements sound odd, they are. Emotional turmoil has underpinned my entire life to date. I was married twice by the age of twenty-one. Divorced at thirty-one, then in another long-term relationship (which broke up acrimoniously), followed by yet another marriage. Friends who are still married to the same man say, enviously, 'But it sounds so interesting . . .' That's one way of putting it.

Mostly, my life experience has been one of enormous emotional suffering, caused by the fall-out from all these relationships, beginning with my first divorce – that of my parents when I was still a child. Unable to manage my feelings, I drank excessively, as soon as I was able to: drink was my friend – I worshipped it. Nine months ago, I went to AA and stopped drinking and, in so doing, stood my version of the known world on its head. Addiction to alcohol, it almost goes without saying, has shaped the entire landscape of my emotional life.

I look at this view every morning as I put on my make-up, using the swivel mirror on the chest of drawers just to the right of the window. The whites of my eyes are whiter than they used to be. I roll them from side to side enjoying the fact that this is now a pain-free activity. Nine months ago, my eyes were bloodshot, and when I moved my eyeballs, they hurt. I spent a lot of time trying to decide how yellow they were, or whether it was just my imagination. This is what drunks do: they bargain with their health. If a doctor says to cut down, they take that to mean keep on drinking, just not quite as much. If I decided my eyeballs weren't yellow, I could keep on destroying my health, and my mind.

I go downstairs to the basement kitchen to make coffee. As I'm doing this, I hear footsteps on the kitchen stairs. To my surprise, it's Arabella, who's doing her master's degree, or is supposed to be. I'm astonished to see her this early, as she was out last night at some event to do with her course, and these events inevitably mean drinking, something she's pretty good at. Academic life, in common with so many other activities in our society, is built on a platform of booze. Everything is underpinned by booze. There's a word for this, apparently, a rather inscrutable hard-edged little word: 'alcogenic'. Basically, we live in a culture so saturated with booze that we scarcely notice, until we are forced to. I know that Arabella drinks a lot – who doesn't at her age (see the alcogenic-ness of that assumption)? – however, until this point, I have managed to deny to myself quite how bad it is. She drinks differently to me; she binges, then stops for days or weeks. I was a daily drinker. I'm still new enough in AA to not fully understand that alcoholism takes various forms; some drinkers are like me, some are like Arabella, others have different patterns still. We're all different and all the same.

'Mum,' she says, dramatically, standing in the doorway, 'I think I'm an alcoholic . . . ' She's trying not to cry. She's clearly had a heavy night. Her long hair is unbrushed and slightly matted over one ear and she hasn't taken off her make-up. She's wearing a grey baggy T-shirt and sweatpants. Her rather dirty feet are bare.

'Do you? Are you sure?'

I feel ambushed by this declaration. *I'm the alcoholic round here*, is my first thought. *This is my illness, not yours.* Me, me, and more me. At the same time, I feel deeply shocked and disturbed. Is this also my fault? The answer to that is both yes and no, but I won't understand the ins and outs of it all for a very long time. I know *I'm* an alcoholic – a former compulsive daily drinker – but the illness, as above, comes in many different guises. *She can't be,* I think . . . *she simply can't be* . . . God alone knows why I'm so certain about this. I'm an alcoholic, her father is too, and he's still drinking. It's all over our family but never discussed. Alcohol is. It. Just. Is.

But there is another fear at work here: as my first sober year goes by, the extent of the damage I've inflicted on my child is just beginning to dawn on me. Sometimes, like now, I just want to deny it. *Is it catching*? The answer to that is complex, but, yes, in certain ways, it is. *Is it my fault*? That question again … I just don't know the answer,

'Yes,' she says, 'I am sure, it was so awful.'

'What happened?' I don't really want to know but can't stop myself from asking.

'Don't ask,' she says. She's crying now, really crying, snot and tears mingling.

'Oh,' I say, floundering, 'that's awful, but look … why not wait and see about meetings and all that?'

In retrospect, I have no idea why I said that. Was it a last desperate attempt to put off the inevitable inter-generational reckoning with this illness that runs through our family like a dark thread from generation to generation? The tapestry of our family tree is tightly embroidered with those dark threads. The Scottish and the Irish (my family on both sides) have the alcoholic gene baked into them like a curse. My grandfather on my father's side and many, many more going back from him into the dark, the father of my children, and now my daughter. My father's middle wife was an active alcoholic who actually died of the illness, as would Arabella's father two years after she got sober. As the child of two alcoholics, what chance does she have of escaping the dread illness? All I can say is that, after years of lousy single-parenting, I really don't know where the boundaries are, and in spite of nine months' sobriety, I'm still having trouble processing what's going on.

The fact that my marriage is clearly falling apart does not help, and Arabella living with us has made everything ten times worse. There is a dreadful atmosphere in the house and my husband and I can barely exchange a civil word. It feels like the whole place is strewn with broken glass. Quite frequently after one of these encounters, I am filled with a rage so intense that I'm terrified I might inadvertently press what is known in AA as the 'fuck-it' button. I have to do something – anything – else instead, so I go upstairs and sit at my desk. As I do this I can literally feel the froth of rage rise in me like an Alka Seltzer in a glass but then – and this is sobriety – instead of having a drink, I wait for the fizzing, dizzying feelings of rage to subside. This much I have learnt: *wait*. Every time I do this it makes me stronger: *look at me*, I think, *having a feeling – a really unpleasant one – but not drinking*. I must be doing something right. I feel the way I do when I've thrown up: empty, relieved, scraped out. I can have a horrible, poisonous feeling and survive its scorching flame. Feelings will not kill me, apparently. Sounds daft, but I never knew that before.

At the same time, where Arabella is concerned, years of alcoholism and self-absorption has had the effect of stiffening and inhibiting my reactions, as if I am somehow covered in scale: *I am not a good mother*, I think. Much later, I will come to believe that what I am, in fact, is a loving mother with an illness, but this insight will take years to shape itself in my mind. I now think that it is precisely these dark and unfairly punishing feelings about myself that constitute such a large part of the mental illness of alcoholism, or my own particular version of it. *Mea culpa, mea culpa, mea maxima culpa.* The truth is, however, that I'm finding it hard to feel compassion for her situation and her very obvious pain, in spite of the fact that only a few months ago, at the end of my drinking, I blacked out at a dinner party and insulted everyone, or so I was told. I remembered none of it, only coming to as we were leaving, aware that people were giving me shocked looks. The excoriating memory of that shame is with me still, but I don't recall it at this moment or empathise with the way Arabella is clearly feeling this morning. I'm more annoyed than anything. She's getting in the way of my morning with her drama. Haven't I got enough problems already? My relationship with alcohol is the longest and deepest relationship of my life, longer even than the relationship with my daughter. My actions and thoughts on this morning show how very damaged I have been. Nine months' sobriety is amazing but it isn't enough to compensate for a lifetime of drinking.

Getting sober means coming to terms with this, but not all at once, *please*. It's a process. That thing about one day at a time comes in here: *Don't try and solve all your life problems at once*, goes a line often quoted in AA. Coming to terms with all this will take me a very long time, as above, and I understand nothing of it this morning when Arabella's declaration smashes up against me like an immense wave that will drag me down into the depths, if I let it.

'Wait and see what? What do you mean?' She wipes the back of her hand across her nostrils, a habit she's picked up from me, one that my mother tried to break and never succeeded.

'Well . . . ' I continue, irritated in spite of myself by the endless drama that always seems to surround her every move, 'are you sure you're an alcoholic? I mean, I know you drink, but not every day, surely? Not like me.' Me, again.

In fact, I know perfectly well there is something wrong with Arabella, but I just don't know what, or don't want to know, more like. She quite frequently goes out at night and comes back in the morning. Sometimes she doesn't come back at all. There are clearly men, but I never get to meet them. And then there are days when she will be lurking in her room without appearing at all, either sleeping or watching *Grey's Anatomy* on her computer. If I knock on the door, she either won't answer or will give me short shrift if I put my head round the door. Her room smells of stale smoke and dirty clothes with something else rather repulsive underpinning it all. Later, I understand that this is the smell of the vomit she washes down the sink.

What's wrong with her? Depression? Who knows? When she was doing her undergraduate degree there were sinister flurries of trouble, but she did incredibly well, so she can't be an alcoholic, can she? She's also made it quite clear she doesn't want me to interfere, and our boundaries are so messed up by my patchiness as a parent during my drinking that I don't know how or where I stand or what to do about her and there is no one who really knows her that I can talk to about her sensibly. Her father is an active alcoholic who won't speak to me, and my old boyfriend, the artist, whom I was with for most of her childhood, has adopted the tactic of blaming me for everything that goes wrong in Arabella's life, as a way of punishing me for leaving him.

The area surrounding the maternal figure is supposed to be the deep litter of utter safety where you can be yourself; both heard and held. I haven't provided this, far from it. Because of my own drinking, my daughter doesn't come to me with her problems, or she hasn't until now, because she knows from long experience that I would either be angry with her or despairing (indulgently blaming myself for everything that had gone wrong in her life, as I am still tempted to do this morning) and absolutely no help at all. And she's right. I am being absolutely no help at all. I lack compassion for her, but I also lack compassion for myself. I still hate myself, mostly. You can't love other people properly if you don't love yourself, or so I've been told in meetings. I nod and agree but inside I think it's just really annoying bullshit. How little I know!

'What happened last night was so awful,' she says, 'I can't go on.'

'Look,' I say, 'let's go upstairs. Go back to bed for a bit. We'll talk later.'

Arabella's room is on the ground floor behind my husband's office. He appears in the hall just as we do.

'What's wrong?' he asks, coldly, looking us up and down, mother and daughter. By this time, he thinks of us as interlopers in what he regards as his house rather than our house.

'Nothing,' I say, hastily opening the door of Arabella's room. 'She's not feeling very well, that's all.'

'*Plus ça change,*' he says, going back into his office. With enormous difficulty, I manage to prevent myself from replying. God, my life is exhausting.

Arabella's room stinks. There are clothes all over the floor, and a full ashtray by her bed. I kick an empty bottle by mistake, which rattles across the floorboards.

'I'll get you some coffee,' I say, 'and then you can rest a bit.'

'I'm going to go to a meeting,' she replies, 'you can't stop me.'

'I know I can't,' I reply, 'all I'm saying is think about it a bit.'

'I have thought about it,' she answers, 'and I'm going. Don't worry about the coffee, I'll be fine.' The dog climbs back on her bed and she pulls the duvet over her head. I am dismissed.

Fine. A word regarded in AA with polite derision, a cover-all word that tells you nothing about the speaker, a way of evading closeness. Fine not fine.

As I sit down at my desk, it occurs to me that I should ring my sponsor, whom I'll call Susan. Susan got sober in the US and has only just returned to the UK after spending three months in a detention centre in the States. After years of living with the wrong papers, immigration finally caught up with her and sent her home, but not before she was incarcerated. She stayed sober during this incredibly testing time. I asked her to be my sponsor because she's tough and boundaried in a way that I know I need to emulate.

'Arabella says she's an alcoholic and that she wants to go to a meeting,' I say, hoping for sympathy for what I see as *my* predicament.

'Well, that's good, isn't it?'

'I suppose so.'

'Look, Julia.' I can sense Susan getting into no-nonsense mode. 'It's her life, her choice. Nothing to do with you. Pray for her.'

Nothing to do with me . . . she can't be serious. Of course it's to do with me. She's my daughter. I want to say this but something stops me.

'Pray for her,' repeats Susan.

I hate people telling me to pray. I have no real idea how to pray, although I hate to admit it. God already knows everything, what difference will it make? What difference will I make by praying for her? But AA suggests 'conscious contact' with God, and I settle for this. I will attempt to make conscious contact with my distant, deist God who looks very like the red-robed Father figure in Rembrandt's portrait of *The Return of the Prodigal Son*, an interesting image, in fact, as the Father figure's embrace of the son is very tenderly portrayed, something I realise when I actually search for details of this picture on the internet. Perhaps my unconscious mind knows something I don't about the progress I am actually making in my spiritual life. There's a Hebrew word, *chesed*, which means loving kindness and the Rembrandt is drenched in it.

In the evening, I go to my usual meeting. The person I sit next to turns to me and says, 'I saw Arabella at the lunchtime meeting today. She seemed very upset.' Here we go, I think, uncharitably, unwilling to discuss her with someone I don't know all that well, but then this person, as if sensing what I'm thinking, says kindly, 'She's in the right place.' *She's in the right place.* Something inside me gives when I hear this, as if the large and immovable stone that I'd rolled right up against the chamber of my heart has suddenly been set aside.

What I didn't realise at the time was that the fact that Arabella had come downstairs to find me in extremis was in itself a harbinger of the change in me, in spite of the fact that I wasn't much use to her.

'I have to deal with my alcoholism,' I wrote in my journal a year before when I was in the throes of my last disastrous attempt to control my drinking. At that point, I was trying not to drink in the week as a way of proving to myself I couldn't be an alcoholic. Sometimes I could get to Thursday gritting my teeth, hating myself and everything and everyone around me. Mostly, I couldn't. As soon as I began drinking again in those last desperate days, I was off again into the madness. As well as the aforementioned bottle of vodka concealed in the turkey's bosom, I glugged from the bottle of whisky on the dresser before I took the dogs out in the morning, then a glass of wine in a special blue glass that didn't give away its contents, or so I thought, more wine to follow, then vodka to finish off the job. Sloshed most nights, hungover most mornings. Every now and again, particularly for some reason in the basement kitchen of that Oxford house, I'd hear a voice saying to me, *'You're playing with fire . . .'* And I'd think, *Yes, yes, but I can control it*, as I swigged from a bottle at ten in the morning.

Years of wondering what was wrong with me, years of therapy, years of self-searching had not solved the riddle about why I was the way I was. I felt as if I was under a curse. I've recently discovered, however, that my paternal grandfather actually died of alcoholism. It's right there in the family tree crouching like a devil on a branch not far above me, casting its long, cold shadow over his descendants. I never knew. No one told me. Talk about a code of silence. I had no idea.

'Oh, he had cirrhosis,' my father casually remarked one day when we were discussing him. I was astounded. I knew he'd died young-ish but not what he'd actually died of. Suddenly, it all begins to make sense. My grandfather had this illness and died of it. It killed him and it has done its level best to kill me. Now my daughter has it, too.

The fact that she has had the courage at the age of twenty-six to admit that she thinks she's an alcoholic should be a cause for celebration, although on this fateful morning it feels like the very reverse. I can only see the failures that have led to this moment, not the promise and the hope it is overflowing with, although I will eventually come to understand that a miracle has taken place on this rather unpromising, cold late-winter day in 2010.

Chapter Two

Inheritance

Arabella

When I am eighteen, my mother gives me a ring. It was meant to be given to me by an elderly second cousin, but she has died and the inheritance has been sent in an envelope to my mother to pass on. The ring itself is gold with two brackets on either side and a blue stone upon which the letter A is engraved. Its journey to my hand is circuitous: made in the eighteenth century for a woman called Arbel, it was worn on various other hands for almost two centuries before arriving in the custody of a great-aunt and then on to me. This left-turn of ownership out of the maternal line, away from my grandmother and mother, and into the hands of a more distant female relation, confuses me like a piece of luggage left in a train station and carried away by someone else. I struggle to explain why I have the ring to those who notice it on my finger. Yes, it bears my initial, but was I destined to have it? Whose was it before mine? I don't know the answers to any of these questions. For a long time, I don't even wear it; I can't see the point.

In my early twenties, I rediscover the ring when I am moving flats. It is a Saturday morning, and my possessions lie all around me in total disarray as if after an amateur burglary. I am chronically hungover and make no attempt to pack up my things but instead lie on the floor looking at the stains on the carpet: one for wine and one for sick, both mysteriously the same shape and colour. After nearly a year of my tenancy, the carpet resembles a map in which the mountain ranges are shaded darkly. In the other room, I can hear my flatmate detailing her exploits from the previous night; her voice is young and jaunty, and she keeps saying, 'I know, I know,' with increasing speed to whomever she is talking to. I want to tell her to shut up, but she is not speaking to me after something I did when I was drunk – what? – and for once, I know my limits. I am, after all, moving out at her request. Slowly, I get up from the floor and walk towards a pile of clothes from which a small box has been dislodged amongst the great carcass of my things. I open the box and find the ring winking back at me. I feel a sharp pang of guilt as I think about how easily I could have lost this thing that holds such a potent charge of the past. I think of all its other fleeting custodians and their surroundings and the unchangingness of the ring and I start to cry. I do so as quietly as I am able as my flatmate has had enough of my histrionics, she says.

Much later that day, I stand in a different room in a different flat in another part of London. My possessions are stacked around me in black bin bags and a shabby assortment of wheelie suitcases, some with their handles missing, some with wheels missing. On the way up the stairs several books fall out of the bin bags and with them, the childhood photos I had forgotten I had stashed in them. It is the emotional equivalent of being caught stark naked in public. As I bend down to pick things up, I look down at my hand and see the ring. I suddenly feel contained by its story, housed in it as I am not housed in any of these flats. It is who I am: the 'A' initial, I decide, is for me, it was *always* for me. I didn't ask for the ring, just as I can't remember asking for my life to be in such total disarray, but briefly, looking at this object, I feel myself standing in a line of women in which I, too, am meant to be standing. It will take many years before I identify this feeling as acceptance.

***

The random inheritance of the ring amongst the women in my family has always struck me as a decent metaphor for the way another inheritance – alcoholism – has moved down the female line. Like the ring, its movement is random and not necessarily linear: neither my grandmother nor my mother wore the ring but its trajectory across some other branch of the family is something they knew about, just as you might hear whispers of the alcoholic misfortunes of some distant aunt or uncle or hear their unsteady tread on the stairs.

This erratic movement of the addictive gene around my family has always fascinated me, partly because its course is so difficult to map. How do you chart something for which there is over-whelmingly no first-person declaration – until, of course, my mother and me – only consequences? The clues lying hidden in divorce papers, autopsies and bailiffs' letters. How do you trace something as slippery as addiction across family lines when, like the ring, it periodically disappears only to reappear decades later or lies forgotten underneath a heap of other possessions? Crucially, how do you pin down something that everybody, but *everybody*, disagrees on?

If you were to plot the shadowy movement of the addictive gene across my family, it would resemble a map leading to nowhere: the rot appearing to move in no particular direction across a mass of time and space. Perhaps, most of all, you would get lost, since we all disagree on how we got there.

My mother arrives at the junction, misleadingly, with a man, her grandfather, as her guide. Haddy Belhaven, the man she knows from the pages of his books and the things he sold and wasted, the man who squandered his material inheritance and left his descendants something altogether darker and more damaging: addiction. He is her family alcoholic, and she traces her addiction back through him. He was a writer, too, and this tangled knot of words and booze is how she understands herself. It was poured out for her in his cryptic biographies that gesture, obliquely, to a life lived in alcohol's grasp: the endless wandering around Arabia or the way he mistakenly shot himself in the foot. Other stories about him even filtered down to me: his daily trips to buy gin in Castle Douglas, a bottle a day, each day at the same time. Throughout my early life, his book, *The Uneven Road*, lay on her bedside table, the same pages thumbed over and over again. What was she looking for? What did she suspect?

Later, as a teenager, I would do the same thing with her novels, looking for *my* alcoholic, although I wouldn't have known that at the time. Reading them repeatedly for clues, finding approximations of myself in the pages only to lose them again, like following someone you think you know through the streets of a foreign town before they duck out of sight into an alleyway.

Some years after she had got sober my mother's father unknowingly – or perhaps glibly – uttered the words she had been waiting to hear her whole life: 'He was an alcoholic, you know, died of cirrhosis of the liver is what they all said, such waste.' Such a short sentence. Cirrhosis: we all know what it means but it's easier to say than alcoholic, more sterile, more medical, safer somehow. But in that short sentence, my grandfather finally confirmed to my mother what all alcoholics long to know: was it *in the blood*?

Because if there is bad blood, it might not be your fault, like being a haemophiliac. The trouble is, of course, even when you do identify the rot, does it help? Did it help my mother to know that her grandfather was an alcoholic? Maybe it confused her more that the blight had skipped a generation? And yet, when I hear her in meetings, I am convinced that the clues her father rather clumsily gave her *do* help: I can hear it in her voice. I am who I am because of what came before me; wouldn't we all like to be able to say that?

Sit in any AA meeting long enough and you will eventually hear someone trying to trace the map of their illness across family lines. *My father drank*, they might say, or, *I think there's a history of alcoholism somewhere way back in my family, but we never spoke about it so I can't be sure*, or even something much vaguer, *It's on both sides, this illness*. In these words, I hear the crackle of guilt. Because to cast around for someone to shoulder the burden of your alcoholic behaviour with you – particularly someone who can no longer defend themselves against the claim – goes deeply against the credo of self-accountability that AA preaches: it's my shit. It's all there in *The Big Book*: 'Acceptance is the answer to all my problems today. When I am disturbed, it is because I find some person, place, thing or situation – some fact of my life unacceptable to me [. . .].' Acceptance will be mine if I just stop looking, if

I call off the search altogether. There's a simple beauty in there: it doesn't start with someone else, it starts with me.

And so, alongside these genealogical investigations you might also hear someone correct themselves: *but the reason I drank is because I'm an alcoholic; I was born that way.* Yet the forensic urge persists, because if you inherited this thing then it might make more sense to you. It might absolve you, even. Sometimes, the search becomes frantic: trace back the rot, find out where it started, scrub the past clean, scrub yourself clean. Purged, you may sit back: the genealogical pipes cleaned. Until the other question starts to whisper itself in your ear: will it end with me, or have I given this to my children too? I'm not there yet but I can't rule it out.

It's a bit simpler for me. Or Is it? I am the product of two alcoholics. There is no doubt as to how I ended up this way: I have a double dose of the gene. For years, the narrative ran like this: my mother drank, yes, but my father was *the* drinker. All my friends knew it, and all my friends' mothers knew it. *He* was my alcoholic, his blood pulsing through my veins even before I had left the womb. He drank in ways that are specific to his class and generation: stiff whiskies in his office in the City after work, martinis at the tennis club, hip flasks full of grog at the top of the mountain before the race, Sancerre before a business lunch. As I see it, these were cultural and generational drinking habits but they are also particularly masculine ones, carried out largely amongst other men and coded with all the privilege of sex: the freedom to drink unencumbered by children or domestic life, the permission granted by a society that encourages men to drink as proof of masculinity, the freedom to earn and the independence to do as you please. As his daughter, I struggled to see how any of these habits could be passed down to me; it seemed unnatural, impossible even. It is far easier, as a daughter, to blame your mother, to look back through her. And, unfairly, I did just that.

I look at my mother and I know that I am her daughter. I am always shocked to discover just how similar our ways of existing are: the way we fall asleep amongst a tangled underlay of books and magazines, our poor sleep patterns punched through with bouts of insomnia, our almost identical palates, a robust brute physicality that means we are never really ill. There are darker likenesses too, that weld us together with an unmistakable glue: a certain sharpness of voice, flashes of rage, a tendency to just give up, a disdain for any kind of due process; all these things I know I have inherited from her just as she might say she inherited them from her mother.

But what does an alcoholic inheritance look like in two women? Unlike the ring, it can't be held in your hand, or put away in a box and forgotten. When we first went into the rooms of AA together, the question hung thick in the air: was our drinking the same? Inevitably, the answer is confusing. It was the same and it was different, just as we look hugely alike to some and not at all to others. As women, we drank in the same domestic spaces and places: the first drink I ever had was in my mother's kitchen just as her first drink was stolen from the drinks cabinet in her mother's house.

Generationally though, we drank in different ways. As a teenager in the late sixties, drink was available in excess but the binge attitude and 'ladette' culture that I came of age as a drinker around was many years away for her. In AA, these discussions are moot.

They're too clever and too wily: *Take the cotton wool out of your ears and stuff it in your mouth*, I heard someone loudly say in a meeting once. They're the sort of questions you start asking if you're looking to relapse, what old-timers call paving the way for a drink. That AA can contain not just my mother and me, but millions of others proves that it doesn't matter which decade you drank in or which kitchen cupboard you stole the bottle from. I know this but still it doesn't stop me asking because how many people share the rooms with a parent? *More than you think*, I can hear a voice say and I stop myself.

When I was eighteen, my father invited me to join him on a trip to Madagascar, a place where he had often brokered insurance and where he had many friends. It was, he said, a chance for him to introduce me to some people who might give me a job after university, and to speak French. It was also a chance for him to drink exactly as he wanted to away from my stepmother. But I didn't know that. I jumped at the opportunity, flattered by the offer from this distant but revered figure.

From the airport onwards, it became apparent that we were not alone in the way that I had envisaged. Between us loomed the giant brick wall of alcohol, blocking any communication. On the plane, my father sat in a different cabin, consigning me to the back. It was only when I walked up the aisle that I could see why: slumped in his seat, his lips reddened from wine, he was clearly in a state of alcoholic blackout. Appalled but not surprised, I retreated to my seat and immediately ordered a drink myself. Much of the trip would play out in the same way: long, alcohol-heavy dinners after which he would disappear with no explanation given, tense silences before the first glass was delivered into shaky hands, the faux pleasantries exchanged over breakfast designed to paper over the unsayable. Ironically, it was only when we spoke French in a group that I felt I could communicate properly with him; each of us dissembling the other.

It was my first prolonged exposure to his drinking with adult eyes, having lived for most of my adolescence with my mother. It was also the first – and last – time that I would spend so much time alone with him before he died. But what shocked me most was not the blackouts or the silences, or any of the other deeply bizarre alcoholic behaviours that he went in for, but the bond that fizzed between us when we drank, a liquid power line that connected me to him after years of separation since he had divorced my mother. Fourteen years apart reconnected in an instant; the lights back on after a power cut. The relief!

Up until that point, I had considered myself my mother's faithful apostle, believing that it was from her that I had inherited what was becoming, even at eighteen, a heavy legacy. Whenever I had looked to my father, I felt sure that his drinking could not be, would never be, my own. Its shell was hard and unfamiliar, conducted in foreign and muscular places, nothing like the known quantity of my mother's addiction drawn out in the domestic playground of the home behind the kitchen door, under the bed, bottles stashed behind clothes that smelt of mothballs and soap.

This is dangerous territory for any alcoholic: *I'm not like that*. It's remarkably easy to do with friends and acquaintances. 'I'm not like her, am I?' you ask someone quietly in a moment of sweaty panic. 'No! Nothing like her,' your co-conspirator (usually someone who is also drinking with you at the time) says silkily.

I once watched someone at a university party rock herself in a corner, her crotch darkening as piss began to stain her dress while we looked on and whispered. How many people were holding her up as the danger line then? More than I could know. I certainly was, even though I would do the same thing not two years later.

My mother, by her own account, asked people all the time whether she was an alcoholic, most of them telling her what she wanted to hear and what they wanted to say: 'No, Jules!' Who, after all, wants to call someone out? I even heard my father describe *his* alcoholic to someone once: 'It's the bottles he hid, you see. Wouldn't go to the meetings apparently . . . ' he said, nodding vigorously and drawing heavily on his cigarette while we listened, stunned.

Making these judgement calls in the context of your parents is a lot harder because, try as you might, you can never disassociate yourself from them. That's the great fantasy. You grow up and you say you'll never be like them. You *know* you'll never be like them because to turn into that would be horrifying, you couldn't possibly. Although in fact, I'm not sure the feeling is even that distinct: you don't think it's horrifying because it's from the deep tissue of home, and whatever that looks like, it's still home, it's where you come from. No, it's subtler and more complicated than that: I won't be like them, you say to yourself; I'll be me instead.

Except being you is harder than you thought because you keep coming up against a huge monolith of something else, if only you could name it. And then you do start drinking because you're a teenager and everyone else drinks and you don't want to be different because you've had it with being different. It's fun and it's nothing like what you have seen your parents do. You're also very good at it, you can drink a lot, you're an *adult*. And then one day, now you're just about old enough, your father offers you a drink and the great unsayable, unknowable pain of old lodges itself in your throat, except now you're drunk too.

Julia

Inheritance

Sometimes in the early morning, when I glance in the bathroom mirror, I see my mother looking back at me reproachfully. This fills me with an inexplicable sense of doom. But why? I am her daughter, after all, why would I not look like her? And why the sense of doom – the powerful feeling of being trapped by that likeness – the idea that however far I've run from her I'm still back where I started?

That early-morning me in the mirror, that reflection, is like glancing into a series of mirrors all the way back to the very inside of my mother's being. It is a glance, a look, that binds us together ineluctably. And that's what scares me and makes me feel trapped by the sight of her now, long after she has died. She is still with me, still tugging at my hem. And I don't want her. I don't want the burden of her reproach. At the same time, I realise that this hostility towards the sight of her keeps me tied to the painful memories of my relationship with her. Is there a way of acknowledging how difficult things were between us and making peace with her?

I am hoping to find an answer here by investigating these dark and shameful feelings. I need to let them out of their cave into the light where they can evaporate on the breeze like my mother's ashes did when we scattered them on the sea in south-west Scotland on a high clear day in June 2012. I felt the most terrible sense of doom that day, a kind of infinite feeling of something broken that could never be mended. The sadness I felt circled round me during the hour afterwards when we sat on the rocks at the beach she knew so well, looking out to sea; I'll never forget it.

At the very end of her life, I went with Arabella to visit Mum in the nursing home where she was living. We were confronted with a shocking sight. My mother had refused to allow anyone to cut her hair, which had grown almost to shoulder length. She no longer wore her bridge, so her jagged, discoloured teeth were fully on view. She was naked under the rug covering the lower part of her body as she also refused to allow them to dress her. The room had an undertow of stink.

My instinct was to flee, but I couldn't. We sat there and tried to make conversation. I looked at Mum and I felt guilty. Guilty that I'd been instrumental in her being here when she didn't want to be, guilty that I didn't love her enough, guilty that the sight of her like this repelled me. The whole situation was just unbearably sad and depressing.

When I was a child, grown-ups would say to me: *You're so like your mother*, and I used to hate it, even then. I felt, without being entirely aware of it, that being like her physically meant I was also like her mentally.

But a physical likeness is a very powerful thing to share. It's more than just a 'likeness' – it's closeness on a cellular level. I have the same annoying, fine, floppy hair, the same nice legs – below the knee, anyway – the same thick, dark eyebrows, the same hazel eyes; those eyes with their slight look of surprise in the early morning – the startled deer in the thicket – which remind me so painfully of Mum.

The older she got, the more trapped she became in the dark wood of her life, unable to escape from the jostling army of resentments and grudges that hedged her in on all sides like the sharpest of thorns. Each way she turned she became impaled. She was utterly a slave to her thoughts. For Mum, a thought was a fact, a tendency I have, too. Very often, I have to stop and look at my thoughts, step back from them to get some space.

The knowledge that she felt like a victim is intensely painful to me because, all her life, particularly as she got older, she wanted me to save her. And I couldn't save her. I was too busy swimming away from her as fast as I could. She used to say, 'I don't want to be a burden,' and that word 'burden' made me wince.

I once said to her – apropos of quite what, I forget now – 'We grow old in our own image.' And she almost shrieked, '*No*, don't say that . . . don't say that.' Cruelly, I allowed her to squirm in her own pain. I said nothing. And I knew she was aware of it. I might as well have hit her.

I remember it so clearly because it was one of the rare occasions when I actually got an honest response out of her. Most of the time, she hid behind a very high, daunting wall of denial. She could never, or hardly ever, be wrong about anything. Once she had made up her mind about something or someone, that was it. She would rather fall on her sword than admit she was wrong. And fall on her sword she did, many, many times, even to the extent of not seeing three out of five of her grandchildren because of a poisonous dispute with my brother. Sometimes when we drank together, we could gingerly touch on certain aspects of the past that were less unsafe than others: my first stepmother, Rosemary, for instance. She was so awful, it wasn't a problem to listen to my mother's denunciations. Rosemary was a piece of the past that I could happily fling on the toppling pyre of my mother's grievances about her life; then we would move on to my father, and there, things began to get complicated. I wasn't really up for nuking Dad and everything he stood for, and when it came to my brother, I thought it better not to speak at all – even when drunk, I knew this.

Sometime in my early forties, our relationship became utterly stuck in emotional pack-ice. Beneath the surface, gigantic forces of resentment were churning but she was also ageing, and ageing badly. The stress of her dark feelings literally began to pull her physically under. 'Arthritis is a stress disease,' she said to me once, without seeming to understand the enormity of what she was saying. I have to admit I didn't ask what she meant, because I had a pretty good idea of what she would say about the source of that stress, and I just didn't want to hear it again.

She had one hip operation, and then another, and another. Her back gave out. Then her knees. Her mental state began to fracture, and she became more and more angry with everyone, including me, whom she saw as a traitor because I had simply refused to allow her the moral high ground about my brother, whom she had wronged. We had nearly come to physical blows about him one ghastly Christmas when I was alone with her. That was when the pack-ice really started gathering. I refused to speak to her for a couple of months, but then she wrote to me saying she would like it if she could see me and, of course, Arabella. She didn't apologise. That wasn't her style. If she could have said sorry – just once – for all the damage, things would have been different. One 'sorry' would have been enough to melt all that ice. It never came.

But who was this strange, tormented person who turned out to be my mother? Born in Australia to elderly parents, her father, Colonel Arthur Moseley, had fought at Gallipoli and then lost a leg in France fighting in the Ypres salient. He was a hero, like so many men of that benighted generation, and to my mother he was always 'the one'. Her mother, Bessie, was from a distinguished family of Australian pioneers, women who had crossed the Blue Mountains in crinolines and survived to tell the tale, but my mother loathed her mother from the beginning, or so it appeared.

The trouble with looking for clues to one's inheritance is that with grandparents, however well documented, the trail begins to grow cold. Who was my grandmother, apart from the gigantic old woman of my childhood who wore pink satin stays bought from Harrods? I have no clue. But I imagine that she was a wounded soul who in some way passed on her own sense of incompleteness lock, stock and barrel to my mother, and then to me.

My mother was extremely critical of her mother. She felt unloved by her and rejected and yet at the same time, she could feel the role of spinster daughter and carer being made ready for her and she was determined to escape. She managed to flee physically, but her mother was with her to the end of her life, kept alive by my mother's burning resentment towards her. As I write this, I realise that I am doing exactly the same thing. Just before Mum died, she was still grumbling about Granny to me on the telephone.

There is a photograph of my mother at Randwick Races in Sydney in the late 1940s with her best friend, who would later become my godmother. Both young women look fresh and fun, with tiny waists and jaunty tight-fitting velvet hats, two shining girls emerging from the ruin fields of the Second World War ready to take on the world, or so it seems in the picture. My mother is smiling in that photograph. She had a lovely smile, like a burst of sunlight on a dull day, and there was a gaiety about her, which married life quickly snuffed out.

Mum came to this country, so she told me, to escape from Bessie, although it had meant leaving her beloved father, Arthur. There was a family house in this country, a kind of centre of operations in Monmouthshire at Cefn Tilla Court where my great-aunt and uncle presided and this was where my parents, second cousins, met in the early 1950s. My extremely *grande-dame* of a great-aunt arranged a marriage between them – a really bad idea, as it turned out. Sometimes I wish I could have intervened in their dreams and said to them both individually: *Just don't do it. Please don't do it.*

At the time of her marriage, whatever was wrong with my mother mentally was starting to emerge. The honeymoon in Paris was blighted by illness and from this moment on, illness would become a leitmotif in her life. As a very young child, I remember her being 'off-colour', like some Victorian heroine, not well, suffering in some mysterious way. There was always something nameless going on in the background about her health. I think she started taking sleeping pills then.

After I'd got sober, I wondered if my mother was an alcoholic. She certainly had what we call the 'isms' of alcoholism: she was

often in a rage for no particular reason; she was insanely controlling (everything from the kitchen cupboards to her desk was
locked and the keys hidden) and also a perfectionist. She suffered
from paranoia throughout her life, absolutely certain that people
were out to get her, but sometimes went to the opposite extreme
where random people were absolutely marvellous for no apparent
reason. Towards the end of her life, she had fallen out with almost
everyone, even her very oldest friends. Quite often people would
say to me, 'I don't know what I've done but . . . ' And I would reply,
'I don't know either. This is what happens with Mum.' And we
would shake our heads in sad acknowledgement of the fact that
my mother was a sinking ship firing on her rescuers.

Now, when I think about Mum and her tragic, embittered
life I think she might have been a manic depressive. The sauce-
pan-crashing tyrant of my childhood had moments of joy, too,
when all was well; moments of kindness when she asked me how
I was feeling. They were rare but they were there.

As her marriage fell about her ears (and mine – I was home
alone) her sense of victimhood grew and grew. Everything was
my father's fault: the chaotic finances, the inability to make a go of
anything, the debts he had run up. On and on the list went. I began
to hate her more and more. When we three had supper together
Mum was almost always in a cold rage that was impossible to
penetrate. I remember trying to make polite conversation like some
stranger who just happened to have dropped in from outer space.

And it was from this fractured background that I rushed into
what I call my 'starter' marriage, then rushed out of that and into
another marriage a couple of years later with a man much older
than me. My reinvention of myself had begun, although I had

no clue then that I was using men to fix myself. On my better days, I just felt I was this glamorous, doomed figure, leading my glamorous, doomed life. Very quickly, second time around, I became aware that I had married the wrong man, again, but I couldn't deal with that idea. I just drank more, trying to keep the truth from myself.

Nevertheless, having a husband and children protected me from Mum. I'd jettisoned my old self, safely stashed her in that sealed container on the ocean floor. Or so I thought. The fact that I was an alcoholic was something I preferred not to think about. I sort of knew it, but I kept the idea at bay in the same way as I kept the memory of my broken self at bay, or the fact that my marriage was already collapsing.

As soon as you have children, however, your past starts to catch up with you, however you deny it. The hormonal surges of pregnancy and motherhood disturbed the thin crust of my sanity. Every now and again I became aware of something vast, unknowable and frightening banging up against me, a kind of submerged mass of feeling. Naturally, I turned my back on it.

What sort of a mother was I to my daughter? Of course, I wanted to be the best mother ever. I definitely wasn't going to do it the way my mother had. I was different to her. I had a completely different kind of life. I was a writer, a bohemian. I lived in a world of writers, literary parties, intellectual discussions. Once Mum found a novel by William Faulkner on my bed. She tried to read it, she said, didn't understand a word. *You're so clever, I envy you.* I didn't admit to her then that I couldn't read a word of it either.

I had Arabella when I was twenty-five. I was already an alcoholic and had been since my drinking started in my teens. Alcohol was welded to me, entwined around me like a serpent, constantly whispering in my ear: *Nothing a drink won't fix, you deserve it,* all the usual clichés, or should that be lies? I think of the words of baptism in the Catholic Church: *Do you deny Satan and all his empty promises?* Drink was always an empty promise for me, I just didn't know it. I drank whenever I could get away with it. It was always on my mind, but I hid it. It's quite easy to hide in our society, which considers alcohol the solution to all life's ills. But it made me hungover and neglectful, a lazy, resentful parent, in hiding both from myself and the needs of my child. I loved her deeply but, just as I had with my mother, she picked up the darkness in me on that same cellular level; in other words, what she was experiencing and what was embedding itself in her was intergenerational trauma.

My restlessness continued throughout my thirties and forties when Arabella was growing up. My drinking continued, too, always worse, never better. I kidded myself that I was hiding it successfully from my child. I wasn't. And as she became a teenager, she began to imitate me.

I remember driving past a pub in Old Church Street, and seeing Arabella standing in the window holding a cigarette in one hand and a drink in the other. She was fifteen and just at the very beginning of her career as an alcoholic. It's a vignette that has stayed with me, a kind of snapshot of my mothering, or lack of it. I was in a car full of people and we all roared with laughter. Like mother, like daughter, ha ha!

Without knowing it, I was descending into the depths, the never-ending flight of stairs that goes down into the dark if you're an alcoholic. When I was forty-two and Arabella was sixteen, I left my relationship of twelve years and rushed into yet another marriage, my third, or fourth, really, depending on whether you counted my recent relationship. I'd managed not to marry him, though I'm not quite sure how. The new marriage to another writer from a very similar background to mine (aristocratic, impoverished) was, predictably, a catastrophe, a period of profound unhappiness for me right from the word go. Now, I realise it was my last gasp at reinventing myself: I would ditch my own extremely unsatisfactory family, including my child, and graft myself onto another. I'd show them, whoever 'they' were.

Yet again, I would become someone else. Not a mother, not a daughter. I would be a bohemian member of the large bohemian tribe I was marrying into. I'd published quite a few novels, after all. I was definitely one of them. Except I wasn't. I was just a lonely, mad, alcoholic woman. Only a professional fantasist could have come up with something so bananas. It was like standing with outstretched arms on the edge of a cliff with jagged rocks beneath thinking you can fly.

Arabella was at university by now, and rumours of her crazy behaviour drifted back to me like flakes of ash borne on the wind from a forest fire. In spite of what was going on, however, she distinguished herself by getting a very good degree. *Ha*, I thought, *all is well*. Nothing to worry about after all, panic over. Just a bad dream. Next thing I knew, she was hospitalised for her mental health and under the supervision of a crash team at the Charing Cross Hospital. It was true, after all. This was the dark fruit, the poisoned chalice of her inheritance from me.

The time of reckoning was approaching for both of us, although we did not know it yet.

Chapter Three

Shelter

Arabella

'Where do you live, dear? I just need to pop it down on the form so we can admit you . . .' It's a good question. Where do I actually live? For the purposes of the kindly nurse's form, I live in a dark room in a small basement flat off the Fulham Palace Road with a friend from university. But I don't really live there. I don't really live anywhere. That is how I have come to end up in the Mental Health Crisis Unit of the Charing Cross Hospital, as luck would have it, just a stone's throw from the flat in which I don't think I live. It is the spring of 2009, and I am hanging by a thread. Hanging, in fact, by the thread of a thread.

In addition to my perceived homelessness, or rather, my inability to find a physical home no matter where I wash up, I can find no shelter in anything I do. What is a shelter? In my mind, it is the place where you shield yourself from the storm. It is a fragile structure, but still, it is something. It is a place to catch your breath, a place to push your hair behind your ears and still yourself, a place to stop your hands shaking. It is, by definition, temporary.

In alcohol, I find a temporary shelter every day. From the first sip to the last shaky gulp, I hover gratefully under its tarpaulin roof. The problem is, the roof blows off every day, and every day I find this appalling. Every hangover feels as if someone has pushed over the last thing that was protecting me from the elements and left me to the pouring rain and lashing wind. Still, I persist because it is better than no leaky tarpaulin at all. In my cheap bottle opener, grubby glasses and Laurent Perrier ashtray stolen from my father's house, I shelter. But the patch upon which I pitch my shelter is getting smaller and smaller by the day. Sometimes I think I am not so much in need of shelter as asylum. In the end, that is where I wind up.

I think I know I am unravelling. But it is hard to unpick this trouble from my mother's current troubles – which are profound and marital – and the trouble I have experienced my whole life: a sense of desolation and homelessness that I can never understand. I sense, somewhere deep down, that I am caught up in some kind of dreadful reciprocal dance with my mother, but I am powerless to stop it. Or maybe I just don't want to. Increasingly our phone conversations take place when we are both drunk; a dance we know well and to which we are excellent partners. I don't know what I say to her, but I know that I feel compelled to call her all the time; it is another addiction in my ever-tangling web. And so, we sit, glasses in hand in different cities, and shout at each other down the phone. I don't know if she shouts, actually. I am told that I do by my friend from university with whom I co-exist in high dysfunction (mostly my own). I shout and then I cry and then I drink some more and then it is the morning and the tarpaulin is nowhere to be seen and I must go to work.

It is at work that the great crisis begins to unfurl. The crisis has been unfurling for a long, long time but it is in this adult arena that it gathers speed at a shocking rate. If I haven't found rock bottom yet, I certainly come close to it there.

When I leave university I realise, with some horror, that I must get a job. It is not that I think that someone will pay for me – everyone is alarmingly clear that there is no money, ever, for me – but I cannot think what I am qualified to do. My ambitions, when I voice them, are either wildly unrealistic (write a book) or ridiculously mundane (just get by). I have, after all, never seen either of my parents go to work. I saw my mother writing her books early in the morning and late at night, seated at her enormous Amstrad computer, yes. I remember visiting my father at his office in the City as a child, my eyes watering from the cigarette smoke in his office, yes. But by the time of my coming to consciousness with the adult world, neither of my parents went to an office in any kind of routine way.

So what? Plenty of people had parents who didn't work, and it never stopped them, you might reasonably say. But in a lifetime of mirroring my parents, I find it hard to strike off in a new direction. Instead, I do nothing of the sort and end up in a poor approximation of my father's erstwhile career in business. At the very least, I think, as I accept a job in financial PR, I am walking the same streets as he did. Sometimes, when I have had too much to drink in the pub next to the office, I think I catch a glimpse of him. But he is nowhere near those alleyways, he is far away in a remote house in Wales, and he is drinking himself to death.

Financial PR is a curious profession. Neither banker nor journalist, the PR exists in the parasitic space in between the two, their calls eternally unanswered. Naturally, this is not what they tell themselves. No, no, the narrative is very different: PRs are the ones with exclusive access to the clients without which the entire system will fold; PRs are indispensable operators greasing the wheels between the press, the clients and the bankers. The young recruitment agent who gets me the job is well versed in its benefits and tells me I am just the type of person to 'get along well' in the industry. I am unduly flattered. I have never got along that well in anything, I don't think. I sense somewhere within that I am making a huge mistake, but plenty of people seem to encourage me – it is perhaps rare to see me get on with anything, let alone well. As a profession, it promises great financial reward. As a young, burgeoning alcoholic, I am extremely interested in anything that will earn me money without having to expend too much effort; something that won't get in the way of my real job: drinking.

Two long months into the job, I realise that I am not at all cut out for the work, which involves the analysis of balance sheets and company accounts alongside a diligence and care for the work that I cannot muster. This is in part because my mathematical literacy is so poor and in part because my emotional literacy is also impoverished. As many alcoholics may relate to, I consider myself to be either wildly too good for the job or hopelessly bad at it and can find no middle ground without some kind of emotional short-circuit. I am, in short, a child masquerading in the body of a young woman. I have not understood that there is no shelter for people like me in the adult world; that we are either ejected from the functioning world or simply fall out of it. I try to quietly fall out of it but in the end become forcibly removed from it.

On any typical morning in the office, the juniors are expected to be at their desks at 7 a.m. From the dark basement flat off the Fulham Palace Road to the office in the City, this start time requires me to be up at 5.45 a.m. Very often, I have woken only two hours before to swig wine from a tooth mug in order to put me back to sleep, a fugue state I cannot stay in for any restorative amount of time. I know my mother does the same as I have seen her guard a dark blue glass next to her bed with her life. *If she does it, I can do it*, I think, not for the first time. When the alarm goes off, I am in a deep fog of intoxicated sleep, somewhere in the lost fields between a dream and blackout. I levitate upwards before shoving a fag in my mouth and getting dressed in the regulation black trouser suit I wear to hide stains and burns.

All the way to the tube station I smoke furiously, each one as if it were my last, like a victim on the way to the guillotine. Once on the tube, I sit with my head resting on my chest and feign sleep. When I look up, I think I see other passengers laughing at me, laughing at some part of myself that is protruding or collapsed. Years later, in a meeting, I tell the room this and I can hear a chorus of assent; we alcoholics are persecuted, yes, but by ourselves most of all.

The morning of the great crisis begins much like any other. I am flushed out of my lair by the usual alarms and beeping and make to propel myself onto the tube. I am more fragile than usual on this particular morning, as I have been drinking with my mother the night before in a depressing pub near Notting Hill Gate tube station. *Her third marriage is collapsing*, she says, *she does not know what she will do*, she sobs. She is very drunk as she relays all this information to me and I feel the deep ache of premature responsibility, an ache that has pointlessness shaded all around its edges. I have been drinking since I left the office at 5 p.m. and I don't know how I can help her. Instead of offering advice – or, at best, staying silent – I start to become angry and remind her how much I begged her not to marry him. I remind her of the time I stood crying in the street outside school begging her to leave him while she reassured me that she had landed on her feet this time. I remind her of the day they sat me down and told me they were getting married and how I had stormed out of the café and disappeared for hours. I remind her that she married him not six months after she had left the artist, of how everyone thought she had taken leave of her senses.

I think she will get angry with me but instead she says nothing because she is used to it. After some period of silence, I think she must be crying but I can't tell. Drunk, I am insulated from my cruelty, insulated by self-righteousness. Eventually, we reach stalemate and stagger off into the night, she back to Oxford and me to my lair. Our mutual unhappiness must have radiated across the whole sorry pub.

The next morning, I am more jagged than usual. The daily ritual of rebooting myself is harder than ever. People really do look at me on the tube as I sit and sob indulgently before getting off at Embankment and walking the rest of the way to the office so that I can smoke. I feel dangerously foreign to myself, as if a stranger has taken over at the wheel and could crash into a wall at any point. I have forgotten, because I take no care in my job, that it is the morning of a big pitch to a brewery for us to do their PR. In my current state, I am the anti-PR for any such business, an embodiment of how dangerous drink is. But such musings are by the by. There is work to be done, or rather grunt work: pitch documents to be printed, share-price graphs to be calibrated, last-minute rehearsals of the brief. On any other day, I would skulk and hide around the disabled bathroom but on this morning, there is no shelter. My boss, a portly man who wears braces and speaks in a loud voice designed to let you know that he went to public school, has sent me sixteen emails by the time I turn my computer on at 07.10 a.m. As soon as he sees me at my desk, he walks over, his gait quickening.

'You're late and I need all of the documents detailed in my emails to you in the next hour,' he says with what I detect as glee but could just be exasperation. He is, after all, just trying to do his job with the most insubordinate of employees. I look him in the eye and burst into tears. After some period of loud sobbing, I look up and see him walk back to his desk and make a phone call, his head bowed into the receiver so other people can't hear.

I used to think about him a lot when I first got sober. His name was D and he was one of the few people who held a mirror up to me during that time; one of the rare few whom it felt deeply uncomfortable to disappoint. I didn't give a fuck about lots of other people, some of them very close to me, but for some reason I did care about letting him down. I would feel ashamed whenever I thought of him, my cheeks blushing involuntarily, and I would press my fingers into my palm in an attempt to distract myself with some other, more literal pain. At eight years sober, I wanted to make amends to him; I desperately wanted to say sorry for that day and for it all. But I never did, and I still think about it.

***

'It's Arabella, yes? What a lovely name,' a different nurse says, writing something on a blue clipboard. I suppose Arabella is a lovely name; everyone always says so. But everything else about me that evening isn't lovely. My face, red and swollen from prolonged periods of hysterical crying, stares back at me from the mirror opposite the bed on which I am sitting. I don't remember taking off my clothes, but I must have done since I am wearing a hospital gown with a split down the back, my bare back gaping out of it like a mouth.

'Your friend brought you here,' she continues. 'I gather there was some crisis with your employers, and you left your place of employment abruptly, sometime in the morning?'

Employers, place of employment. Careful, measured, terms for what was certainly an unmeasured episode. As far as I can recall, I had appeared before my bosses at work. There, in a glass office with the blinds drawn, they enumerated the charges brought against me: rudeness, insubordination, leaving too early, arriving too late, disappearing at certain times of day. I had listened, sullenly, before storming out, past the rows of desks, past the screens, past the shocked faces, into the cold air of Fleet Street. I wanted to drink it in, to blow the cold air into my head, to blow away the rot inside, but I couldn't. I went into the nearest pub and ordered a drink. A drink that blew me like a leaf all the way from Fleet Street to the mental health unit in the Charing Cross Hospital.

The mental health unit was the wrong shelter for me, as it turned out. But I didn't think so at the time. At the time, it felt like the perfect place, as if the tarpaulin was finally, firmly secured above my head. I knew my lines well: I had suffered depression from my early teens, I explained; it was a family affliction, I went on, a family affliction that was most pronounced down the maternal line. I gathered pace here; it was, after all, a story I had told many times before: my grandmother and mother were depressed and they had passed it, through some dark cellular alchemy, on to me. It was not my fault and there was nothing I could do, I finished with a flourish. I certainly could not be expected to work in any normal, office-going capacity. I simply wasn't well enough, I reasoned. I was in a mental health unit alone on a Tuesday night for Christ's sake, was that not enough?

I do not think, to look at me, that you would have disputed a diagnosis of depression, my ringed eyes and bruised limbs acting as visual accompaniments to the more nebulous diagnosis of psychiatric unrest. I *was* depressed; I had been on anti-depressants since I was seventeen and had been in and out of NHS therapy provision for much of that time. Most of the therapeutic relationships I had made, I was fired from for failing to turn up because I was either drunk or hungover. As the psychotherapist (and recovering alcoholic) Carl Erik Fisher so lucidly puts it, 'We describe mental illness as if it's an entity, a clearly demarcated state, or at least a state with some sort of checkpoint or transition, but I passed no such gate.' I, too, felt that I had passed no such obvious threshold with my depression. I was clinging on to enough, if not many, vestiges of a normal life: I had a job, I shared a flat, I had a mobile phone. No, drinking was not the problem. Instead, I would court female madness – specifically the inherited kind – as my malady: pills, therapy, institutions, bed rest, isolation; I courted it all with some success until even I couldn't stomach my own hypocrisy.

If I had to find a moment when my drinking entered a different phase, or took on a different colouration, I would name this one. When you tell your story in an AA meeting, the problem is how to narrate the twists and turns, the reversals and straight lines of addiction. How to tell the story. Do you begin with the first drink, the very first time alcohol trickled down your throat, activating a thousand twinkling stars? Or should you start with the first time alcohol made you do something so alien to your sense of self that you struggled to look at yourself in the mirror? The time you woke up next to a man you didn't know in a strange house? Or maybe the first time you lied about your drinking? Like so many female alcoholics, I have plenty of these moments to narrate. I could tell you all of them, I could really shock you, but I won't, because, tragically, the turning point for me wasn't any of these. It was the first time I sat in a hospital gown in a mental health unit in the middle of the night, sobbing.

Writing about this episode, I think of stories. I think about how stories are all in the telling, about how this story was a house in which I could live, a place to wait out the storm. In delivering myself to the mental health services – and I had, according to my friend R, been adamant that that was where I needed to go – I see that I was trying to write myself into a story of depression, a story of lunacy and female hysteria and asylums. The story of alcoholism did not, then, feel like a shelter for me. How could it? Far better, I thought, to live under the cover of depression. Depression wasn't your fault, after all. It was passed down in a chromosomal time bomb across the generations. My mother was depressed. Her mother had been depressed. I sought out depression like you might seek out a place to live, inspecting its rooms and windows, imagining myself within its walls. It would take me many more years to realise that this refuge was wholly not mine, to accept that I was simply squatting in it, hoping not to be found out.

Julia

Shelter

I remember saying to the woman doing my nails somewhere in Kensington, 'I'm getting married tomorrow.' It was February 2001. Purposely, I didn't add in the word 'again'. 'Oooh,' she squealed, predictably, 'that's so lovely.'

I felt the uplift, the warmth, the sense of achieving one of life's goals that getting married was supposed to bring. It lasted for a second; there was a tiny surge of dopamine, that feeling of being on the inside, for once. But it had vanished by the time she got to my toes. This was also someone who didn't know me, almost the only person to whom I could make such a seemingly innocent remark.

To anyone else – my daughter, for instance – such a statement would have been met with outright hostility at worst, or, *Yeah, right* . . . at best. She had tried to talk me out of it but had run up against the marble cliff of my resolve to *change my life*.

I was unhappy in the relationship I had been in, but I had no idea how to fix it and neither, it seemed, did he. We were at an impasse. I was fed up. I decided I wanted out. Never mind the fact that I was leaving a man I had loved more than anyone and who had been around during Arabella's childhood and to whom she was intensely attached. I knew this. I had witnessed her tears when he came round to collect some of his stuff, but I was absolutely determined to leave him. It overrode every other thought in my head.

I took an inventory of his faults constantly: *bad tempered; broke; no help; on a different wavelength; no understanding of me as an artist, writer or whatever.* The relationship was all about him: his needs, his career, his goals. His endless problems with art dealers, which went on and on. Always their fault, of course. I had tried to be supportive, but you can't give what you haven't got.

Active alcoholics spend a lot of time trying to do the right thing and failing for obvious reasons: hungover, self-absorbed, self-pitying. I was all three with knobs on. He loved me, I knew that, but why didn't he show it more? Why didn't he try to hold on to me? The fact that he made no effort to do so strengthened my resolve to reinvent myself as someone else. Little did I know that this was my illness talking, the serpent alcohol whispering in my ear. I wanted to change the way I felt about my life and getting married again seemed big enough and dramatic enough to make the wholesale change I sought. With glorious hindsight, I should have tried to repair the relationship, but I was also an active alcoholic and my judgement was profoundly unsound, just as it always had been about almost everything. I was an impulse-driven, chronically hungover, professional fantasist trying to make a serious decision. Of course I got it wrong.

I hadn't actually been married for a while, I reasoned, and now that I was at the beginning of my forties, it really was time to get all that sorted out, find someone, and then marry them. Simples. I had someone in mind – a target, in other words. A man I already knew, a writer, who longed for a child, he had told me. I pricked up my ears at this. I could do that, I thought. I've done it once, I can do it again. This was wrong on so many counts, I feel ashamed to admit it.

One of the huge perils of drink, dare I say it, for writers in particular, is the way that it's glorified by its creative sufferers: its injuries are seen as badges of honour, as darkly glamorous, as the exploits of 'real men', or amusing, mad women. Lunacy is normalised. Just read Hemingway or Fitzgerald or Dorothy Parker if you don't believe me. It's an illness that comes complete with its own awful pantheon of broken, tormented gods and goddesses. I fantasised about my new marriage – it was part of God's plan for me, obviously. I even assembled the music for the church ceremony, which never took place because, although my first marriage had been annulled, my husband-to-be's first marriage hadn't. We were Catholics adrift. Even that can be glamorised, if you try hard enough.

At the time of my wedding to this husband, I did not yet think of myself as an 'active alcoholic'. Far too clinical a phrase, and not entirely applicable to someone who just drank too much some of the time, in common with almost everyone I knew. *Yes, OK, I probably drank too much, but, hell, I would deal with my drinking sometime in the very near future*, I told myself. If I got pregnant, I would have to stop drinking, I reasoned (although 'reasoned' is the wrong word – perhaps I should say, 'I told myself'), without understanding that my drinking was now so far advanced that I couldn't stop, even if I wanted to. Unwittingly, I was about as far divorced from reason as it is possible to be. It never occurred to me that I should stop drinking *before* I conceived.

I had yet to accept the enormous but simple underlying fact that alcohol controlled my life and every thought I had and every action I took. I was in the grip of a monstrous, escalating mental illness but I couldn't see it. Alcoholism is so clever: it weaves itself into your life so subtly and then, even more subtly, it melts into you. It becomes indivisible from your thinking. I could not see that my thoughts were twisted out of shape, that I was driven by fear of being alone, of being left behind, of being abandoned, basically. In order not to be abandoned, I would become the abandoner. This is alcohol talking. Acting out this fantasy nearly cost me my life and everything else I held dear. No wonder I felt so stuck and powerless, no wonder I suffered such torments. How I got free is a miracle.

Only my mother approved of this new marriage, sort of, and that approval was an essential element of the black comedy that was one way of describing my life to date. She had looked up my husband-to-be's family in *Burke's Peerage* – what she referred to rather hilariously as 'The Good Book' (shades of Sir Walter Elliot) or *Burke's Landed Gentry* or the *Almanach de Gotha* or all three, and there, in each edition, in print, was his family, page after page of them, prominent for centuries, Catholic for centuries and centuries: '"Recusant" is the word, Ma,' I told her grandly. 'Well, they're certainly very PLU,' (an acronym used by her generation and class for 'People Like Us') she replied, defensively, uncertain, I think, about quite what 'recusant' actually meant but unable to admit it, and I took this remark for what it appeared to be: a gigantic seal of approval from someone whom I had been trying to differentiate myself from all my life. This is a perfect example of the lunacy of the active alcoholic. Mum didn't really approve of Catholics, but my new family weren't bog Irish Holy Romans, after all, they were the rarefied English (or in his case, the even rarer Welsh) variety, married and inter-married for many centuries inside a small pool of their own kind with the occasional foreign grandee thrown in to spice up the mix a bit. My husband-to-be's great-aunt had been married to a German prince, and there was much talk of a Hapsburg connection – they were 'the per-Hapsburgs' went the family joke. Oh, how I loved it. I was going to be a completely new me, different, better, totally reinvented. I was going to join the 'per-Hapsburgs' and become one myself. Per-Julia, perhaps.

My mother's approval meant more to me than I cared to admit, in spite of an entire lifetime spent trying my best not to be like her. Nevertheless, the inescapable truth was that I had been branded like a heifer with the desire to please her since I was born, and so this latest flourish in my tangled and, frankly, utterly disastrous love life, seemed finally like the 'right' one. It was my time, I reasoned to myself. At last. The One. More bonkers thinking, which went unchallenged. The fact that Arabella didn't want me to marry him was extremely painful for me, but I told myself she didn't understand – how could she? I still felt deeply resentful at her lack of understanding. I needed stability, for God's sake, and so did she. Why couldn't she see that? Stupid girl. All I was doing was trying to give her a secure base upon which she could stand. She saw through that at once and hated me for it, understandably. I was choosing someone other than her as my compass, doing exactly – more or less to the letter – what my father had done to me. History was repeating itself, as it has the habit of doing in families where nothing is ever discussed frankly. The fact that, yet again, I had chosen someone whom I could never be happy with was not lost on some of my friends, several of whom tried to warn me. I ignored them. 'Out of the frying pan and into the microwave,' said one of my oldest and closest friends, but I brushed it away.

But with one part of my mind, I knew he wasn't right in any way. I wrote down things about him in my diary that rang very loud alarm bells and then ignored the evidence. Some of his observations and certain reactions he had to everyday life were not normal. He once asked me if I wasn't too literary to have a car, for instance, which even in my early besotted-ness I realised was a bit off-beam. The way he lived, too, was extraordinary: untidiness doesn't begin to describe the chaos in his flat. I was shocked that anyone could live like that and get anything done but in another way I loved it: I was going to save him from himself, so instead of running for the hills I decided that I was going to be the one who would tidy up his life and allow him to function properly. It never occurred to me that he lived like this because he liked it. It suited him. He got things done, had undertaken important, demanding jobs and written several excellent books on the Middle East, upon which he was considered something of an expert.

On the emotional front, I knew that he had an alarmingly che-quered history when it came to women, but I hadn't quite worked out at that point what was going on with him. But he loved me, I told myself, and I loved him back; everything would be all right. *Amor vincit omnia* – always room for another cliché with a drunk. And I myself had had a long history of failed relationships. Who was I to judge?

For a very brief period right at the beginning of our relationship,

I was the One for him. I could do no wrong. It was the first time
this had ever happened to me. He wanted to be with me all the
time. I was perfect, a goddess, a genius; this attention and praise
was like a powerful narcotic, and I swiftly became hooked on it.
I wasn't an addict for nothing. We got engaged after a few weeks.
A middle-aged whirlwind. *How romantic, how sweet.* I continued
to live in my flat with Arabella but went to and fro. Quite often
I wasn't there when she came home from school.

Very swiftly, however, this relationship upon which I had staked
my life (and Arabella's) came apart at the seams. I still clung to the
myth of perfection that our first few weeks and months had been.
It was a bit like clinging to the myth of what drink would do for
me. I was always trying to get back to that elusive and euphoric
sweet spot and I was doing it again now. In other words, I was
behaving like an addict. One day, a few months in, I suddenly
found myself in the middle of a vicious argument with him; it felt
like I had been spun around by a gigantic unseen hand and I had
no idea how it had happened. I was devastated but I soldiered on,
clutching the relationship even harder.

What I didn't realise was that I was engaged in a psychological
process that I had no understanding of, which went like this:
idealisation, devaluation, rejection. That argument seemed to
me to be the beginning of the devaluation phase: I was no longer
a goddess, no longer a romantic figure, merely someone whose
sell-by date had expired, destined for the rubbish heap. I can
still feel the shock of that apparently random betrayal, even now.
I think it's Freud who says when you go to bed with someone
there are six people in the room: the two of you and both sets of
parents; all unwitting, I was engaged in yet another variation on

a theme of transactional love, something that was second nature to me, so much so that I couldn't even see it.

After three months, he called it off, but then I got pregnant. It was on again. My only value to him now was as a broodmare. I knew this but ignored it. It went in the sealed box at the bottom of the sea, along with my alcoholism. I felt desperate almost all the time. *It had to work. It had to work.* If I clung on tightly enough I could ride this out.

We went to Cairo for Christmas. Friends came out to join us. We walked all over Islamic Cairo, miles and miles every day. One night, in whatever restaurant we were in, I went to the loo and discovered I was bleeding. Spotting, it's called. Nothing serious, probably. But I returned to the table in a total panic. I had never bled at this stage before. All my worth to him was now tied up in the child I was to have. I wasn't Anne Boleyn but I felt a bit like her. I couldn't lose the baby. If I lost it, I would lose the marriage, too. How bonkers can you actually be? It would have been a very good thing if the marriage had never taken place, but I just couldn't see that. I was going to change my life and it had to come off. Had to. The fact that my ex was waging a campaign against me amongst our common friends made me even more determined to 'prove' that I'd made the right choice.

In the night, I woke up with a terrible crimped line of pain low down in my abdomen, like a period pain, only worse. I stumbled into the bathroom and sat on the loo and when I got up and looked into the bowl there was something there, a tiny crescent of a human, outlined against a mess of dark black blood. The brilliant, unshaded light was harsh. Perhaps I was hallucinating.

When I sat down on the loo again, a great gout of the same

dark jelly blood fell out of me, followed by more blood. I felt totally unhinged, like some demented figure in a play by Aeschylus, seeing my fate coming towards me but unable to stop it, unable to save that poor little homunculus I'd given birth to under that gruesome bathroom light. Not knowing what else to do, I went back to bed and somehow slept. In my hazed and fantastical dream, the child was beckoning to me to follow but I was so terrified I couldn't move.

In the morning, I told him what had happened. He wept. To be fair, he was stunned by the news. One of our friends suggested, rather tactlessly, that he had made me walk too far. In another row, too desperate to care what happened any longer, I raised this as a possibility. He said I was accusing him of killing his baby. I wasn't, of course, but we were both in shock. In a weird way, it bound us together. We would try again. There would be another baby.

It was January and our wedding was scheduled for 2 February. Would he call it off, again? I closed my eyes, crossed my fingers and hoped for the best. For some reason he didn't. Why not, I shall never know. Suddenly it's 1 February. Here I was with my newly done fingers and toes and a nice shell-pink Max Mara outfit to wear, plus one of the most uncomfortable pairs of shoes I've ever owned.

I went to the house of my future sister-in-law in Oxfordshire where the reception was to be. He went to a very plush hotel in Oxford. I spent the evening before putting out chairs and counting cutlery before going to the house of an old friend nearby who'd been a bridesmaid at my starter wedding in the Hebrides, where, having vowed not to drink, I ended up plastered. I woke up the next morning with a hangover, as usual. I looked at myself in the mirror with a feeling of doom in my heart. Why did I always, always do this? I still had no idea.

It was a glutinously cold February day in Oxford. The pub next to the register office sold me some vodka, which I downed, and let me have another little bottle for my handbag. Friends assembled, the deed was done, interrupted by my mother dropping her stick with a loud crash at the *moment critique*, a deliberate ploy, I felt, to attract attention to herself. How typical!

As I left the register office, I noticed a sign forbidding alcohol, and the thought crossed my mind that I could have scuppered the thing I most wanted by getting caught. But it had seemed such a good idea – what a stupid rule. Anything that got in my way was stupid.

The sun came out as I entered the house where the reception was being held. Glasses full of champagne gleamed and glistered with small bubbles. *What a beautiful sight*, I thought, helping myself to one and then another and another.

The reception went on. *Where was the groom?* people asked. No sign of him. I wondered if he'd done a runner. I wouldn't have put it past him to be on a plane to Jerusalem. It would have been better if he had. Eventually, he showed up, having stopped off at Ede & Ravenscroft on his way back to the hotel to buy the matching waistcoat for his extremely natty Gatsby-esque white linen suit, all of which had taken some time. Of course it had. This was the man whom I was hoping would shelter me from the gathering storm. What could possibly go wrong?

Chapter Four

Love Me, Don't Leave Me

Arabella

Before too long, I was back in a mental health unit. That's where I met him. Evidence enough for most people, but not for me. You see, we were at an Alcoholics Anonymous meeting in a hospital. Patched-up sick people coming back to the hospital to remember why we wanted to stay out of it. To remember why we had to stay well.

It was an early evening in late August and the sun shone across the manicured lawns of the grounds long enough for you to forget where you were, just for a moment. We filed into the room slowly, people exchanging greetings and commiserations. The plastic chair felt hot against my legs, and I looked down at my shoes so as to avoid conversation. I had been sober for three years, I knew the drill – *talk to people, that's how you get better* – but that day I didn't feel like it. I felt like being anonymous, disappearing into myself. We were in a hospital, after all, the most anonymous place on earth, a place where you could be reduced to mere polarities. Dead or alive. Mad or sane. Sober or drunk.

I first saw him out of the corner of my eye. A taste of what was to come: things only ever seen out of the corner of my vision, imperfectly. He was wearing shorts and flip-flops, his tanned legs muscular and firm. He spent a lot of time in shorts wherever we were and whatever the weather; shorts in the Boston fall, shorts in the cold spring mornings in New Hampshire, shorts on rainy days in London. It's funny that I remember the things he wore, sometimes more than I remember what we said to each other, or who we were with. Maybe it's because I felt that I could only ever snatch the superficialities. Green Bermuda shorts, yellow Havaianas flip-flops. When I did eventually look up, I saw that he was wearing yellow glasses. Yellow and black Ralph Lauren glasses. Glasses that he fiddled with when he was driving or reading something. Glasses that he would eventually lose in a restaurant in New York, even though we went back to find them the next day.

Hush descended on the room as the meeting was about to start. Phones buzzed away in bags, Styrofoam cups of coffee pushed under chairs, legs crossed and uncrossed. The room was oppressively hot with only one fan pointlessly whirring away in the far corner. The heat made me feel drowsy and I thought about slipping out, biking away into the warm evening across the plain, my legs moving beneath me. But then I saw his face properly for the first time. Blonde and square with a scar across the right cheekbone. He was sitting directly opposite me in my line of vision, looking right to the back of the room as he began to speak.

I can't remember much of what he said to the room that evening, partly because I wasn't listening and partly because I only heard the bits I wanted to hear. He had a flat, London accent that hardly fluctuated in cadence or tone as he spoke. I know he said something about playing Monopoly because we laughed about it afterwards. Everything else has gone, like it used to in a drunken blackout. As he spoke, I felt his gaze rest upon me, long and cool. I looked straight back at him and nodded my head at some of the things he said in encouragement. He would mock me for that later, telling me I was seducing him from the minute he opened his mouth. I smiled when he said that, but it hadn't felt that way to me. I think I had nodded at him because I felt uncomfortable for him, because I wanted to take away any nerves he might have felt. I always wanted to protect him.

I looked up at the clock. Twenty to seven. The meeting would end at seven and I started to feel desperate in case he disappeared into thin air afterwards. People vanish at the end of meetings, slipping away back into their lives as if the confidences shared meant nothing. That evening, though, I hung around, clearing away chairs and collecting cups so that I didn't have to loiter too obviously. He was surrounded by people when the meeting dissolved, young and old, people who wanted a piece of him. I scanned the group to see how many women were talking to him, feeling the spirit level of jealousy rise within me. After there was nothing left to clear and no obvious reason to stay in the room, I gave up and walked away out of the room down the winding staircase of the old Victorian building. Not that it looked very Victorian from the inside any more; plastic rails jutted out from the staircase to help the infirm and the automatic doors clicked open and shut to prevent inpatients from wandering into areas they shouldn't. As I walked through the final automatic door at the front of the building and into the late-summer evening, I felt a hand touch my shoulder. I flinched, almost theatrically. I knew he wouldn't forget me. I just knew. Sick people have a magnetic force field of attraction to one another, one that permeates through far more than automatic doors.

'You're Arabella, right?' he said adjusting his yellow glasses and shuffling idly across the gravel towards me.

I swung round. 'I am. And you're B. I liked what you said in there . . . '

I fell silent. I couldn't think of any way to stop him vanishing from the moment, vanishing from the evening and leaving me without him. I felt my cheeks burn and my hair fall across my face. Later, much later, he would tell me that he thought I seemed very nonchalant. I'm amazed he thought so.

'Listen, I'm biking back to town. Let's bike together?' he said, starting to unlock a giant padlock on his yellow bike. More yellow. How did he know I even lived that way?

I biked behind him, down the hospital drive and along Morrell Avenue, struggling to keep up, trying not to let my bag fall out of the basket. Every so often he would look back at me, smiling, his glasses and the bike coalescing into a ball of yellow, like an amber traffic light in the dark. Should I stop or go? I couldn't remember what amber meant. Either way, it was ambiguous, like that evening, like him.

We drew to a halt outside the graduate building on Parks Road and he got off his bike.

'Well, this is me. Come to the Friday meeting. I'll be there.'

'I'll try,' I mumbled, dodging another mad, student cyclist.

Later that night, I thought I should have said something else as I lay awake with the window open. Something funnier, jauntier. Or maybe I should have declined altogether, said I was busy. He had given me his number, punched into my phone on the last dialled list. I hardly dared save it, in case I would lose it altogether or, worse still, dial it accidentally, so I kept it there like an electronic love letter. Numbers not words. Hieroglyphs that I would spend the next year trying to decipher.

I didn't see him at the Friday meeting, although I went expectantly, hoping to see him again. The weather had turned as it does at the end of August, rain falling day after day, sandals left discarded under the bed, sweaters dug reluctantly out of the cupboard. I biked across town in the rain, the hood on my raincoat constantly falling back, leaving my hair to get drenched. Ten minutes from the meeting, I nearly turned back and went home but decided against it. The meeting room smelt of wet clothes and old books, the AA banners lying forlornly in a corner, a leaflet on drinking and substance abuse poking out of a box. The usual suspects were there, people who go to meetings because they have nowhere else to go, people who go to meetings because they're scared of drinking, people who go to meetings out of habit. I fell into none of these categories. I was at that meeting to find B, and if I couldn't find him, I would disappear.

The room filled up slowly and with every opening of the door, my eyes would dart across in expectation. Chair after chair became occupied as the clock moved round towards seven. He hadn't come. I felt as deflated as I had ever known, and foolish, to boot. What a fraud I was to hare halfway across town in the pouring rain to meet a stranger I had met once. As the meeting wore on, I tried, half-heartedly, to connect with the speaker. Drugs, drink, rock bottom, recovery, relapse. The words bounced off me. I spent the latter part of the meeting trying to work out if I should text him, only roused from my reverie by the person next to me trying to hold my hand to say the serenity prayer. I prayed silently and furiously for him to come back to me and dashed out of the meeting into the cool street. The rain had stopped but the water sluiced through the gutters and across the pavements.

By the time I knew him well enough, I fully understood why he hadn't come to the meeting that evening. Lying in bed together a couple of months later, I brought the subject up. He leant back against the single bedhead and threw his arm out to find his yellow glasses. Once on, he stroked the scar on his face, something I would come to know as a prelude to dishonesty, as if he was comforting himself even as he hurt another.

'I went away at the last minute. Decided to go surfing in Cornwall.'

'Ahh. I went looking for you. Biked there in the pouring rain and everything . . . ' I said, hoping this would elicit – what? – guilt, a sense of obligation? I didn't know.

'You win some, you lose some,' he said, laughing, and pulled me towards him, the yellow glasses falling onto the brown carpet of the college room.

At this point, he could have said anything, and I would have, if not believed him, then accepted it. Just like the unruly and messy aspects of my drinking, I simply swept away anything that didn't look or feel right. A year before I found sobriety, I had stood in an alleyway outside Earl's Court tube station every morning on my way to work pushing down a can of Gordon's gin and tonic to settle my shaking hands, furiously smoking a cigarette. For the addict, the abnormal quickly becomes very normal. And that's how it was, even at the very beginning, with him. I washed away pangs of confusion or discomfort with the things I wanted to see, papered over the cracks with my wishful thinking. *Tomorrow I'll stop, tomorrow it will be different.*

When we eventually did have our first proper meeting, I was due to fly back to the US that day having secured a fellowship to study for my PhD one year into sobriety. An unknown number flashed up on my phone.

I should have said no to meeting and no to everything that went with it. But I didn't. I laughed at his jokes and let him ask questions and eventually agreed to meet him when he was back from wherever he was going that week. After I put the phone down, I felt as if I had had a drink. My cheeks were flushed red and my hands shook faintly. The feeling – the one that I had chased unceasingly when I was drinking with diminishing returns – was back.

We met at the Carluccio's in Terminal 5 at Heathrow. When we had been together long enough for the first encounters to be referred to, we always laughed about that airport lunch. I arrived just after I had checked my bags in, scanning the restaurant for the yellow glasses, given that I always saw them before him. But this time he wasn't wearing them. It took me quite some time to recognise the figure seated at the back of the restaurant reading the menu while stroking the scar on his face absentmindedly.

'We meet at last . . . ' he said, kissing me on both cheeks, the exchange lasting just long enough for us both to look away awkwardly.

When I had passed through security and into departures, I scanned through our meeting in my mind like someone looking at pictures on their phone. Over and over I scrolled back and forth through the conversation, enlarging bits and minimising others, changing the filter on the images as if I was about to post a picture on Instagram. Much of our relationship would be like this: the business of alteration, deleting bits of information and accentuating others. Right from the start of our liaison, he bombarded me with text messages and phone calls. Sitting by the gate about to board the plane to JFK, he texted me several times, mostly with reference to things we had spoken about, the last one typically oblique: 'See you in NYC. B x' He hadn't mentioned anything about coming to the US over lunch, so I presumed it was a joke and turned off my phone, the runway gliding past my window as I left one world for another.

Back in Philadelphia, my other life took over as it always did. England took on the quality of memory, made small by its American counterpart. People joke that everything in the US is bigger: bigger coffees, bigger buildings, bigger sidewalks. I always felt this enlargement emotionally, as if the expanse of American life benevolently dwarfed my unhappy childhood and difficult family relationships, allowing me to turn the telescope on them, to watch my family like Borrowers scuttling around a shoe.

The fall semester was due to start a few days before Labor Day that year, but it still felt like high summer. Freshmen who had arrived on campus early to enrol for classes wandered around taking selfies in college sweatshirts, drinking ice tea under the large willow canopies on Locust Walk. I felt glad to be back and busied myself with preparation for the classes I was to teach and work I had to present on my thesis. Waking early in the mornings, I would go to the diner near my apartment and drink bottomless coffee, making careful notes in the margins of my texts. I picked up one of those texts the other day, my handwriting neat and pointy, noting the use of alliteration in a poem by Baudelaire. I scrutinised the page, looking at the way the letters looped around one another, examining the pages, amazed at the care I took. The work I did in that fall semester was mostly rushed and under-researched, my focus being so completely elsewhere, but there was something about those notes I made in the early mornings in the diner that made me feel sad, some enthusiasm that became extinguished once my life became entwined with his.

During this time, he emailed me constantly, never asking how I was exactly, but writing in such an intimate way that those sorts of preliminaries seemed unnecessary. Without the stutter and flow of telephone conversation to restrain us, our email exchange took on a life of its own, both of us writing carefully edited replies to one another. Ironically – although I failed to see this at the time – I was teaching Laclos's *Les Liaisons Dangereuses* to my sophomore class that semester. My students found the interweaving of letters between Valmont and Cecile unrealistic, a form of epistolary combat that they couldn't understand. But I understood it perfectly as I heard my voice ring out in the sunny lecture auditorium. What I failed to grasp was that I was engaged in exactly the same sort of business with B; narrating my life unreliably and passing off others' stories as my own.

***

I read somewhere once that addicts in particular are experts at ignoring warning signs, driving through a series of red lights on their way to a perfectly calibrated, perfectly specific disaster. I had form in this department, serious form. And so, like a good addict, I did it again. I ignored all the warning signs – the obsessive emailing, the questions I had, the faintly barbed insults about people we knew in common – and carried on, driving far into the distance where there were no lights or signs, just a yellow wasteland.

Being addicted to a person can take on all the hallmarks of substance abuse: high intoxication, denial, huge collateral damage, loss of identity, pointless bargaining, relapse. Sometimes, as with drugs and alcohol, death. As I crawled out of the rubble of this relationship, at four years sober, I had to admit to myself that it was every bit as intoxicating as a drink. The incredible, unbelievable thing, of course, is that I conducted the high drama of this relationship without a drink or a drug in sight. I even went to meetings throughout all of it, and sat there, pretending to be honest – *wanting* to be honest – before walking out and going through the motions all over again. I have no one to blame for this but myself. After it had ended, I had to admit that I had been drunk on this person, that I had sought him out as I had sought out alcohol again and again, despite the immense damage to myself and, I am certain, to him.

I don't know what has happened to him in the years since we parted, but I suspect that he is far happier without me in his life. I wish him well, although it has taken me some years to be able to say that. Some years ago, a friend in AA told me that he had married and had gone on to have two children, and I could feel the addict in me walking up and down: I could sense the heavy tread of its feet on my pride and the prickly feelings of nostalgia one has for old lovers. But these are just feelings, nothing more.

After over a decade in the rooms of AA, I have seen many fellows form happy relationships and marriages. Some even go on to have children together and form families of their own, so different from the ones they had grown up with. There is so much to admire in these relationships: the mutual honesty it takes to conduct a romantic and sexual bond under the spotlight of the Twelve Steps, the bravery required to admit to your partner all the tawdry details of the addicted past, the commitment to rigorous, spiritual change amidst the pressures of family life. For a long time, before I met my husband, I coveted just that: a relationship within the safety of AA, the place where I really grew up, the first place I called home. What could be better, I thought, than to have someone who truly understands the life you lead? Someone with whom to share the solitary road of self-discovery?

I tried it out, many times, without success. As an old-timer said to me early on, 'The odds are good, but the goods are odd,' which is a coded way of saying that getting into relationships with people you meet in the rooms – otherwise known as the Thirteenth Step – is a notoriously bad idea. There are other sayings like this in AA and they're all true: 'Under every skirt, there's a slip,' or 'It's called the Thirteenth Step for a reason,' or 'Men with the men, women with the women,' all of them designed to communicate the fact that AA is not a dating agency but rather a place where people with a serious illness come to get well. Forget this at your peril. I laughed when I heard them in the early days, but I didn't in any way take them seriously. I was young and considered myself deprived of the primary channels young people have to meet each other: alcohol and drugs. Who could blame me if I chose to meet people in the place where I spent most of my time? As it turns out, I was the one with the most to lose, the one who lost out on precious time in recovery because I was distracted, the one who set herself back so much. I could have relapsed when the emotional pain became too great, as I have seen so many others do.

A few months after B and I had parted for good, I went back to the meeting where we had first met. The room still held the charge of that first encounter, and I felt sad and irritable, unable to listen to what others were saying, my leg twitching against my bag. At first, I thought of walking out, but someone in the corner caught my ear as they shared: 'I needed to be in a relationship with myself before I could enter into one with someone else,' they said calmly.

A relationship with myself, I thought incredulously. How about it?

Julia

Love Me, Don't Leave Me

I'm nine years sober, but I'm beginning to realise an extremely uncomfortable truth. I might have given up alcohol, but I'm still an addict. Something is off with me. I know you're never cured of this stuff, it's part of who you are, I bloody *know* that – in my head, that is. My heart, my marrow is telling me something else. My life is OK, sort of, but I still feel a chill and unwelcome emptiness at my centre. Sometimes, when I'm alone in my house, the silence takes on a dangerous, suffocating quality, as if something awful is about to happen. It makes me really anxious. I absolutely hate this feeling – it terrifies me. Actually, it makes me feel suicidal, so I do my level best not to have it.

I shop on the internet. Looking at clothes soothes me. This is another addiction, I know that, too, but I do it because it numbs me. I remember as a teenager cruising along Knightsbridge or Kensington High Street doing exactly the same thing, years and years before the internet was even a thing. I shop, I read compulsively, and I've got a new addiction now: looking for men on the internet. You can shop for them now, too.

On the surface of things, my quest is a common one: I'm looking for love, like half the population. It's normal, except I sort of know that it's not in my case. I feel the furious need to fix myself with a man, an insatiable hunger, not necessarily for sex but for connection, someone to make me feel safe, to look after me, to protect me from the vicissitudes of the world. I feel unsheltered with just myself, adrift.

I stalk the ghastly looking middle-aged couples – the men in sports clothes (North Face has cornered the upper-middle-aged market) with salt-and-pepper beards (I hate beards), accompanied by their women in corrective Mary Janes and fleeces, shopping together in my local Waitrose, wondering what their secret is and feel my painful aloneness, my singleness. I've never been single before, and I hate it. Friends say to me, 'What do you need a man for?' and I feel shame at my lack of feminist credentials, at my inability to feel like they do. Why do I want a man? All of the above. To protect me from me, from my needy, mad inner child. In other words, my search is not really for romantic love at all, but something deeper and more profound, a way of integrating a lost but very dangerous part of myself through love. No relationship, be it with a man or a woman, can do this. A dog is the best compromise, but it's still not enough and I already have a lovely dog.

As in *The Inferno*, hell is at the bottom of my being, and it is frozen over, still, after all this time. The Twelve Step Programme of AA has done a great deal for me, but it hasn't thawed out the ice in this part of my heart – or not yet, anyway. I have admitted I'm powerless, that my life is unmanageable, I've accepted I'm insane and need a God of some description to keep me on the straight and narrow; I've made a moral inventory and apologised to people

I've wronged; I pray, I meditate; but a vital part of my real self is still trapped under that ice, the needy, desperate, lost part of me, part child, part young adult; the person I turned my back on in my late teens in my first desperate quest for reinvention. She's my Bertha Rochester and any minute now she will set fire to the curtains and burn the house down. I need to integrate her into my everyday life but I don't know how to and I'm too scared of her to want to think about it. So I look for a relationship to distract me, just as I've always done.

Dating websites are dangerous for addicts because they activate all the old reward pathways that sobriety is supposed to have flattened out. Like tyre tracks in the desert, though, those pathways remain. Scrolling through dating websites for me is the equivalent of having a drink. Each time I pause over the photograph of a likely-looking candidate (having ruled out all men wearing Lycra and cycle helmets, those engaging in any sporting activity whatsoever or holding a drink in one hand – which means about 98 per cent of the middle-aged/old men on any website) I get a rush of dopamine. I'm playing with fire, because what this behaviour is doing is inflaming the wound which, even under the ice, throbs and pulses, flooding me with fear of abandonment, and another, as yet unidentified but powerful feeling of being utterly, utterly worthless.

At nine years sober, I'm back in this place again, but in a way, my sobriety has clouded my judgement and made me a bit arrogant. I must be all right, surely? I mean, I've done the work and now I'm fixed, right? Wrong. At this point I've been in therapy for about eighteen months. The therapist, with me in tow, is leading me towards the 'wound', the place inside me where a volcano of fear erupted as a teenager, causing the emotional equivalent of third-degree burns that have never really healed. Nevertheless, in spite of having initiated the therapy, I'm secretly not sure I want to go there. I'm afraid of what it will mean to have to go down into the caldera (the large depression caused when a volcano erupts and collapses), or even to look over its edge. But that seems to be where I'm headed. The therapist is intent on taking me to that place. I'm afraid if I go into it – the abyss, the crater – I won't come out again. Once or twice, he's led me to the edge, and I've climbed down a little way but I'm terrified. These experiences leave me shaken and tearful, absolutely ragged inside. The aim of therapy is to make the patient feel better, but I don't feel better, I feel worse. He had actually told me this would happen, but I've conveniently forgotten. What I can only understand with hindsight is that this process is coaxing the volcano buried at the bottom of my being back into action. I have to relive it to let it go. Or something. Random pieces of masonry are beginning to fall off the building; there are regular tremors under the mosaic floors. The fountain in the courtyard sometimes flows and sometimes doesn't, for no apparent reason.

At this precise point, I find the solution on a dating website (the thankfully now-defunct *Guardian* Soulmates) in the shape of the exact man I've always been looking for. Funny, that. He's a bit older than me, tick, a writer with a Booker Prize nomination in his CV, double tick, and he lives on a Greek island. So many ticks I go off the end of the page. A Greek island, in my mind, is paradise on earth. If I hook up with him, I won't have to go down to the bottom of hell like poor old Dante, or into that ghastly crater, no, I can skip that bit and go straight to heaven on a Greek beach with what's-his-name in tow. If there was such a thing as a madometer, I'd be right off the scale.

We rapidly go rogue and start emailing one another – exactly what most dating websites warn you against doing too quickly. *Never mind that*, I think. *What do they know?* I'm drunk already on dopamine. My excitement rises exponentially with every email. We decide to have a Skype call (this is pre-Covid, no Zoom) so that we can see each other in the virtual flesh, except that the connection is so awful I can only really discern the top of his head – at my request, he has removed the hat he wears in all the photographs – which is shiny in the bad lighting of the upstairs room in the café where he is taking the call, not having an internet connection in his apartment, I will later come to realise. Writing pays badly.

After the call, I immediately receive an email from him saying he is in love with me. Bull's eye! I'm in love with him, too, I decide, seeing as he has sweetly gone first. I'm now completely convinced that this man is the answer to all my prayers. He is my everything, never mind work, family, my small Airbnb business. All that can take a running jump. And never mind the rather important fact that we have yet to actually meet.

Arabella is, needless to say, deeply disapproving. She lectures me and asks me if I'm going on another of what she calls my 'sex holidays'. I'm outraged and tell her so. How dare she! We seem to have swapped roles, Edina/Saffy style, and now I'm the unruly daughter doing rash things. I brush aside her disquiet, book a flight to Athens at once and email him to say I'm coming. We agree to meet in a hotel selected by him and paid for by me.

The first thing that goes wrong is that I don't fancy him and he has weird teeth. But, the room, the bed. It won't be the first time I've slept with someone I don't fancy. Literally, what the fuck? He thinks I'm great, which helps overcome my seething feelings of uneasiness at the whole shoddy situation. I'm a grandmother, for heaven's sake! I can just see the headline in the *Daily Mail*: *Rogue granny shags Booker nominee*, like one of those ancient female tourists who goes to some impoverished country and marries a man forty years younger 'for love'. I try not to think about that. My grandmother was practically in black bombazine and a lace cap, like Queen Victoria, not larking about in Greece with unsuitable men.

The next morning, I look at him across the café table in Piraeus where we're having breakfast and decide that I'm going to do this. I've come this far, and I've already walked into my own trap. This has to work, *it has to*. I summon up all my old expertise in fantasy and denial, failing entirely to see that I am doing exactly the same thing as I'd done when I last got married. As a result, my spirits rise. Hell, I'm in Greece! How great is that? I love Greece. I've always loved Greece. We go on a ferry to his island, which is of course beautiful, even in November.

The sight of the entrance his apartment dents my high: a part of the ceiling has collapsed in the hallway. Not a good look. In the apartment itself, the bathroom is unspeakably awful, like something you might find on a roadtrip in India, but I ignore my misgivings. I look over the balcony where hens pick about in a neighbouring patch. The next morning, this balcony will be seething, literally, with the hundreds of cats the writer feeds on a daily basis. I'm also in receipt of disapproving and rather unsettling WhatsApps from Arabella, which I don't mention to the writer. *Send photos*, she demands. I attempt to fulfil my brief and send a photo of the writer in his kitchen with his back turned. Of course, she's not convinced by my bright tone or by the photograph: as far as she's concerned, I'm on some gigantic shagathon. She's been to Sex & Love Addicts Anonymous (SLAA) in the States. She can clearly see what's going on.

The week goes on and my madness deepens. We go for long, long walks in the day, and I survey my fiefdom, because I am going to come and live here, of course I am, with Spotty, my Dalmatian. At night, the writer cooks elaborate vegetarian meals, and we watch films on his laptop swathed in rugs like old ladies. The flat is freezing and it's winter outside, even if only the Greek version. I start mainlining Papadopoulos chocolate creams, cramming them into my mouth every time the writer goes into the kitchen to check on the supper, a sign of my inner turmoil surfacing in my old adversary, sugar addiction. A day or so later, I start hoarding them, hiding them in my suitcase. I may not be drinking, but I'm definitely using. Food was my first addiction and it's still something I turn to when I'm feeling uneasy.

I return to Blighty after ten days. He comes with me on the ferry to Piraeus and we stay in another of those cheap hotels, once again paid for by me. In the evening, we go to a restaurant where the remnants of a wedding party are dancing to a bouzouki. They are all completely smashed. To describe this party as a bacchanal would fail to do it justice. I have rarely seen people so drunk and still upright. It really is a scene from some circle of hell. I primly drink Diet Coke. My own internal bacchanal is hidden from sight and coming to an end, anyway. Talk about being stark raving sober.

Back at home, my spirits plummet. I have an emotional

hangover. I look for a way of getting a hit. *I know*, I think, *we should get married*. Of course, how sensible. But I don't tell anyone, certainly not Arabella. The cracks are widening but I ignore them. He thinks getting married is a great idea and immediately starts to plan the party he'll throw in my house when he comes over in January. We vow to talk every day. I have to ring him because he can't afford to call me on his pay-as-you-go plan.

I go to see my therapist, but I stop off in the multi-storey car park of the local shopping centre on the way. I lose my car. I've never done this before, even when drunk, but I can't find it when I return, and I get hysterical. Luckily, the ANPR locates it. It's on a different floor to the one I thought. I've not only lost my car but my mind, it seems. This is symptomatic of what is going on inside. More masonry is falling off the building.

I tell the therapist about losing my car and about the time I've spent in Greece, keeping a number of salient features back, like the writer's sexual weirdness and the fact that his flat is a shit hole. I find his endless critiques of the books he's reading boring, but I don't say this either. I'm in love. This is meant to be. The therapist tries to get me to talk about how I feel about the work we were doing before I went to Greece, but I don't want to go there. I begin to wonder if I should sack my therapist. He doesn't seem to understand what's happening to me.

The following week, I'm sitting in the local Waitrose car park. I decide to call the writer to get it out of the way and clear space for the evening ahead. He doesn't answer his phone. I ring again. And again. And then again. I keep calling him. He keeps not answering. He's doing it deliberately. This is his way of telling me it's over. I sit in the car crying hysterically. I go home and google suicide websites. The pain I am feeling at this perceived betrayal by someone I scarcely know and don't even like all that much is off the scale. I can't bear it. If I had the means, I would kill myself.

A couple of hours later, the writer rings. He went out to a bar, got drunk, came back and fell asleep. His phone was in his jacket pocket and he didn't hear it ringing. I'm so worn out by this point that I can scarcely even register relief, although he is incredibly tender and sweet to me. Perhaps marrying him is the right thing to do. He seems to understand my pain. Nevertheless, what has happened has really shocked me. The feelings of abandonment and worthlessness have swept through my insides like a wave of acid. I dimly perceive that these feelings are nothing to do with the writer but that my relationship with him, coupled with my therapy, has set everything alight. The house is now burning and I – or at least a version of me – am still inside. In my next therapy session, I talk about what has happened. The therapist suggests that I envisage a safe place where I can sit quietly with this damaged child-woman part of me and make her feel welcome. *Don't turn your back on her*, he says. *Perhaps this is what you've been doing for most of your life*, he adds, knowingly.

It's Christmas and then New Year. I go to meet the writer at Heathrow. A crushed-looking figure carrying a rucksack and wearing a woolly hat appears. Is it really him? It can't be, but it is. He looks different and seems smaller. Maybe it's the climate. *What am I doing?* My doubts have returned. It's as if the incident in the car park erased any romantic feelings I have for him. He's full of the idea of the party to celebrate our forthcoming nuptials. I can't bring myself to tell him that I haven't told anyone yet, including Arabella. The idea of the party fills me with horror.

We go to London so he can meet Arabella and then my father and stepmother. Arabella is polite but tense, holding her baby close to her. She grills him about his work and his life in general. Again, it's as if she's the parent and I'm the child. I catch her expression as she turns away. She looks grim. We leave and slink off to the V&A to look at Indian miniatures, for reasons I can now no longer recall. They were lovely, but why were we looking at them? I feel numb and peculiar and am finding it hard to be polite to the writer. Why am I doing this?

The writer comes from Northumberland and is wearing a flat cap. My father appears to think I have brought a Galloway hill farmer to see him and looks puzzled. He starts to talk about the many, many diseases of sheep. My stepmother is also bemused but kind. Soon enough, they all start drinking whisky. I take the opportunity to look at my mobile phone and I see a message from Arabella that takes my breath away. She says that she will never speak to me again if I go on with this relationship and that I will not be allowed to see her child.

She's staging a kind of intervention. On the drive back to Oxford, I tell the writer what she's said. He's hurt and upset, poor guy. He wants me to choose him over my daughter, but I can't do that. It's not even a contest. *Can we still have the party?* he asks, pathetically. I dither and then say, *No, you'll have to cancel it.* I feel like a beast, as I always do when I get real and set boundaries. The writer hangs around for a few more days until his flight. It's agony for both of us. He can't afford to pay to change his flight and I don't see why I should. I put him in the spare room. He spends one of the days he has left going to Brighton to meet someone new he's discovered on *Guardian* fucking Soulmates. By mistake, he sends me a message meant for her, ending with the immortal line, 'I'm an active pensioner.' I feel sick.

I go back to therapy and talk through what has happened. I feel chastened and humiliated. Rob, my therapist, gently points out that I have faced my fears and survived; I didn't kill myself, sanity did prevail, in the end. The volcano inside me erupted and I lived to tell the tale. I also learnt that I must talk about this stuff and try to look after that desperately frightened, wounded child inside me by making contact with her. If you mention 'the inner child' people groan; I groan, but there's truth in it, too, especially for addicts like me whose addiction started so early on when I was still that child. The experience humbled me – I didn't know everything, after all – but I learnt from it because, luckily for me, I'm part of a community of recovering addicts who help one another. Without that help, I wouldn't be here now.

PART THREE – WOMAN

Chapter One

Starting Over

Arabella

When I think back to that late summer, I think of iced coffee from the diner and frozen yoghurt from the store outside my apartment, of Big Gulp Dr Peppers bought from the 7-11 two blocks west of Pine Street, of bagels bought at the Wawa on the way to campus. I think of how new everything tasted – how new I felt – as if I had bought a new life and was busy eating it, bit by bit. After a year of co-sobriety with Mum, I did the best thing I could have done for both of us: I left. I didn't leave to go to London or even to live in a different house in the same city, I moved across the Atlantic to America to study. Did I know how far away it was? Not really. Did I understand anything about Philadelphia, a large and divided city in which not many English people live? Not at all. Had I ever actually been to America for any prolonged length of time? No.

At times, when I was preparing to leave, the plan seemed to take on all the hallmarks of my drunken travels, which were without exception always aborted and always disastrous. Time and again after these aborted attempts at reinvention – so classically alcoholic if only I could have seen that at the time – I would return home exhausted and ashamed; some drunken catastrophe having propelled me home penniless and haggard. As I sat in the US embassy waiting for my visa, I swore to myself that this time it would be different. *I have been sober for over a year*, I told myself, *I am a different person*. What I did know was this: one drink and the entire plan would come crashing down. Turns out, that was the only thing I needed to know. Everything else took care of itself, more or less.

Like most British people, my knowledge of America was constructed largely through television. I had spent my adolescence watching *Friends* and my twenties watching *Sex and the City*. Because I had also spent a great deal of my early addicted twenties lying in bed hungover, I had watched all of *Grey's Anatomy*, a medical drama revolving around a group of young doctors in Seattle. From these years of early-onset convalescence, I discovered that sober alcoholics existed in Seattle: *Grey's* featured a statesman-like Black doctor, Dr Webber, attending AA meetings and talking about AA recovery in flashback, set to sad and emotive music. It was Dr Webber, really, who convinced me that life in America would suit a sober person. I took his word for it.

Distance is a strange thing. In America, I found it, but it telescoped and changed the longer I stayed sober. Alcohol gives you the illusion of distance, the silky feeling of being far away from yourself, or the sensation of watching a version of yourself in a mirror across a room. *I am that person*, I used to think a few drinks in, *I am a person who dresses and behaves in a certain way; I am a person with a sense of who she is: I am brave; I have suffered*. In fact, I was nothing of the sort. Part of the shock of every hangover was, I believe, the realisation that I had traversed no distance whatsoever from myself to the person in the mirror. And that's the depressing fact of drinking alcoholically over a long period of time: the downfall, when it finally comes, is severe and dramatic, like a bankruptcy. But what of the stasis, of moving no distance whatsoever, neither down nor up or even sideways, the years of simply staying still every day?

When I was drinking, I could see that truth in my mother but not in myself. *If only she would leave that husband*, I would say, disloyally, to her friends behind her back at parties. *She's stuck in her own drunken psychodrama*, I would say to my father or the artist, rolling my eyes. 'It's not that easy to divorce someone,' my mother would snap when I asked again and again why she wouldn't just leave the Blue House and Number Three and start over. 'You need to start again, for God's sake,' I would snap back. But no snapping at each other ever revealed the basic truth to either of us, which is this: if you drink alcoholically, you stay stuck where you are. Stuck in the argument with your mother, stuck in the marriage with your third husband, stuck in the whole sorry mess. Distance travelled: zero miles.

America is the home of Alcoholics Anonymous. Bill Wilson, its illustrious founding father, began to meet with other alcoholics in 1935 in Ohio, desperate to cure himself of his chronic alcoholism. He could not possibly have known then that he set in motion one of the most successful self-help movements of the twentieth century or that he had changed the shape of American vernacular forever. *Grey's Anatomy* had taught me that Alcoholics Anonymous was so woven into the fabric of American society that a medical soap opera could casually use alcoholism as shorthand for other narratives of honesty, community and belonging. 'Oh, you'll find a meeting anywhere in the US, sure,' the Americans that I had met in meetings before I left would assure me. A quick glance at the online directory convinced me of that. What I hadn't been prepared for was the cultural shift in the addict's visibility.

Wherever you go in the world, you'll always find another alcoholic just like you, AA promises. As a promise, it's important: we are linked by our commonalities, we are a tribe. But it's also not quite true because, culturally at least, we are an uneven tribe. To be an alcoholic in America is to have some weight of cultural understanding behind you, some generations-old acceptance of your condition. Say to someone that you need a meeting in America and people will nod in a way that conveys understanding but also a kindly form of disinterest, about as interesting as saying you need to go to the post office. Tell someone you need a meeting in Britain, and they will look at you with high suspicion, even mockery. I'll never forget nervously admitting to someone at one month sober that I had stopped drinking, only for him to burst out laughing before saying loudly, 'But have you started going to the meetings?!' – a phrase designed to bring a roomful of British people to a comedy standstill.

But my new life was about more than iced coffee and television shows on cable. If I wanted to maintain the fragile grasp on recovery that I had, I needed to actually go to meetings. Somehow, through sheer luck rather than advice taken, my apartment happened to be in the part of downtown Philadelphia where several meetings a day were held. My excuses – of which there were many – were wearing thin. I must have checked the location of the first meeting I went to about thirty times before I set off. Expecting to make a long journey worthy of Scott, I was dismayed to see that I arrived at the appointed church basement in less than two minutes flat. I knew I was in the right place because I had often seen people standing outside the church as I shuffled back from campus in the early evenings. When I looked at the assembled group, I knew I was of their number: the uneven way in which people were aggregated, the number of cigarette smokers, the uncommon range of young and old in the same place. I badly wanted to join them, but some diffidence kept me in check, the same diffidence I had experienced at outpatient group therapy in the hospital. Within me some concrete-like resistance held firm, welding me to myself like a statue with its arms and limbs flattened.

I didn't speak to anyone that first meeting. Picking my way down the church steps, I found a chair far enough away from the throng of young people that I could see sitting in the middle rows of the semi-circle. As the room filled up, I calculated that at least seventy people were there. In England, the biggest meeting I had ever been to must have been of about twenty people. I felt certain I would never be able to open my mouth amongst such a large group, let alone speak in a British accent, a novelty that had already piqued so much interest that I found it better to exist mute, only speaking when absolutely necessary. At the same time, I knew that this carapace of cultural sensitivities was doing me no good. In the self-absorption that always comes over me when I stop going to meetings, I had begun to feel as if I was too special to speak.

Luckily, other people spoke for me in that meeting. From across the room, a middle-aged woman spoke of her fear of not being good enough at her job, her voice trembling as she described the pain of chronic low self-esteem. Two seats away from me, a man in a suit began speaking about his marriage and the difficulty of staying sober when your partner drinks, and although he began in clichés – *I needed every drink I had to make it here* – he ended in his own voice: 'I guess I'm just lonely.'

Just before the meeting ended, a young girl raised her hand to speak. I could hardly believe she was old enough to be in AA at all; I would have guessed her to be of college-age, maybe younger. She spoke without hesitation about her relationship with her mother, describing how the boundary between the two of them had been broken: 'We're glued together in all the wrong ways,' she said before looking down into her lap. At this, something deep rose up within me. It was, I suppose, a part of me that I had been suppressing for as long as Mum and I had reinvented ourselves in sobriety together.

That evening, I gave myself permission to write my own story, one in which I wasn't Julia's daughter or part of a generational pattern, or even anyone particularly special. You could say I started over.

With the clean slate that I had granted myself came the inevitable desire for reinvention altogether. I could be anyone I wanted, anyone at all. For an alcoholic, this is explosive ground, not least because you could reinvent yourself to the extent that you don't need recovery at all, so that you disappear right down the rabbit hole altogether. I didn't go that far, but I wanted my story to dazzle. When I did eventually start speaking in the meetings, I couldn't stop; it all came tumbling out in one long drawl. I wanted it to be brilliant, eloquent, spectacular. I wanted to be the best British alcoholic to ever come to America to tell their story, I wanted to be me but with enhanced CGI features and add-ons. Fortunately, in a room full of people also preoccupied with themselves, my story was nothing special; *common garden or alcoholic,* my friend T said to me, smiling in the diner after a meeting. I was annoyed, of course. *The only person I'm like is my mother,* I replied, not really as a joke, and he smiled again. He relapsed and killed himself a year after I left the US. Sometimes I can picture his face smiling like he was that day and I think how lucky I am to still have a story to tell that looks and sounds just like anybody else's.

That's AA for you: a story that you know the ending to, a story that is necessarily full of clichés, a story in which, as Leslie Jamison puts it, 'you are meant to relinquish your ego by authoring a story in which you star'. It's a high-wire act and I'm not sure I managed it very well in my first five years of sobriety; even now, I have to watch my desire to narrate my experience performatively, hoping to make people laugh, hoping to get the timing just right at the point that the meeting will respond. In those moments, I am high. I am the girl standing on a chair in front of her father and his wine bottle, waiting to be rewarded. But how do you simply erase a lifetime of believing that distinction matters? The answer, I think, is to go to lots of meetings; sooner or later the chorus will become more important to you than the solo.

The chorus of a meeting is a sacred thing; like genuflecting before Mass or saying the rosary, it primes the room for our central belief: we speak in the same voice. Yet in those first days in America, the chorus didn't sound the same to me at all. The readings came in a strange order and I felt slow to understand the cues to stand or sit. Worst of all, for me at least, was the hand holding. At the end of every meeting, or every meeting I went to in the US, fellows are invited to stand in a large semi-circle and hold hands before saying the serenity prayer. I thought of home and the mumbled incantations of the serenity prayer said while still sitting down, faces turned resolutely downwards to the floor. I thought of my mother and her theatrical faux-horror at having to hold hands with people she didn't know. Mostly, I thought of slipping out before the end. But something kept me there in spite of myself, some electric current running hot and blue between me and the others.

The palms, when they came, were always different. Some rough and calloused from years of work in the Rust Belt, some papery and liver-spotted from a lifetime of sun on the Jersey shore, some cold and smooth from a day in the air-conditioning downtown. *Let the circle represent how strong we are together*, the meeting leader would shout, and I would raise my hands up and grip my neighbours' tightly and feel brand new.

On the bitterly cold January day my father died, over a year after I had moved to America, I stood in a meeting in downtown Philadelphia and held two strangers' palms and mouthed the serenity prayer. Three thousand miles away from the bed in which he had died, I gripped the hands of two people I hardly knew who held them tightly back. What should you do when you have just found out that one of your parents has died, on the day when your life forks in two? Most people have a drink. Or a cigarette. Or both. I went to a meeting and decided on the way out that I deserved to start smoking again. My friend S, permanently cheerful after discovering AA in her late sixties, handed me a cigarette and stroked my hand, her crepey fingers covering mine. I wept for all the times I had wanted to cover my father's hand as the cigarette ash dropped into the snow. Back in my apartment, I booked the next flight to London and chain-smoked cigarettes out of the window vaguely wondering if it had been the fags or the booze that had killed him.

A year before my father died, we went on holiday together. He was nearing the end then, not that he would have admitted it. His heart, always a source of anxiety to him, was weak, he explained. He couldn't possibly exert himself, he said, moving painfully slowly from the hotel restaurant back to his room each night. His body made the explanations he wouldn't: his face had both a grey and red hue, his eyes deeply lined. Always an athletic man, his clothes hung off him, his legs pitifully thin. Although he still smoked and drank in quantities that would shock most people, he looked as if he could hardly remember why any more. Each cigarette sent him into violent coughing fits, each drink visibly pained him before he turned away to retch. Not once did we speak of any of this, not once did I ask him if he was OK.

In staying silent, I was participating in an ancient ritual that children of alcoholics know well, a ritual that has loyalty and betrayal as its sparring rites, permanently out of sync. To say what you see would be a monstrous betrayal, not just of the alcoholic but of the entire family that has upheld the status quo for so long. And so, you say nothing. It is completely normal for you to witness these things after all. *Normal.* I want to howl with laughter at the word were it not so sad. The problems with staying silent and upholding this pact of darkness are legion. All I can say for my part is that it engendered a kind of colour-blindness on the level of toxicity: I simply couldn't see it.

It was on this holiday that my father did something highly unusual. One hot afternoon after lunch, when everyone else had gone swimming, I sat with my father on the terrace and smoked cigarettes with him. He had had a lot to drink at lunch and was struggling to stay awake. For a long time, we sat in silence, punctuated only by his dreadful rattle of a cough; it wasn't an uncomfortable silence, but neither was it truly companionable. 'Do you still go to those meetings?' he asked finally, his hand grasping for the lighter as he did so, his gaze fixed firmly on the horizon. 'They say they work,' he continued. Stunned, I replied that yes, I did still go, that I needed them even. 'It's good to keep it under control. Alcoholics have to,' he said eventually before getting up and walking unsteadily back to his room.

That was the first and last conversation I had with my father about my drinking. But it wasn't just a statement of my addiction, it was plainly one of his as well. In the first few weeks and months after he died, I thought about that exchange a lot: I fantasised about lengthening it; I daydreamed about what a longer conversation with him would have looked like; I romanced a scenario in which he would have admitted how profoundly alcohol had shaped his life. I longed for a conclusion to the conversation in which he had told me how proud he was of me instead of simply staggering off. In therapy sessions with a college therapist in a tall skyscraper overlooking the Schuylkill River, I wept for all the endings that were left to me to imagine, the loose ends that I could only weave with conjecture. 'Do you think it's possible,' my therapist – a tall, thin man named Dr E – ventured, 'that you have in fact been grieving both your parents for some years?' The mood of the room shifted, and I sat up in my seat. Here, at last, was some advice. 'Living grief is common amongst children of alcoholics,' he went on, looking more animated than I remembered seeing him for some time. 'This period of actual grief must be confusing for you,' he said just before the session ended. 'Be sure to reach out to me when you're back in the UK for the funeral.'

I got a cab straight from his office to the airport. As the car moved across the city to the speed of the freeway, I felt the strange sensation of being pulled in two directions: between the old and the new, America and England, and perhaps, most deeply, between my mother and my father, between the competing feelings of grief for both parental relationships. I wondered if now my father had died, a new beginning might dawn for Mum and me, too. My phone rang repeatedly in my bag and I scrabbled to find it. It was Mum: 'I've got some dreadful stomach bug but I'm definitely coming to the funeral, don't worry,' she trilled, with a flourish. She always did like funerals, more than weddings, she often said. 'OK, Ma, if you're sure, but don't forget that all the wives will be there.' I suddenly felt very tired.

When the plane took off, I watched Philadelphia become smaller and smaller until it disappeared from sight altogether. It was a long way back.

Julia

Starting Over

I was only a few days sober when I went with my then husband to what he had told me was a dinner party in London, but which turned out to be a drinks party instead. I've always disliked drinks parties – even when I was drinking, I dreaded them, and this one – full of people I only half knew – was an ordeal newly sober, to put it mildly. Without alcohol, I simply couldn't think what to say to anyone. All the other guests seemed to know something I didn't. *What the hell were they talking about?* It was exactly what Sylvia Plath described when she wrote about 'the shrill tinsel gaiety of "parties" with no purpose, despite the false grinning faces we all wear'. I'd lost my grinning party face that night for sure: I felt unattractive, lost, wooden, bored, as well as boring, as if I'd suddenly turned into an alien.

These were some of the deeply uncomfortable feelings alcohol had masked for so long. I was the wallflower, the left-out, the left-behind one, childish thoughts that still held sway. I was in the habit of thinking my thoughts were facts, instead of merely thoughts, as ephemeral as clouds. All I wanted to do was go home and hide under the duvet. At the end of the party, we were given a lift by someone to the station, and we had to share the back seat with a middle-aged woman who was clearly drunk: she wasn't making much sense and was strident in the way drunks are. It suddenly occurred to me that I was sharing a seat with myself: I could be like that after parties. For the first time in years and years I wasn't that tedious drunk in the back seat. But it was cold comfort. I felt as if I'd swallowed broken glass or as if someone had punched me in the chest, without warning. I was stunned by this sudden and unwelcome recognition of my new place in the world; I was no longer of the drinking party, not in that gang any more. After decades of active alcoholism, I had to find a new way to be myself, whoever the hell that was. The whole prospect was exhausting and frightening, or it was that night. I was going to have to reconfigure myself as a sober person, although what that entailed I had absolutely no idea.

When you first get sober, you can't quite believe it, and neither can anyone else who knows you well. Occasions that I had used alcohol to get through were now obstacle courses to be navigated, ordeals to be borne, somehow. Lunch at my then-sister-in-law's house a few doors down from ours was a classic example: one of her daughters, when informed I wasn't drinking, said, 'Oh, yeah . . . ' and rolled her eyes, making no attempt to disguise her astonishment and, it must be said, contempt.

After a chronic alcoholic stops drinking, other people are entitled to be sceptical. I was told to seek humility. I knew what the word meant, obviously, but to be humble in a situation where someone else had hurt you – surely not? I must be entitled to a little flounce at the very least, a slight temper tantrum? *Absolutely not,* says AA. *You're the alcoholic, it's your problem, not theirs.* This was a way of thinking that I'd never even contemplated, and the fact that I can still recall that unkind remark shows what a struggle it was. The next moment, her mother, my sister-in-law, enquired in her very loud upper-class voice, 'Are you really never going to drink again?' Somehow or other, out of nowhere, I had the presence to reply, 'Just for today,' and, miraculously, she shut up.

I couldn't possibly have done even a few days' sobriety at this point without the support of AA. Recovering alcoholics need to swarm together. The collective noun for recovering alcoholics should be 'a fellowship' of drunks. I'd tried in the past to stop drinking on my own and failed every single time. There was a man I got to know in AA, an Irishman, who would always say to me, 'Just keep it in the day, Julia, that's all you have to do.' Sometimes I felt I owed him my life. I could keep it in the day, just. Without entirely realising what was going on – you don't when you're newly sober – I was beginning to feel supported by AA. A tap root had gone down into the well of loving kindness that exists in what's known to its members as the 'Fellowship'. I was lucky in this respect. Putting down that tap root was a vital part of accepting my new reality because it nourished me. I was parched and desperate. As an active alcoholic, I hadn't gone out with a tremendous bang – there hadn't been one, final definitive event where I reached rock bottom – but I had been spiralling downwards for years. Nothing sustained me any more: not my work, nor my collapsing marriage and family relationships. My spiritual life was a desert, too. I wasn't writing, just doing hack work on the fringes of the writing world. The marriage was a farce, but a painful farce I couldn't see a way out of that didn't involve total penury and humiliation. My mother, always tricky, now had dementia and my father wasn't speaking to me. My daughter regarded me as an embarrassing burden. I woke up feeling terrible about everything every day and went to sleep in a stupor. It was an awful life.

But something else beckoned now – I'd seen it, heard it, smelt it in meetings – there was hope and there was that deep pool of loving support that I was being lowered into every meeting I went to. I don't like talking about God because it all seems so personal; perhaps that's a vestige of the old British stiff upper lip, but I was encountering something way, way outside of myself – a kind of wild joy like the bright sparks from a bonfire or some marvellous zigzagging form of spiritual electricity – that was beginning to transform my life from top to bottom. I'd tried to stop drinking before, every now and again, and managed with great difficulty a day here and there, but I couldn't manage any more. I was physically addicted to alcohol, wretched with cravings for it even when I was hungover; there was also the mental and spiritual agony to contend with: dark feelings of loneliness and a doom-laden sense of being a failure on every front that would soon overwhelm me and once again I'd be back where I'd started. I felt my inability to stop drinking was a moral failure, rather than the symptom of a horrible mental illness, and I lashed myself about it daily before self-loathing made me throw in the towel again, and again, and again. I was trapped on my wheel of fire.

In hindsight, getting sober for me had to be done with support and not just an alcohol counsellor – I'd had one of those – a well-intentioned, electrifyingly young girl who asked me why I thought my desire to drink 'was bigger than me'. I couldn't answer her at the time, but once firmly established in AA, I realised the answer to her question was quite simple: I felt alcohol was bigger than me because it was. I just couldn't get sober by myself with an occasional visit to her. I still didn't understand that I was suffering from a mental illness, not a moral failing, or defective willpower, but an actual illness, one that had immobilised me in its coils, like a vast serpent. She didn't understand that either and this is the problem with being counselled by people who aren't themselves addicts. They don't understand. They say, 'Cut back.' No real alkie can do that. They tell you to keep a drink diary. I mean, come on: all alkies lie about how much they drink, particularly to themselves.

Six months or so before I actually got sober, I wrote in my diary: 'I have to do something about my alcoholism.' I'm repeating this because it was so, so important. This seemingly small act was the beginning of the absolutely vital process of surrender and of acceptance for me. Not long after this I read an interview in a Sunday newspaper with Hjördis Niven, David Niven's second wife. As I recall, she said in that interview (which I can't find anywhere online) '… he controls me [meaning her husband] … and *alcohol controls me* …' And I thought to myself, *It controls me, too.* I couldn't go anywhere or do anything without planning how I was going to get a drink. It seems so obvious, but I suddenly understood this at the deepest level of my being. Alcohol was something outside me that was running my life. It wasn't a part of me, after all. It was a delusion, a form of madness I could escape from if I did it right.

Weirdly, the group thing suited me; I found I liked being with my fellow alcoholics. I had a feeling I'd come home and began to feel a sense of recognition that this was where I belonged. We were comrades in arms, united not by our virtues but by our failings. That was a new one for me. All the things I'd concealed were our common currency in AA. There was always someone who'd done or thought what you'd done or thought or, pretty often, something much, much worse. I found it so liberating. I hate the word 'empowering', but it was just that. I began to feel hope. *When had I last felt that?*

Very quickly, I began to look forward to going to meetings in the same way as I used to look forward to that first drink. In the morning, I would wake up and say to myself, 'What meeting am I going to go to today?' and that simple idea of making a date with a time and place where I knew, without question, that I would feel happy and welcome began to push aside the craving for alcohol. At least, I think that's how it worked. In reality, at the time, it was a bit of a blur. I was just feeling my way forward, taking any suggestion anyone made. I was absolutely desperate not to go 'out there' again.

I was also living through the dying throes of my marriage. My then-husband who had quite rightly urged me over and over again to drink less, was completely thrown when I stopped altogether. He didn't know how to cope. In retrospect, I realised that he felt he had lost the moral high ground. I was going to meetings regularly and talking to people who helped me; my focus was turning outwards. People went through the most terrible situations in AA without picking up a drink. I heard their stories all the time, much worse stories than a mere divorce, too. Without entirely understanding what I was doing, I was building a life raft that would sustain me as the marriage collapsed.

One of the biggest changes in my everyday life was that what had once been my darkest secret was now turned inside out. I was an alcoholic and it was amazing to say it to people. Honesty cauterised shame, I found. It was heady. I got a hit from dropping my little bombshell. *Are you sure?* people would say, looking at me with shock, as if I needed dissuading from such a radical path. *Totally sure*, I'd reply.

Fairly frequently, people would then tell me they were worried about their own drinking and I, stark raving sober as I was, would counsel them as to what to do. I look back on that now with amusement: it hadn't yet dawned on me that even when you give up drink you continue to behave as an alcoholic. That was too advanced a concept for me during those early days. All I knew was that, day by day, I wasn't drinking.

Towards the end of my first month of sobriety, I shared in a meeting that I was twenty-nine days sober: murmurs of 'well done' rippled through the room. I felt a powerful sense of achievement and, yes, joy, actual joy, that I could do this. After decades of alcoholic drinking, I could become a sober person. Later, I realised that nobody, literally nobody, had approved of me for years: not my husband, not my daughter, not my mother or father, no one. I had become a pariah due to the workings of this awful illness. This shaft of approval in the meeting that evening warmed me inside and gave me the courage to keep going.

One of the biggest challenges came at yet another drinks party in London fairly early on. It was a gallery opening and there was nothing non-alcoholic to drink except orange juice. I absolutely hate orange juice for all sorts of reasons, and I particularly hate being offered it at parties. Just as I turned down the offer, a person

I really disliked hove into view and I started to panic. At exactly the same moment, a waitress with a gleaming tray of full wine glasses stopped next to me. My hand went out and then returned to my side again. I was flooded with adrenalin and all I could think of to do was to take flight, which I did. I rushed outside and down the street, my heart hammering. I felt as if I'd narrowly avoided a true calamity, which picking up a drink would have been at this stage, but my old impulse to shield myself with booze had come out of hiding briefly before sliding back into the dark again.

It gave me a real shock to truly understand how vulnerable I was, and that I had to think through my party tactics very carefully. Early on, I was told to always know your exit strategy. Arrive late, leave early. Avoid weddings: a wedding for a newly sober person – especially modern weddings that go on all day – are pretty much something to swerve at all costs. I realised I could take charge of myself. I went from being the last guest to leave to being the first or one of the first. Getting to bed sober was the great prize and it still is today. I still feel grateful to wake up without a hangover, all these years later.

When I was nine months sober, Arabella followed me into the rooms of AA. By that time I felt I'd been sober a lot longer than I had and having my daughter suddenly appearing at meetings threw me. AA was *mine*, I felt, and I didn't want her telling her version of events to people who knew me first. AA was not mine and she was entirely free to do exactly what she wanted but I felt I had gained some moral high ground (finally) around my daughter and I wanted to keep it that way. Ignoble but understandable, given the circumstances.

One of the first things Arabella did in sobriety was to start having an affair with one of the other members. This is known as the Thirteenth Step, an addition to the normal Twelve, but also very common. Put a load of newly sober people together and it's going to happen. The problem with affairs in early recovery is that they get in the way, rather as landmines do in war zones. You think you see the path ahead and suddenly you're blown off course by an emotional debacle and you drink again. I told her in a finger-wagging way that this wasn't a great idea, but she didn't listen. Of course she didn't. I mean, why would she listen to me? I grumbled to my sponsor about it, and she told me there was nothing I could do. I didn't like that much: *Surely I could give my daughter some good advice*, I enquired. *The only person you can change is yourself*, she said pointedly.

A few months later, the three of us – me, Arabella and this first boyfriend from AA – went to Provence together to stay in a house in a village near Uzès borrowed from a friend. My husband didn't want to come, but I was desperate to get away and the idea seemed a good one. It really wasn't. *A little jaunt to France, that's all it was*, I told myself, but it wasn't entirely true. This was a part of France I'd spent a lot of time in with a previous artist lover who had friends there. The place was saturated with memories of him and of drinking. I mean, what else does one do in France? The long, boozy lunch under a canopy of vines is a staple of every artist and writer's idea of *la vie bohème*, and I'd indulged this romantic fantasy to excess from the very beginning of my long love affair with France in the summer, witness the photograph on the cover of this book. Returning as a sober person was painful. I felt hollow and desperately empty inside now the booze was removed, feelings I'd drunk to conceal, although I pretended I didn't.

Sitting in the tranquil old house that had once belonged to the local priest listening to the clink of glasses and the low whirr of conversation in the restaurant next door made me intensely uncomfortable. How long the hot French days were without alcohol to fill them. How clearly, though, I remember the poetry of small details: the fig tree in the front garden by the wall bursting with fruit, walking along the rutted, grassy track to the farm at the end of the track. Standing high up on a rock I had once sat on with my old lover looking out across the slow, pastoral landscape beneath. Sitting on a windowsill reading the psalms from the King James Bible: *thou anointeth my head with oil; my cup runneth over.* My cup certainly wasn't running over in any spiritual sense, let alone a physical one. I was in mourning for what had once been, for an old life that had gone forever. It felt like it had to be done.

I took to eating catering packs of crisps, lying on my bed in the pulverising heat of the afternoon, crunching away, reading book after book, escaping my painful, jagged feelings in the only way I knew how. I'd always used books to escape with and food was an old helpmeet of mine, too. I used it to displace the discomfort of being me. I wasn't drinking, but I was still behaving like an addict. The difference was, however, that I was aware of my feelings. I didn't like them and I tried quite a lot of the time to avoid them but I knew with absolute certainty that alcohol wasn't the answer. This was a start, even if I did put on about seven pounds in as many days. I must have eaten some proper food, but I can only remember the crisps. Recovery from

addiction is a process and if you've been an addict for most of
your life it takes time, lots and lots of time. Give time time, they
say in the rooms.

In retrospect, this was an act of utter folly. Three newly sober
alcoholics, all with under a year's sobriety, setting off to a place
with such a loaded history for at least two of them could have been
a catastrophe but I did it to exorcise or cauterise a part of my old
life, to see if I could do it and survive. Without alcohol, France was
still beautiful but tearing away the romantic myth of drinking in
hot places where wine is cheap was unbelievably hard; I still find
it hard today but now I recognise how deep the romanticising, if
not the idolising, of booze had gone inside me, how much and
how deeply I had bought into the myth of its transfiguring powers.
Spiritus contra spiritum, as Jung had so wisely observed in his letter
to Bill Wilson all those years before. I had to dig out my alcoholism
root and branch to get to another level. My spiritual awakening
couldn't take place unless I did this. This little but perilous trip to
France was a part of the process for me. I needed to learn to trust
in God, not in the bottle.

Somehow or other, day by day, good days, bad days, obstacle
by obstacle, I reached a year's sobriety. A whole year of not having
had a drink. It felt more like a decade than a year, but it was a year,
nonetheless. A whole year. In many ways in my new, booze-free
life I felt returned to the eager innocence of the eight-year-old
girl I'd once been, before my world fell in, when I'd wandered
about by myself in the Scottish landscape, hardwiring my brain
on the beauty of what I saw. The return of that forgotten feeling
was an immense gift, and one I never expected to receive, one of
the fruits of sobriety. We give up so much when we stop drinking

alcoholically, but what isn't mentioned as much as it should be is how much we gain.

'What do you do when you reach a year?' I asked someone.

'Start the next year,' came the answer.

And so I did.

Chapter Two

Shame

Arabella

'My name is Julia and I'm an alcoholic.'

'My name is Arabella and I'm an alcoholic.'

It is October 2011 and we are sitting in an AA meeting in Oxford. In fact, we are doing much more than just sitting in the meeting; we are its centrepiece, like curiosities in a museum, both of us poised at the table in front of the rows of chairs assembled in the church hall. There should be a glass case around us. I am here to tell 'my story' and Mum is here as the meeting secretary, to keep time, make announcements and open and close the meeting with the readings from the shared text. She is not supposed to comment on the content of the speaker's share, but we are way past that.

Plenty of people assembled in the meeting know that we are mother and daughter, a few don't. Another few know but don't care. Anonymity, the spiritual foundation of all of AA's principles, has wafted out of one of the church's modern folding windows, never to be seen again in our case. For my part, I can't decide what I want people to know or not. The real question, I suspect, is how much I want Mum to know. And anyway, it's not exclusively my story to tell, since its fabric belongs to both of us. After a year of joint sobriety, the fabric is delicate; if you pull at it in the wrong way, it will completely unravel.

It is a Monday night, and I am in an extremely bad mood when I arrive; all day, the prospect of the meeting has loomed over me, triggering an extreme, debilitating lethargy from which I feel I may never recover; I am *nothing* if not a serious drama queen at one year sober. For those versed in AA speak, this is a sure-fire sign that you need a meeting. *Hungry, Angry, Lonely, Tired?* Then HALT. Stop. Yes, stop whatever you are doing and go to a meeting. In the very early days of sobriety, I follow this acronym religiously. I like it, even. Recently, a newfound scepticism has crept into my practice, and I find myself unwilling to go to meetings. Is this because my mother is there, in every single meeting, telling 'her story', too? Or is it because the boundary lines between her story and mine have become contested, their demarcation unclear like Yugoslavia after the First World War? I rather think the latter. Either way, I feel tired and would prefer to be in my room smoking cigarettes, alone, in a canny repeat of my drinking days, although now *sans* booze.

The room fills up steadily; the Monday-night meeting is well established and, unusually for an Oxford meeting, full of both old-timers and newcomers. People process into the room via the tea hatch where they may gorge on biscuits and sweet tea, the short-term replacement therapy for those new to the immediate effects of alcohol withdrawal. You can't smoke in the meeting room any more, but a sizeable crowd of smokers is always outside any meeting and is, I have found, the best way to locate an unfamiliar meeting in a new place, acting as a beacon of toxic welcome hiding in plain sight. I recognise some of the faces before me, making mental notes to myself about how well they know Mum and whether they have been to the Blue House or not.

Plenty of people have been to the Blue House, of course, their anonymity splintering as they walk through the door and into the peculiar details of our shared, bi-sober life there. Husband Number Three dislikes the new status of the Blue House as a destination for sober alcoholics with their tea and cigarettes and bonhomie and often hangs around asking leading and provocative questions about 'just having one', and saying loudly 'everything in moderation', while pouring himself a drink in front of them. To the credit of all our sober guests, no one ever hits him.

On the floor in front of the table is a selection of laminated slogan posters; 'One Day at a Time', 'Think, Think, Think', or 'Keep It in the Day'. On my way in, I slip on one, damp from the spilt tea held by a trembling hand, and nearly fall over. 'Whoops!' Mum says before rearranging them in a rainbow motif. I can tell she is nervous from the jaunty tone of her voice that she uses with other people. I feel nervous, too. I have spoken to large groups in meetings before with Mum present, but tonight feels different. There is something about the way we are both sitting at the front of the meeting that makes me feel both uncomfortable and unhinged at the same time; I have no idea what will come out of my mouth. But I know full well that an Alcoholics Anonymous meeting is the least critical audience you can find. God knows I have already said a number of strange things to various groups of assembled sober alcoholics and the reaction has always been of gentle and loving acceptance.

No, this discomfort springs from the murky business of the

secrets we keep and the stories we tell. In short, from shame. *You're as sick as your secrets.* You hear that a lot in AA. It's one of the first aphorisms that made sense to me because it felt in the early days that my secrets and lies were slowly twisting their way around my vital organs, constricting my movements, my very breath. I would wake up in the night drenched in sweat and breathless, a refrain ringing in my ears: *who will find out, who knows?* The body keeps the score, said Dr Bessel van der Kolk and he was right: the body betrays its secrets in a trembling hand or a pounding chest, a headache that won't shift or the plague of insomnia. In active addiction, my alcoholism was a secret that formed part of a larger code of silence within our family; a thread of secrecy that ran from my parents to me. More than anything else, the secret was how I knew who I was; it felt like home. In my teens, I romanced it like a lover. I initiated myself in its codes and silences lovingly. Like a good student I watched its guardians carefully and reverently. *Pour this, do that, say nothing, more, repeat, keep quiet.* For a long time, I felt that the secret kept me safe, not sick.

For my mother, the decision to turn the secret of her alcoholism into a story of transformation and recovery was not met with unanimous approval. This was inevitable. Her friends, in an attempt to correct what they saw as the most desperate slur against her name, wasted no time in telling her she was talking absolute rubbish. *Really? Are you sure? I mean, I know you like a drink, Jules, but AA, really?* Mum, annoyed and feeling misunderstood, persisted. Yes, she was sure. For our family, who had witnessed the issue at closer range, airing the secret publicly caused a great deal of confusion. This was, in large part, to do with my father; **he was our token alcoholic. My mother couldn't possibly match** him, not even close. For her to declare, aged fifty-three, that she, too, was an alcoholic engendered a profound confusion that stank of treason, or worse still, a lie.

In large part, this suspicion was to do with mum being a writer. And not just any old writer, a novelist to boot. Her job was to make things up. But she didn't just make things up, she was far cleverer than that. Everything is copy, Nora Ephron said famously, and Mum took that to its logical conclusion, using every inch of her past to inform her novels. She had always got into trouble for it within the family, but she didn't care. *Where do you think fiction comes from?* she used to say, blithely. But the trouble with playing roulette with fact and fiction in your professional life is that the blockbuster confessions – divorce, addiction, sexuality, and so on – when they come, are treated with a scepticism that verges on contempt.

Luckily, Mum didn't care about what they thought. If she had, I might not be sitting next to her in the meeting now. That's one way of looking at it; she gave me alcoholism and then, in a stranger-than-fiction plot twist, she gave me recovery. But she's only 50 per cent of my gene pool. What about Dad? Why, when he drank himself to death, should he get away scot-free with the chromosomal blame-game? Tonight, as I clear my throat to speak, he's still alive, lifting a wine glass to his lips with shaking hands in his house in Wales. I'll start with him; Mum would probably prefer that, optically.

'My name's Arabella, and I'm an alcoholic. Thanks for taking the meeting, Julia, and for everyone who does service here tonight. I'll start from the beginning and tell you what it was like, what happened and what it's like now. I'm not sure exactly where to start, so I'll just see what happens, I hope it makes sense and I'm sorry if it doesn't. I grew up in an alcoholic household where alcoholic drinking was the norm, but my parents divorced when I was three. From the age of four, we saw my father only at weekends. Typically, he was in alcohol's grasp during these visits. Often, he would forget we were coming and stagger out of his front door to greet us in a state of intoxicated confusion. Time spent with him would revolve around alcohol and the getting of it: in pubs and restaurants or going to shops to buy it. Until my stepmother arrived when I was five, I don't remember other people being around to take care of us. It felt lonely and I remember waking up screaming in the night in strange and unfamiliar houses.'

As soon as I start speaking, I feel like I've fucked up, like I've opened the wrong door to the house. Lots of addicts say this, that it's hard to tell the story of your addiction chronologically, partly because it's always a story that has been told before and you risk pre-emptively boring your audience, and partly because I'm not sure anyone is ever very good at thinking in neat arcs of before, during and after. I've tried to do it just now – 'I'll start from the beginning' – but that's just me rattling off stock phrases to soothe my nerves and get the juices flowing. I don't really want to start at the beginning at all. What I want to do is to get the audience to like me. This is hardly a newsflash in an AA meeting; all addicts, everywhere, at any time, want people to like them. I also want Mum to like me after this meeting and to do that, I need to keep her on side. We still live in the Blue House together, after all, and I have nowhere else to go. Even in an AA meeting, I'm still playing my parents off against one another. Truly, children of alcoholics never leave the emotional casino. The combined energy Mum and I are now radiating could power the National Grid several times over. Like a cameo in a film, I can sense she is waiting to be called from the wings onto the stage, but we are both without a script in some wild improv experiment. I look at the clock: twenty minutes left.

'You know, my Dad isn't the reason I'm an alcoholic. I believe I was born this way; I know a lot of us say this. Every drink I had was one step closer to coming here, to getting to this chair tonight. I don't remember my very first drink – I had access to alcohol from such a young age that it wouldn't have been a noteworthy occasion – but I do remember some of the feelings that made me feel like I needed to drink when I was a teenager, when I was about fifteen or sixteen. I remember once I had a disagreement with a friend at school over someone's boyfriend, some stupid teenage argument. All day at school I was on the verge of tears, engulfed by what felt like a terrible darkness, and when I got home, I stole a bottle of my mother's wine from the fridge and drank the whole thing in my bedroom lying on the bed. Nothing terrible happened, although I'm sure I felt like shit the next day. But what I did do that night, and for a long time after that, was to cement the connection between drink and shame or drink and sadness in my mind. For the ten years that I drank alcoholically, this seemed the most obvious truth to me, that drink and sadness were welded together. Welded makes it sound mechanical or ugly, but I don't think I mean that. I think I thought it was a beautiful thing, like a picture or a poem.'

I try not to look at the assembled faces when I'm speaking but I can see some people – women, mostly – nodding their heads when I talk about sadness and drinking. In my very first meeting I heard someone talk about the sadness of drinking alcoholically and it unlocked something within me; some large and mossy stone became uncovered in my heart. I always want to mention the sadness when I speak; it feels like my special subject, the one thing I actually know about. Everything else has the hollow, tinny feel of fraud. Out of the corner of my eye, I can see Mum's head nodding. Sadness is her thing, too. Mum sad on the school run; I can see the tears streaming from her eyes in the rear-view mirror. What had happened to make her so sad? I don't think I ever really understood. Mum sad in the afternoon; her face glassy from drinking and tired, something Dad had done maybe, some problem with money. Mum sad at the school gates; she didn't look like the other parents, she stood apart from them. Tonight, I feel a huge surge of compassion for her. Mum, sitting next to me, trying so hard to change the legacy of hurt. That's new in sobriety; I never felt compassion for anyone when I was drinking, least of all for myself. Pity, certainly. Compassion, never. I'm getting into my stride now, but I need to wrap it up in ten minutes. But how on earth do you close a story like this?

'I didn't stop drinking when things got bad. I pressed override and went way, way past that red traffic light. So far past it that I went off the road altogether. I didn't stop drinking when things got really bad either, when I had been fired from my job and my friends wouldn't speak to me. I didn't even stop after I had been admitted to a psychiatric ward. I stopped after a pretty ordinary night of alcoholic chaos, one of any number of nights that all looked exactly the same: delusion, blackout, shame, remorse. On repeat until the end of time. I guess that's what we call grace, or the grace of God as we understand him. But I think it also illustrates **the madness of this illness, that you can be doing something so** destructive for years on end and it's a small detail that crashes the entire edifice; an empire burnt to the ground by a fag butt tossed carelessly out of a window. I'm aware of how lucky I am. I found AA early, and I've been given another chance. To do what, I don't know; I'm still figuring that out. Thanks for listening.'

When I eventually stop speaking, I feel like I need a cigarette. Even though I don't drink or take drugs any more, I'm still wearing the addict's security blanket: feel anything, immediately take a drug to change the way you feel, draw your blanket around you as tightly as you can. This is normal, apparently. It will take me many years to take the blanket off in sobriety. At one year sober, I'm not even close, although I consider myself to be well. I look round to Mum and smile at her, hoping that this gesture will be seen and interpreted by others in the meeting as a sign of hope.

That's why we're here, I think. And there is hope, so much hope, in our relationship now. But that's only part of the picture. There are other parts of the picture that are indistinct, sketched out in dark outline in the background. These outlines are the messy, unfinished fault lines of dysfunction that run right down our family through the women, those lightning rods for generational blight. There's a Rembrandt I like in the Ashmolean, an early sketch; the contours of the mountains behind the central scene are unfinished but it is to them that my eye is primarily drawn, mad stabs of thin pencil that portend a storm. A part of me feels like I've left the best bit of the picture out.

People from the meeting begin to share back. *Share*: how I used to cringe at that word. But it's the only word that really captures the exchange of emotional truth from one stranger to another; we give of ourselves willingly. Mostly, people talk about my age.

At twenty-seven, I am normally the youngest person in the room by a country mile. My youth – abundant, although I don't know it – works in reverse: other alcoholics look at me and wish, not that they were younger, but that they could have had those sober years. Time regained, or maybe just time reframed; *I wish I'd known then what I do now.* Sober time operates differently, like dog years maybe; every sober year worth seven civilian ones.

It's nearly the end of the meeting. An American woman raises her hand to speak. She's been sober a long time, over ten years maybe. She's often in meetings but she rarely shares back, usually sitting somewhere near the front, her clothes muted neutrals, her expression inscrutable. I hardly know her but when she's there I feel seen, held in an embrace of fellowship that borders on the deep fug of long-forgotten childhood safety. I'm always struck anew by the strength of this feeling every time it happens, how a relative stranger can trigger the same feelings of profound intimacy as a parent, a triangulation of some long-forgotten parental bond. It's also perfectly possible I have no idea what parental intimacy even feels like. She thanks me for my story in a restrained way, alluding to my youth and the promise of a long and sober life: decisions made in earnest, happiness and pain mingled together, held in both hands.

'I'm looking at you both sitting here, and I know there's healing. I see proof that things can change in families. But I also know how much pain must have brought you both to the Fellowship and I want to call that out,' she says, her eyes fixing on both of us squarely. 'I guess what I'm trying to say is, things look different outside the meetings. These realities are hard to bring out into the open, families are hotbeds of silence. I'm glad I heard you tonight, thanks.'

Generally, speakers don't respond to the people who share back, bar a nod or a smile. There aren't rules in AA but there are traditions, ways of doing things that have been carefully grooved like pebbles in a stream over decades, ever since Bill Wilson first held a meeting in his house in Ohio. Sharing back is one of these sacred pebbles; a communion between the speaker and the fellow. In this moment, I'm glad I don't have to respond directly because I feel a vast wave of emotion breaking over me. All that silence, for so long, only for me to respond to its naming with yet more silence, with a nod.

Mum drives us back to the Blue House in the dark. At a set of traffic lights, she turns to me. 'I did look after you, when you were little, you know. I wasn't drunk all the time. I just want to say that.'

'I know, Mum. I know. Look, it's OK. I'm sorry.'

When we get back to the Blue House, I go into my room and light a cigarette.

Julia

Shame

I'm sitting in an AA meeting at the Catholic Chaplaincy in St Aldate's, Oxford. The meeting takes up one end of the vast, cavernous room with a circle of chairs and a table for the urn, mugs and biscuits. An enormous, colourised photograph of Cardinal Newman dominates the empty space at the other end of the room.

Glancing at his amused but somehow remote expression in this portrait, his enormous nose, the bags under his eyes, makes me feel uneasy and strangely lonely. Newman, I feel, would not have approved of me or my rackety life, or the alcoholism which has brought me to this place. I am, in fact, a Catholic convert and although I revere Newman for his intellect, I find myself thinking what a cold fish he was. Looking at him in this way reminds me that on becoming a Catholic myself in 1996, it didn't occur to me to confess to the priest that I had a problem with drink; I'd never have told anyone that, not even God.

As I look away, I see Arabella entering the room and I wave with a jauntiness I don't really feel. I didn't know she was planning on coming because she'd vanished to the library by the time

I came downstairs this morning. If I'd known she was going to be here, I might not have come. Although I'm insanely proud of her sobriety, it makes me uneasy to hear her sharing. I kind of want to just leave it there: she's sober, that's great, over and out. I suppose I don't want to hear her confession, if we're on the subject. I've hidden from the truth for so long that confronting it in daylight, even in the sacred spaces of an AA meeting, still makes me uneasy.

Please, can't we just push it all under the carpet again?

I also find it almost impossible to reconcile Arabella's view of me as a mother, as heard in previous meetings, and my own view. *I wasn't that bad, was I?* I tried so hard. Or maybe I *was* that bad. There's another thing, too: I've forgotten so much. *Did I really say or do that? Is that normal, or is it my alcoholism?* Listening to her is painful and sometimes humiliating, and this lunchtime I'm really not in the mood. Perhaps she won't share. Reliving the shame from an illness I didn't know then was an illness doesn't help. It just keeps me stuck in feeling what an awful person I am. And I have to move on from that. I can't keep dragging the past around behind me like a dead cow. But here is the past and it's called Arabella.

The meeting starts promptly. I know the woman doing the share and don't particularly like her. I'd once asked her to be my sponsor and when she hesitated, I'd felt an acute sense of grievance, a fact I immediately recall when she starts to speak.

The sharing back starts, and I hear, with a mixture of curiosity and animosity, if I'm honest, Arabella saying, 'My name is Arabella and I'm an alcoholic.' Oh God, here we go. I watch her across the room with pride and apprehension. Objectively, I can see without any difficulty how attractive and funny she is. Subjectively, somewhere inside me, I also know that she's a little girl with a big grudge. She's an absolutely brilliant mimic and raconteur with the ability to put her own spin on things that weren't quite exactly as she describes them. According to me, anyway. The parent/child relationship is turned completely on its head in here and I find it confusing and sometimes infuriating. I feel like a beetle on its back, legs cycling in the air listening to her: absolutely and utterly powerless. A further reason I don't like going to meetings with her is because she quite often tells the assembled company things I didn't know about her and I realise with a pang how vulnerable she was and how I failed to help her. Sometimes, I think what a stranger she is to me, how much of her life I've missed because of my addiction. How much I've simply forgotten. I joke to my friends that I'm tracking her through the rooms to find out the truth about her life, but what I don't say is that it's actually quite painful for me to listen to. I'm in the habit of making jokes about serious things in an attempt to draw their sting.

In active addiction, a lot of my waking time was spent thinking about where and when the next drink was coming from. I was quite good at disguising it – or so I thought – but now, listening to my daughter, I realise I wasn't as good as I thought. I remember one occasion when I'd returned from the off-licence round the corner from our flat in London, only to find Arabella hanging out of the first-floor sitting-room window saying, 'Sarah called' – Sarah was my literary agent – 'and I told her you'd gone to the offy,' she added, casually. I shrank then and I shrink now. *Did Sarah know I was a drunk? Did my editor?*

'Alcohol was freely available,' she is saying, 'I can't even remember my first drink . . . ' She adds something about my attention, as well – how I was always hidden behind the spine of a book. *What*? Now she's criticising me for reading. Reading is my life and hers, too. I gave her a love of books, I read to her every bloody night. I sit and seethe, trying not to roll my eyes.

But I'm an addict: I use things – books, shopping, food, men – to change the way I feel. The great difference now is that I no longer use alcohol, but I'm beginning to realise how saturated with addiction the rest of my life is, witness the comment from my daughter about reading. A lot of the time – as is clear from what Arabella is saying – I may have been physically present as a mother, but mentally, I was elsewhere. I tried to pay attention to her, and I did. I drove her to school every morning until she was fifteen or so, when she started to take the Tube. Well done, me. Big tick. I took her on holiday. I turned up to sports events, at her junior school, anyway. The trouble is that our joint alcoholism has blurred the boundaries of what was acceptable and what wasn't. I have to leave it to her to decide now. It's humiliating. But, apparently, it's good for me to be humiliated, or so AA says. In fact, it doesn't say exactly that: that's my current spin on it this lunchtime. AA wisdom decrees we don't always have to be right, and we don't always have to have the last word. My God, is she *still* talking?

The trouble with sharing the Fellowship of AA with your daughter is that it's always your fault. It's true – it *is* my fault I didn't pay her proper attention – but I just don't want to hear it said in public. It's also true that I was almost invariably hungover in the morning on the school run or, if not actively hungover, then definitely below par. But I kept it a secret. I would never *tell* anyone I was hungover. And because I wouldn't admit it, in a bizarre way I could convince myself that I didn't really have a problem. Yes,

I drank 'a bit' too much, but you'd drink like I did if you had my life. It was my lifeline, my prop, my beloved. It's only been a year and a half since I formally acknowledged my alcoholism and got sober, but today, listening to my daughter, I'm acutely aware of the wreckage of my past and the shame is corrosive. The worst thing of all is that there's nothing I can do about it except stay sober myself and attempt to make amends for what I've done. Amends to children are ongoing – living amends – and not finally done until death, or that's what I find myself thinking. I feel sorry for myself, second nature for an alcoholic.

Part of the shame I feel is because, as a single parent, I felt I had to be the best. If I'd still been married to Arabella's father, I reason to myself, I would have been able to share responsibility for her, but we parted when she was four. She's never known us as a couple. That's a terrible loss for her, but even now, I feel he gets off too lightly. He's Daddy, Daddy, marvellous Daddy, and I'm her drunken mother, or that's how I'm being depicted. What about his misdemeanours, which were legion? Her father is at this point living in Monmouthshire, drinking himself to death. I'm the sober one. Shouldn't I get a fistful of Brownie points for that? Apparently not. I feel my sense of grievance building inside me. It's just not fair. I'm on a roll now, not paying attention to what is being said. Luckily, Arabella has finally shut up. Her father abdicated any accountability for her and left it all to me. He never attended either of her schools once or the university where she did her undergraduate degree. He stopped paying for her, too, and I had to chase him through the courts for years. I felt put upon and extremely resentful towards him. Money was an endless, ever-present worry. I'd been brought up like that and I inflicted that mindset onto my child through my lousy choice of a husband. It didn't have to be that way, but it was. The absurd thing was that Arabella's father always had plenty of money. He was good at making it; the plutocratic gene runs in his family. But once he'd cast me as the enemy it didn't seem to occur to him that he was depriving his child, too. That made me gnash my teeth. It still does when I think about it. And yet it's my fault, apparently. *Mea maxima bloody culpa.* I'm so sick of my thoughts. I'd like to leave but I can't. It wouldn't look good. No, I have to sit it out.

Arabella's father was seventeen years older than me and already had two children by his first wife when we met. He was going through a nasty divorce, and I felt that I could help him. I got it. I was young – twenty – but I felt older than my years. I'd lived through the emotional turbulence of my parents' divorce and I'd already been divorced myself by the time I met him. Divorce runs through my family like a recurring virus. It's not a great subject to be an expert in, but I already was. We intuitively understand the things we know, even if they're negative. His parents had divorced in flames, too. Divorce and alcoholism bound us together, not that I would have put it like that in those days.

One of the wonderful things about him was that he drank even more than I did. My drinking looked nothing beside his. He was thirty-seven when I met him, and given that alcoholism is a progressive illness, a lot further down the road than I was. Morally, it was already devouring him, but I couldn't see that. How could I have done? I didn't have the wisdom to understand the bigger picture of his rather tragic life: like me, he was a child of a rotten marriage with alcoholism running in the family, like a background refrain. By the time I met him, booze had made him greedy and cold and only interested in me because I burnished his sense of self. He liked having a much younger wife who was a writer, a world utterly different to his own. I was a trophy wife without even knowing it. He was a narcissist, of course. Alcoholism fosters it. All alcoholics are narcissists to varying degrees – *including you,* says the voice in my head. With him, all I could see was a very attractive, older man who had the means to protect me from the world and who liked having a good time. I liked having a good time, too. I felt I was owed it after what I'd been through as a child.

Although the biggest thing we had in common was drinking, we never discussed it, not once. But this is the problem with alcohol: it isn't discussed, it's just *there*, like a bloody serpent coiled in the corner of the room. There's a code of silence around it, particularly amongst the Baby Boomers of my generation who grew up in a world where nobody ever talked about booze and its attendant perils. Instead, alcohol was the prize you got when you entered adult life.

Now I can see that alcohol controlled our married life right from the beginning. When I first met him, he would frequently turn up after hours at the office I was working in, brandishing a bottle of champagne. I loved it. So stylish, so fun. The first night we ever spent together he ordered champagne on room service. I loved the lavishness of the gesture, the idea that ordering champagne on room service was a normal part of his life. I saw a future with money in it: room service, fast cars, lovely hotels, a world so different to my own upbringing that I longed to be a part of it. I was desperate to escape into the glamour of his world. I was using him just as he was using me.

Alcohol, however, very quickly drove a wedge between us; as soon as I was pregnant and then had a baby he started coming home later, drunk, and I didn't know what to do. He was already sleeping around again, I guess, back to his old ways – the bad habit that had helped to destroy his first marriage – and we quickly fell apart as a couple. All my dreams of escaping in safety were smashed to pieces. Arabella went to him for the occasional weekend and would come back cross and tired and smelling of cigarette smoke, her clothes crumpled, her hair unbrushed. He neglected her and it made me furious.

Our society is blind in many ways to the perils of alcohol, but if you're a single mother with a drink problem, you daren't seek help. I was in sole charge, apart from those weekends. If I admitted I had a problem, Social Services would get involved – I'd already had a brush with them after Arabella was born, when I was still married (although I don't recall telling her father about it – I kept it to myself) – and I was of course terrified of losing her, and not only that, but the horror of losing her to the perpetrator of those weekends when she'd come home stinking of neglect. Having a child of my own inevitably revealed the negative of the lost, terrified child that was hiding within me. I was a child with a child, but I just had to get on with it. Her father was bad cop and I was good cop, a ruthless calculation in which I left myself absolutely no margin for error.

Ah, the wisdom of hindsight. To say I was ashamed of my alcoholism doesn't suffice: I denied to myself that it even existed. Crucially, I had no understanding of it as a separate entity, an actual illness, both mental and physical. It was who I was. I also couldn't see how I could possibly live without alcohol. The idea terrified me. I needed it to survive my life.

In AA, you gradually learn that you have everything the wrong way round: that if you give up the alcohol, your life starts to straighten out. Alcohol is not your friend but your enemy. For decades, I simply couldn't see that because I'd started drinking so young that my alcoholism had grown with me; it *was* me. Losing it, I felt, would be like tearing out my heart.

All this passes through my mind as I sit through the meeting: Arabella had talked about how sad I always seemed to be, how separate, how different, for instance, from the other parents at the school gate. I did try to talk to the other parents, I did take her to parties. *Was it really that bad? Was I really that sad? God, I feel exhausted.* My head, as they say in AA, has worn me out. I wish I could just take it off and leave it on a chair.

I don't speak during the meeting, but at the end I go over to say hello to my daughter. She glances at me apprehensively as I approach, and I detect that she's alarmed by how I'll react to what she shared. I want her to know she doesn't have to worry about that. This new way of life has offered me other means to deal with my hurt apart from old-fashioned retaliation: talk to my sponsor, listen to what she says, and not allow what Arabella has shared to sour our relationship. I have to allow her to be free in the rooms, I have to be forgiving of her point of view – this is truly radical – but I must just make sure we don't go to the same meetings.

Chapter Three

Mother Love Revisited

Arabella

I believe that I loved my mother more than anything, and that it came undone all at once. I think it happened when I had my child.

ME & OTHER WRITING, MARGUERITE DURAS

The overhead fan in the church basement was so loud I could hardly hear what the speaker was saying so I looked at the meeting scrolls instead. For the thousandth time, I shifted in my folding metal chair, trying to find a way to balance my weight and elevate my ankles. At nineteen weeks pregnant, I was sitting in an AA meeting. From the reaction of the other fellows, you might think that I was the first pregnant woman to ever go to a meeting: women smiled silently and knowingly, while men avoided me altogether, giving me at least a three-chair berth. I felt painfully and agonisingly different, a newcomer once again. Leaving every meeting I swore I would never go back, only to find myself in a meeting a couple of days later. Somewhere along the way, behind the shield of my pregnant body, I had lost my connection to the group. I kept going in spite of myself because it was where I grew up. Besides, I had already embarked on a journey to a place about which I knew nothing: motherhood.

And what kind of mother would I be? The best, the very best, make no mistake. Nothing at all like my mother, or her mother, or her mother before her. And yet, from the earliest days of my pregnancy a dark cloud parked itself above my head and refused to move. I had become pregnant easily, on my honeymoon, the great fortune of which was not lost on me as friends around me tried to get pregnant with little or no success. I had just finished my graduate work in America and now I was married and pregnant, living in central London in no time at all. I had shapeshifted once again: from East Coast Ivy to wife and soon-to-be mother. People congratulated me on my pregnancy and my marriage, and I thanked them and went home in time to be there when my husband returned from work. Despite my gloom, I felt pleased to be pleasing other people; my life seemed to have taken on an acceptable shape at last.

Privately, I was appalled by my changing shape. From the early weeks of my pregnancy onwards, I would scrutinise myself endlessly in front of a mirror, trying desperately to conceal what I was told to be proud of. Nothing looked right to me, and my swollen frame seemed to indicate that the body was changing, indefinitely. Sometimes I would look in the mirror and hit myself, the act of which pleased me because at least it felt like a literal punishment rather than what felt like the slow judgement being meted out across my body.

Working on turning my PhD into a book while my husband

was at work, I spent long hours alone revising work that had taken me five years to complete and which I now saw as derivative and pointless. Occasionally I would break the deadlock by wandering around the park near the flat where I would watch young mothers pushing babies around in prams, fascinated by the ease with which they seemed to have recovered their bodies and composure. But it was the mathematics of pregnancy that baffled me: one plus one still only made one and yet I had lost any sense of integration. Within me, a split was occurring, and it wasn't delicate.

At seven years sober, I felt that the best solution – the *only* solution – was to go to AA. But I had moved away from the bedrock of sobriety I had created in the States, and I felt on the fringes of the London meetings. When I did go, I arrived late and left early, never once raising my hand to share. Deep down, I felt that drink and all its seductions were no longer the problem. The problem, I felt sure, was my ambivalence towards my pregnancy. I felt as if I had graduated from AA and into real life. In this new era, I saw myself not as an addict but a woman, two modes of being I saw as radically distinct from each other. AA had worked for me by reinforcing shared experiences, but these commonalities had dissolved. I felt unseen and unheard at the very moment when I was physically at my most conspicuous. Angry and disillusioned, I began to feel that the Fellowship had cheated me: the very sayings and prayers that I had been soothing myself with for years now seemed hollow and pointless. Full of venom, I began to tell my mother that I didn't believe in the programme, that I had been worshipping a false god. Patiently, she told me to go back to the meetings; impatiently, I slammed the phone down and went back to looking at myself in the mirror and deleting large parts of my thesis.

In desperation, I went to see my doctor. New to pregnancy, I was surprised by her insistence that she examine me physically first. 'We'll just make sure baby is OK,' she said in a sing-song voice that I now realise is the voice of all maternal health practitioners. '*I* am not OK,' I declared, after I had been returned to the upright position in a chair. Quickly, I gave her a whistle-stop tour of my mental health over the past decade, making sure to point out the many years I had been on antidepressants and my family history of addiction. Young and fresh, she listened with compassion, raising her eyebrows occasionally and nodding sympathetically. 'There are two things we can do for you,' she said when I had come to an abrupt stop, my eyes brimming with tears. 'We can either put you back on a low dose of the antidepressants, but this comes with a risk to baby, or we can refer you to the perinatal mental health team at the hospital, but the waiting list is long, and you may not be seen for many months.' Yet again, I felt as if I was in the wrong place, being offered a sop instead of what I really needed. As I walked out of the surgery into the cold March wind, it dawned on me that no one could give me the fix I wanted: no drug, no person, no achievement, no nothing. Here was sobriety proper and it was the hardest thing I had ever done.

Slowly, the months passed. By October, I could fit into none of my coats or shoes and took to simply waiting in the flat like a prisoner. Every day, I would order the same pad thai on Deliveroo and take it wordlessly from the driver who looked at me barefoot in my linen tent with a mixture of pity and amusement. Every day, I wondered if I might be pregnant forever. But nothing lasts forever and by the time my daughter had been out in the world for a few weeks, I began to look back on my period of imprisonment with sheer amazement that I had spent so long in my own company. Never again would I have the (dubious) luxury of so much time to myself. Never again would I feel the departure from one life into the next so fully and starkly.

Can you ever really pinpoint the moment when one life ends and another one begins? When I went to my first AA meeting, I'm not sure I could have guessed how radically different my life would be afterwards, that the shaky decision to walk into that church hall would alter all the other decisions I would make after it. Luckily, AA doesn't work like that. *Keep it in the day,* they say, or, *You only ever have twenty-four hours. If you knew that you'd never have another drink again, you'd drink yourself into oblivion,* they said, and I could easily believe it. Pregnancy isn't like that; you know, from the second you see the two lines on the test, that nothing will ever be the same again. Life has very few certainties like it, death being one of the only exceptions.

She came at 3 p.m. on a mild October day, lifted above the wreck of my body in an operating theatre I didn't expect to be in. She was – and still is – luminously beautiful with bright blue eyes and white-blonde hair. She looked nothing like me, a fact that pleased and unnerved me in equal measure. The mathematics of birth had overwritten those of pregnancy: one plus one made two now. Except, as I would soon find out, she hadn't really separated from me at all; the sum still didn't add up. Back in the flat and crippled by the surgery, I was amazed by how much she slept and how quiet she was. 'She'll explode soon,' a jolly Nigerian health visitor with bright red nails said to me when I mentioned how placid she was. Disturbed by this remark, I decided she must be wrong; *You've got a good one!* people trilled when they came to visit, and I agreed smugly. I had a good baby, nothing like the terrible accounts of me as a baby from my mother. Things *do* change from generation to generation, I thought, as I read a book on the sofa while she slept in her Moses basket. 'I'm enjoying it!' I texted a friend from AA, sending a picture of her sleeping, head tilted to one side, one eye ever so slightly open. She was waking up.

When she did explode some days later, I adopted a grim acceptance. At first, I remained calm, putting her to my breast and waiting for her to feed. After several hours of her screaming into my chest while I scrolled Mumsnet threads on my phone in increasing frustration, we both collapsed into a half-sleep only to be woken by my husband leaving for his day at work, oblivious to the events of the previous night from the relative quiet of an upstairs room. Soon, night after night took on the same shape: up to six hours of inconsolable crying, while I paced the nursery with her in my arms. I became more and more desperate. Desperate for sleep, yes, but even more desperate for the crying to stop. In the moments when she was actually asleep, I lay rigidly awake like a sentry, cortisol pumping through my veins, waiting for the crying to resume. My face, which I tried not to look at in the mirror, had turned a strange hue of pinkish grey, my eyes bloodshot and watery from too little sleep. Too scared to leave the flat in case she exploded in public, I wore the same stained clothes day after day. The London autumn was turning to winter; I watched from the window as leaves and rubbish blew across the street from the flat. I became thin. Having unravelled before, I knew that I was touching the grooved edges of my sanity.

Did I think about having a drink? Often. The flat was full of my husband's bottles, something which had never triggered me before since he isn't an addict. But as the weeks wore on, the bottles began to speak to me: *Just one*, they whispered, *you deserve it*, they murmured, to a chorus of newborn howling. Doggedly, little broken bits of AA wisdom floated through my addled brain. After seven years in AA, I knew the danger of relapse: I had seen the living ghosts who walked back through the church doors to meetings afterwards, their faces haggard. I had always thought that if I did relapse, I would be simply struck down by the desire like a lightning bolt, that I would automatically abscond all moral reasoning: *it just happened.*

But it hadn't occurred to me that I would be caught in a no-man's land of choice. And I did make choices, that evening. I put my daughter in her cot and in the small window of time before she began to howl at the realisation of my absence, I poured myself a large glass of red wine. The action felt wooden and unfamiliar, an old friend held in the bottle like a genie all this time. From the nursery, I could hear the now-familiar escalation of my daughter's crying, what I took to be the jump from normal to critical: her screams becoming louder, her throat straining. And then, suddenly, nothing. I ran to the nursery and plucked her from the cot, her face red and tearstained in what I understood as reproach.

I thought of my mother, interrupted by me as she brandished a knife to her wrists, her eyes wide; I thought of my grandmother interrupted by her own daughter as she stared into her own depression listening to the gramophone; I thought of myself, trying to have a drink. We were all fatally and eternally interrupted. Moments later she fell asleep on my shoulder. Quietly, I carried her back to the kitchen, balancing her with one hand so that I could pour the glass of wine down the sink with the other.

Where was my mother during this period? True, she came to see me and the baby often, but she lived over an hour away, not nearly close enough to help with the daily crises that come with a newborn baby. Once, I summoned her down the motorway at a moment's notice, completely desperate for her advice, only to accuse her, unfairly, of not being able to help as the baby continued to howl in a corner of the kitchen while we hissed at each other about colic remedies. When I felt I needed her most, as I began the impossible process of finally splitting away from her and towards my own daughter, my mother was deep in another of her addictions. The curtain had fallen once again. She had met a writer on an internet dating website, she said, on one of her visits to see the baby. She would be gone for two weeks, to Greece of all places. When asked if she had any idea about this man whom she had never met and for whom she was about to travel some distance, she became belligerent: 'I have to live my own life,' she cried. Three months later, she was engaged to him. One month after that, the whole arrangement was off, and she would never speak to him again.

Against the backdrop of my mother's most recent abandonment and my daughter's incessant crying, I could only feel rage. Rage at my mother for her dependence on men, but mostly rage at myself for believing I could have mothered anyone in the first place, a conceit I tortured myself with for many months. I could not see, then, that my rage and the baby's crying were directly connected. I dimly understood in rare moments of clarity at the kitchen sink that the thread that ran between me and her had become knotted somewhere along the way, that some dark inheritance was at work, but I failed to understand this at the level of the body. This, in spite of all my hard-won 'self-awareness' in sobriety. It was only when a friend from AA gently suggested that I stop breastfeeding my daughter that things began to improve, even if this raised the bar of my failures higher still in my eyes. Slowly, as I stopped breastfeeding and began to feed my daughter with formula, I found my way back to myself. I started taking antidepressants at a high dose; I slept for more than two hours at a time; I learnt to hear my daughter cry and not feel my hands shaking or my heart pounding. The acceptance that I was unable to sustain her with my own body took longer to come. The belief that she had been unmothered in some way is ongoing.

In the photo that my daughter keeps of me and her by her bed, she sits on my knee and smiles up at me, her eyes tightly closed, while I smile back at my husband who is taking the photo. She is three years old, wearing a dress with strawberries on it, her legs dangling off my lap. You could never guess our tumultuous start; you would have no inkling of the anguish that underwrote so much of our first year together. Having thought that I was exceptional, or that my experience of early motherhood set me apart from others, I now see it as a common, if sad, one. I have joined another fellowship now – that of mothers – and I see and hear stories like my own all the time. The connection that I so craved in pregnancy I have found in motherhood. Occasionally, I meet young mothers like myself who are also sober alcoholics and I am reminded of just how close and how ill-defined the relationship is between addiction and the business of motherhood. I can still remember the first time I read Gabor Maté's words: 'All addictions are attempts to escape the deep pain of the hurt child, attempts temporarily soothing but ultimately futile,' and I can still see myself throwing my head back and putting the book down, desperate to find a pen to underline them and keep them for myself.

After what had happened, I never thought that I would have another child. For five years I dodged people's prying questions and deflected their remarks. I felt angry that my responses smacked of some deep and dark discomfort that I couldn't put my finger on. It seemed cruel and unmaternal not to give my daughter a sibling, but I papered over these worries with hollow justifications of lifestyle and career, justifications that I privately suspected were driven by my own vanity. A peculiar kind of self-loathing sprung up within me. When I looked in the mirror, I could only see the grey hairs and the bags under my eyes, the promise of motherhood draining from my face. Often, I would read Jane Burn's poem 'Only Child', reciting the last verse out loud to an empty room: 'Something broke after you. I tell you how I could never have made something so magical twice, that you grew so tall and strong because you are all my babies born at once.'

But it was no use. I knew I needed to have another child, if only to prove to myself that I could break the cycle of unpurged anger that swelled within me. I set about it calmly and methodically and became, to my surprise, pregnant straight away. I felt pleased, hopeful even; my internal struggle became dimmer.

Immediately, another internal struggle took its place: why didn't I feel any signs of pregnancy? Where had the absolute certainty of the test lines gone? In a strange re-run of my first pregnancy, I scanned my reflection in the mirror for the outward signs of life, this time praying for the very thing I had despised so much five years before. I felt sure I was being punished for some complacency; a criminal convicted after years on the run. When I did eventually fall asleep at night, I dreamt of frantically looking for my daughter in crowded places or watching her move away from me on a train I hadn't boarded. Some nights, I dreamt of nothing at all, presaging the deep black of nothingness to come on the scan. My knowledge of miscarriage was confined to my mother's experience with her third husband in Cairo: the baby had simply vanished in a souk, never to be seen again. She had gone away with a baby and come back without one and nothing was ever said about it. I had no idea how you lost a baby, no inkling as to what this strange brand of disappearance would feel like.

Until I did. Except I hadn't lost a baby so much as suffered an early catastrophe, the doctor said, turning the screen towards me so that I could see the deep black of the womb flecked with small dots. A 'silent' miscarriage she called it. 'The body still thinks it's pregnant,' she said carefully, 'but in fact something must have happened very early on because there is no sign of any gestational sac. You should start to miscarry soon. In the meantime, you need to wait.' The weeks that followed were a blur of waiting rooms and hospitals, blood tests and scans. Most of all, there was the feeling that something had disappeared without trace. When I asked consultants or doctors why, they shrugged and looked sympathetic: *the body is a mystery.* Nobody knows, they say. It's best not to ask, others add. The body can be a garden but it can also be a graveyard; how can any woman stand this fact?

Six months or so after the miscarriage, a submersible destined for the wreck of the *Titanic* disappeared with five crew members aboard. In the week before its fate is confirmed, the papers are full of theories as to whether the crew are alive and when the oxygen might run out. Three days later, all five of the crew are confirmed dead. Experts later confirm that there is a debris field, but no human remains are ever found. My fascination with the tragedy is linked, I am sure, to my feelings about disappearance and the business of remains. I wonder at the disappearance of the miscarried foetus, where it went and who it was, of what remains it has left in my deep tissue. I wonder about the wreckage that lies beneath the sea level of the body before it makes itself known; I think of the ten days in between the diagnosis and the reality of the miscarriage and then I think of the nose cone of the submersible fished out of the deep Atlantic and the remains of anything that lived in the deep if only for a short time.

Two months later, I am pregnant again. By the time this book is published, I have another daughter.

Julia

Mother Love Revisited

The WhatsApp message takes me by surprise: it's an invitation to a party. Arabella is leaving for the USA to study for her PhD. She's going away for five years. It's hugely significant.

What is even more significant to me at this moment, however, is that I've actually been invited to the party. This was by no means a given by the time I'd reached the end of my drinking. By then, Arabella was in the habit of hiding anything important. I would get to hear about it later from someone else: a birthday party I was not asked to; a lunch with my old boyfriend; the cry for help to her godmother rather than me. It was so shaming and hurtful that I ignored it, or tried to, and numbed the feelings with booze and more booze. As a mother, I was the equivalent of a failed state. But how had this come about? When I think back to the beginning of it all, I was going to be the best mother ever, or at the very least, better than my own mother, which wasn't actually that difficult, or so I told myself. How very wrong I was.

There was so much in my relationship with my mother that was unresolved from my childhood, and those issues remained painfully alive in me throughout Arabella's childhood. My resentment of my mother constricted me – it was like a straitjacket. I couldn't get free of her, or rather, I could, but only by being unpleasant, which merely bound me to her with yet more guilt and shame. Those feelings of rage and resentment were like the wrappings of a mummy: it was the past, but it wasn't dead: the fearful child in me was simply buried alive beneath the grave clothes.

It was only very much later on, once I'd been sober for a while, that I could finally understand the conundrum concerning my mother and me: until I made the attempt to understand and forgive my mother for her failings, I would be forever shackled to my childhood and, to a large extent, a child myself. Forgiving her, remitting her sins, pardoning her, freed me from those ancient fetters and allowed me to grow up, at long last. In a sense, as I pardoned her, I pardoned myself, too, and the Gordian knot was finally cut.

As a young mother, understanding nothing of either my relationship with my mother or with alcohol (they were inextricably bound together), I was full of good intentions, but good intentions are useless when it comes to active addiction: alcohol always wins. *I won't do this*, you tell yourself, about drink-driving, for instance, and then find yourself doing it. *I will be nice when she rings,* then you're poisonous. Shift the goalposts. *I won't do it again.* You do it again the next day. *I won't drink tonight*: you start drinking at tea-time instead. And so on and on. I didn't stop drinking, I just loathed myself more and more because I couldn't stop. It never occurred to me to seek help. I was too ashamed. I had to be perfect, don't forget, I had to out-mother my mother, so I denied my imperfections.

This somewhat miraculous WhatsApp message is a part of my new awakening, my actual rebirth. No exaggeration. I feel thrilled to be asked, and at the same time I feel weirdly like some sort of lost traveller in the landscape of my daughter's life. She has friends I've never met, academic colleagues I've only heard her allude to, one or two women who have mothered her. I definitely don't want to meet them. I hope they won't be there. There are quite a few other people who've played a major role in my daughter's life: the crash team at the Charing Cross Hospital in London, for instance, who tended to her when she had a psychotic breakdown and wandered out of her job without telling anyone where she was going. That happened in the darkest days at the end of my drinking when, yet again, I was not called in or consulted. I wouldn't have been any use. I only heard about that, not because Arabella told me – she didn't – but because her flatmate called me in despair.

Because we are both sober now, the party won't be in a pub. Phew! I've spent too much time in pubs in my life and if I never set foot in another, I won't be sorry. Quite often, in meetings, I hear people, newly sober, recounting how they've wandered past a pub garden full of people drinking frosted glasses of lager or whatever it is, and how they long to be able to take their place among them once more, one of the merry crew harmlessly indulging in the romance of alcohol. I drove past an ad at a bus stop only yesterday featuring a member of Gen Z holding a frosted bottle of Peroni as if it was the holy grail, with the caption 'The Taste That Takes You There'. But where is '*there*'? For civilians that's just fine – go there and have fun – but for an alcoholic, it is that remembered sweet spot they can never quite recapture, however hard they try. And, boy, do they try! For me, and for all sober alcoholics, there is no romance in the idea of drinking: it definitely won't take me 'there'. My version of 'there' will be A&E or being wrangled into a straitjacket on a locked ward.

Luckily for me, my capitulation to the knowledge that alcohol controlled me was so complete that this fantasy has almost entirely disappeared from my life – or has it? It must linger in the shadows because it still annoys me how the message that alcohol will solve all our problems goes unchallenged everywhere. *If you spot it, you got it*, they say, annoyingly, in the rooms of AA. I remember all those pub gardens so well: the endless to-ing and fro-ing to the bar because I drank so fast; the drunken waving of the almost maxed-out credit card; the extra drink necked at the bar before I returned; the glasses of wine and shots of gin that were never, ever big enough. Even the doubles were laughably paltry. The loos where I fell asleep. The stumbling home only to find I'd left my handbag behind. That is the reality of the pub garden for me, not some chilled nirvana where I can escape reality for an hour or two. Luckily, it's summer so we're heading to Port Meadow for a picnic.

When the day comes, I arrive alone, tripping across the hummocks of the meadow carrying a basket of food like some elderly milkmaid, with Spotty the dog running in figures of eight just ahead of me. I have to watch her like a hawk, as she is a professional picnic-raider, practised at rushing other people's picnics and helping herself as they scatter. Today, however, there are such a large number of people sitting on a chequered sea of rugs and assorted mats with Arabella in the centre that our party is big enough to keep her occupied and her attention focused only on us.

Arabella leaps to her feet when she sees us, crying, 'Mum!'

People look up and smile, whether at me or the dog, I'm not

sure, but I feel welcome, all the same. The tone of her voice contains a real welcome, not just, *Oh God, it's you,* as the subtext. People shift up. I recognise one or two faces from AA and feel reassured. I sit down and start talking to someone. My head is clear, the whites of my eyes white rather than yellow-ish, my hands steady. I feel what I call a 'gratitude attack' coming on. This feeling of sober life is textural, almost granular, a sense of the present moment running through my hands, like fistfuls of beads. It's the sensation of being in the here and now, I suppose: not the regretted past or the dreaded future, those two states I lived in when I was drinking.

It's wonderful to see my daughter in all her glory, even if it means I am losing her, having just found her. A sudden darkening at this note of sorrow. But then I think that, today, I am able to want what is best for her and this is a very big best indeed: five years' worth of funding at an Ivy League university. This is the girl who wouldn't leave her room for days under a year ago, who would then go out on a bender and come back the following morning managing to look both bedraggled and furious at the same time. This is the girl who was hospitalised for mental illness just over a year ago. The change in her is astounding. All this from stopping the booze and undertaking the programme of moral psychology for drunks that is the Twelve Steps of AA. This is not only sobriety but an enormous, almost incomprehensible transformation in the shape and direction of our family life. The ancient illness that has zigzagged through our family like the knight in chess and that has been suffered in silence from one generation to the next is now named at last. And naming it means you can treat it.

Alcoholism took my grandfather's life. It is taking the life of Arabella's father as we sit here. It nearly took my life, and that of my daughter, who would probably have been dead by the time she was thirty. It played some enormous, nameless role in my mother's life, too, which I never got to the bottom of. Probably, though, it's not that difficult to guess why she drank: it numbed her tumultuous feelings and gave her relief, just as it had for me, until it didn't.

It never occurred to me when I got sober that Arabella, who was living with me and Husband Number Three, would go and do the same thing. It's the greatest gift I could ever have given her – not that I saw it that way at the time – and I gave it without even knowing I was doing it.

Fast forward, and suddenly here we are at Terminal Five. We had to leave the dog in the car and I'm rather wishing she was here to defuse the tension. It feels momentous, wrenching and unbelievable all mingled together that Arabella is leaving. A sober parting is something we've never done. How do you do that? How do you say goodbye without getting off your face afterwards? Sometimes it really is a case of just trying to join the dots in this new, alcohol-free life. Coffee, hell, yes, where's the café? It is possible to be at an airport and not drink, apparently. Not everyone has a water bottle full of vodka. Airports are haunted places for sober alcoholics.

We sit together and neither of us knows what to say.

'I'll walk you to the gate,' I say, and we get to our feet.

I watch as she passes through the turnstile, smiling and waving at me over her shoulder. And then she's gone. Just like that. A vast space opens up inside me. I walk towards the car park, putting on my dark glasses so that my tears can't be seen.

The dog leaps to her feet on the back seat when she sees me. If she could squeeze through the open window, she would. I bury my face in her lovely long, fur-scented neck and weep. She licks my hand and then my face. *All will be well*, she says, *all will be well*, the Mother Julian of the canine world. Or maybe all dogs are like that and that's why we love them so much.

I drive home with Spotty in the passenger seat. At the traffic lights, people stare and then laugh, and suddenly I'm all right. The awful feeling of loss has moved away, and in its place has come something else, something good. Look at me, I'm doing this difficult thing and I'm not drunk. It's a miracle.

Chapter Four

Write It Down

Arabella

She bore a very strong resemblance, he now saw, to her mother: the same cheekbones and eyes set so slightly at a slant. Why had he not noticed this before? She looked old-fashioned and remote, an untouchable black and white beauty, someone he did not recognize. Why had she not told him she was searching for her family? He was filled suddenly with a conviction that this was one of the keys to the mystery that he battered at, like someone banging on a door that was locked and barred to him.

JULIA HAMILTON, AFTER FLORA

It is a warm summer's day and I drop my bag on the hall floor as I come into the house and call out for her. Where is she? I want to tell her about how awful it all is, how lonely and depressed I feel staying in my father's house for the weekend. She doesn't come downstairs, so I go up to find her, pushing the door open. She's writing; it's what she does when I'm not here. When she does finally turn around, I can tell she's elsewhere; the green cursor of her Amstrad computer is flashing; she probably hasn't finished a sentence or a paragraph or a chapter, or even a book. She is always finishing a book. *When I deliver my manuscript . . .* Then. Then we will go away, then we will have some money, then things will come together. But not until then. In the meantime, we must wait for the editor to ring, or the publisher to decide or the magazine to call back. Most importantly, we must wait for the Muse. On the days when the Muse comes, everything is brighter; she picks me up from school and I just know. On the days when the Muse has not been, I also know; we sit in silence in the car and the weight of irritation hangs heavy between us. It could have been some other irritation – hangover, money worries, boredom – but there was a peculiar feel to this one; I can still trace its outline like a scar.

***

What's it like to have a novelist for a mother? People used to ask me that quite a bit when she had a burst of writerly fame in the nineties. It wasn't an easy question to answer because, as it seemed to me at the time, the writerly life is so intensely private. It is a business conducted separately, behind closed doors and prying eyes. It is not spoken of at the breakfast table, or the supper table, or anywhere at all. To mention the book is considered a great insult. For months and sometimes years while the book is being written, there are very few traces of it all. Certainly, there is next to no money given for it, although this is a secret and shameful matter never to be brought up. 'I can't tell you my sales figures, no,' I once heard her saying on the phone from the other room in the voice I thought was exclusively reserved for telling me off.

What exactly did I know? I could tell that it was a thing of great importance, possibly the most important thing in the world. What could be greater or more distinguished than publishing a book? Nothing. But I could also tell that it was a painful thing, a thing not chosen, but bestowed. 'Don't ever become a writer,' she would say ruefully sometimes, 'you'll spend all your days alone,' or, 'No one would choose this life if they knew.' She didn't mean it, of course, but even as a young girl I could sense the feeling of being trapped. I could also tell that being a writer meant spending quite a lot of time doing exactly the opposite and not writing anything at all. 'I'm engaging in displacement activities,' she would say as we went off to the high street to spend money we didn't have, or when she would spend an entire morning hoovering the flat loudly and with some frustration.

I look at my mother's bookshelves and I see a portrait of her over time. 'I will always buy you a book,' she would say to me as a child even when we had no money at all, 'books are sacred,' a generosity that meant I read a lot but also that we had nowhere to house the hundreds of books that accumulated in our house. There are novels, endless novels spilling out of the shelves, plenty given to her to review, plenty that she bought. There are her novels, too, all six of them, side by side in the far right-hand corner. I remember seeing one, *The Good Catholic*, in a Waterstones when I was thirteen and being deeply shocked that my name was there in the dedication. How could something so private become so public, I wondered, before positioning it right at the top of another pile of books so that people might be encouraged to buy it. Lining the other shelves are endless biographies, bought in a panic after she nearly wrote a biography of Mary Queen of Scots in the early

nineties. Elsewhere are the dozens of books on the First World
War, collected when she was writing her first novel based on the
trench diaries of our relation, Ralph. When she got sober, fourteen
years ago, the bookshelf began to change. Alongside her early
fascination with Jung and Freud that occupied her early twenties,
came books on recovery; memoirs but also more theoretical titles
on the nature of addiction and trauma by writers like Gabor Maté
and Susan Cheever. There is no obvious order to the shelves, no
colour-coding or alphabetisation, but the haphazard arrangement
of them seems to represent some truth about a life, some messy
and uncategorised way of reading around yourself in search of
answers.

Lately, I look at my bookshelves and see different versions
of myself amongst the spines. There are the books I studied at
university, every page marking a defiant bit of distance between
my childhood and my newfound independence. I see the root of
plenty of obsessions with different writers, dozens of titles jammed
together before they bleed out into books that look unread or
bought and then forgotten. There are the books I bought at thrift
stores in the States or in second-hand bookshops in Oxford or
Paris: pocket geographies of where I have lived. My mother's books
are all there winking away at me, their familiar spines asking me
to connect the writer to my mother. It is impossible to read the
fiction of anyone you know well enough and suspend belief, even
for a second, because you have glimpsed what lies behind the
curtain and seen the scaffolding that rudely bolts it all together.
I think that the way I read has always been circling around this
problem; I think I have tried to solve this problem with theory
and facts and journalism but I'm not sure if I have ever succeeded.

I began to read her novels as a teenager. I was looking for myself, of course, but I knew that they were also windows to her. 'What are your books about?' I asked her when we were writing this book, trying to find a golden thread that ran through all of them. 'I was fascinated by disappearance, I suppose,' she answered after some time, although she seemed amazed that I would want to include them in my emotional excavations of our past. Broadly, I can see that she wrote and rewrote the plot of her own life. It's all there in her later novels, the thrillers that she hoped would make her money, full of the ghosts of wives, mothers and daughters. It's there in her first novel in the spectral wanderings around the trenches that our ancestor Ralph made, parsed through his letters. It's there in the way she writes about a certain way of life that is coming to an end without knowing it; the Edwardian summer of 1914 or certain customs of class and generation that come apart in your hands like a dried flower.

I didn't notice these things when I first read her books with teenage eyes. Mostly, I felt embarrassed. Embarrassed in case her readers would know that I was the person behind the character on the page, the Chloe or Iris or Amanda; my mother's books are full of little girls. Alongside this ill-founded embarrassment was also the feeling of theft: this life we had, given to everyone else in fictional form, just as I felt she had given herself to plenty of others when my need was greatest. It was another loss.

Writing is a cruel calling. When she was winning, it was clearly the best job in the world. When she was losing, it was clearly the very worst. And there was, definitely, a period of her winning: a time when her books were reviewed and she was on the cover of features supplements and magazines, a moment when her books were in the front window of Waterstones on Kensington High Street. At one point, there was even heady talk of her most commercial novel, *Other People's Rules*, being made into a film. During this time, she was jubilant – alive – living out the promise of higher education that she had been denied as a young woman.

But the winning was also punctuated by enormous stress and anxiety: a bad review of her book could send her into a tailspin for days. Professional neglect by an editor would plunge her into deep depression out of which it seemed she couldn't crawl. Once, reading a review of her book in the *Sunday Times,* she threw the paper at the wall and sat on the floor sobbing and inconsolable, a pall cast over the house for the rest of the day. Whole weeks would be spent waiting for the agent to ring to tell her the fate of her latest book only for her to be dejected every Friday evening as another week passed.

Throughout, there was the drink. A glass by her desk as she wrote, a glass in her hand for when she couldn't. Writing and drinking; drinking and writing. Who would dare to say that the two were incompatible? My mother's circle was bohemian: writers, artists, opera singers, photographers, academics, all descending on our flat and staying long into the night. To a child, it could have looked any number of ways: frightening and chaotic maybe, but also jolly and permissive. To me, it was the latter. I was allowed to stay up and dance to the *King and I* while her French opera-singer friends sang along; I was admired and indulged by friends who would ask me to read passages aloud to the dinner table; I was told that my opinion mattered, and I believed them. The spark that led me to study French at university and later at graduate school in the States began at one of those evenings.

What I could only vaguely perceive as a child under ten years old was the swirling undertow of alcohol. It made itself felt in strange ways, the way a forgotten needle used to pin a dress unexpectedly pricks the flesh. It was there in the way an adult would be amused by a child briefly before casting them off and wrapping themselves in the cloak of adult conversation. It was there when great gusts of laughter would break out and I would join in, unsure as to what was so funny but without a script. It was there when I wanted my mother but got there too late, her face changed by the drink, her eyes glassy and her tone curt.

I carried this atmosphere of exception with me amongst my peers from a young age: I felt as if I knew something that the rest of them did not. In fact, I was certain that I did; after all, I was treated as an adult while my friends languished in childhood. I wanted nothing more than to be a writer. I fantasised about my own books lining the bookshelves in another house. When my school friend Daisy and I played endless role-plays, I was always the writer, on the phone to her agent accepting a lucrative book deal. When I told my mother about my ambitions, she seemed delighted: 'You come from a family of writers,' she said, tucking my hair behind my ear and adding, as she always did, 'I always knew you would be a writer, I just knew.' It was pre-ordained, written for me in advance, just like the alcoholism, you could say. I was *meant* to be a writer just as I believed for a long time that I was *meant* to be a drunk; the two wrapped themselves neatly around the other.

I don't know what came first, my mother or the writing. Whichever way I twist the kaleidoscope, I know that it is because of her that I write; the other elements twirl and change but she is there in the middle of it all. 'Just write it,' she would say when I was trying and failing to write a novel in my twenties. 'The hardest thing is getting started.' When I began to publish my academic work and other pieces of journalism, it was her approval I craved most, her voice I had to hear first, hers the only review that mattered. 'It's brilliant, darling, really, really good,' she would say, and my heart would soar because it is a rare and special thing to have another writer praise your work. It is even headier for that writer to be your mother.

When she married Number Three, her writing fell apart. I know she tried to write because I saw her sitting at her desk, her brow furrowed, glass by her wrist. She would deny there was wine in the glass, but it was pretty obvious. What was also pretty obvious was the fact that the long-held pact she had held between alcohol and creativity had completely broken down. The desperate hunger to publish that she had exhibited in my early childhood was still there, but it was continually thwarted by her drinking.

And what do you do when the Muse becomes deaf to your pleas? You pour yourself another drink because it is all damned and there is nothing else to be done. The multi-book deal that she had discussed with her publisher became doubtful as she endlessly tried and failed to write a proposal. Eventually, the deal collapsed altogether, and she sank even lower. Number Three, also a writer, could have been an enormous comfort to her at this time; he did, after all, notionally understand the cruelties of publishing: the long periods of waiting, the incessant criticism, the endless self-promotion required to push sales. Instead, he turned away with contempt and busied himself with other people because their pact as 'two writers together' had also proved to be doomed. She was fatally distracted. Distracted by her inability to write and her inability to bear another child, the two moving against each other like jammed dials every second of every day. All creation seemed to have halted.

I could have gone in a completely different direction from her and from everything I had seen about writing, but I didn't. I read literature at university and then, after my disastrous stint in financial PR, I read some more literature for a master's. I could have stopped there, too, but I didn't; I moved to America to read a bit more. I read voraciously and keenly but it took me a long time to write the kind of academic prose that was required at graduate school, and I still wasn't a natural. The cool, dispassionate gaze of the academic didn't belong to me, no matter how hard I tried and no matter how much I wanted it. I learnt that graduate school – the playground for baby academics – is also a cruel calling. Against the enormous privilege of the Ivy League education comes the shameful process of 'hazing', a fraternity term used to describe the process of being initiated by way of constant criticism and humiliation of your work.

At only one year sober, I was ill-prepared for the onslaught. Sitting in a tenured professor's office as the snow fell across the campus outside, I wept noisily at my grade, each objection in red pen taken as a terrible slight. 'You're making this far too complicated,' the professor sighed impatiently, glancing up at the walnut bookshelves lined with her own monographs and adjusting her grey bob. 'It's not about you, it's about the text, it's not personal.' What I couldn't explain to her was that writing – in whatever form it took – felt painfully about me. *Writing is the most intimate fucking thing of all*, I wanted to scream, but I didn't. In my mind's eye, I could see my mother sitting on the floor crying at the review of her book. In the end, all you want – all anybody wants – is a good review.

In my twenties, I used to think that being a writer was about the facts. Not for me the strange alchemy of fiction with its blatant thievery of people's lives or the weird magic of poetry. I preferred the cool, angular temple of academia with its facts and footnotes, indexes and bibliographies. I wanted answers and accountability; I wanted it to be catalogued and put in a library, end of story. I didn't want the slippery truth that revealed itself to me in drips and stains and patches across the fabric of my life only when people divorced or died or threw you away. But I could never escape the grubby subject of myself in my writing, it resurfaced everywhere: in the subjects I chose, the way I wrote, and ultimately, the way I wanted to be read. I found it impossible to get out of my own way. From a distance, I had watched a junior professor in my department leave the Ivory Tower to write a column about failure for the *New Yorker*. I later found out that he had the most crippling writer's block and felt incapable of writing the book on Weimar literature that he had started. I began to think that writing about yourself wasn't always something you needed to scratch from the first draft.

After my daughter was born, I began to publish little bits and pieces of journalism from the kitchen table while she slept, each acceptance from an editor a thrill not dissimilar to the high of a drink. I wrote about anything and everything, but my most successful pieces were the ones where I described how things felt to me, however banal: the way a dress in a charity shop had someone else's dry-cleaning ticket in it, or the atmosphere of a diner in New

York. 'Don't fall into the trap of writing about yourself too much,' a male writer friend warned one day, 'or you'll be writing about childbirth for the *Daily Mail* until the end of time.' I didn't want to admit it, but I could see that he was right. Overwhelmingly, editors would only commission me on the proviso that I would write about some trauma, be it drinking or childbirth or even my childhood. I started to feel as if I was guilty of the same theft that I had accused my mother of. What would my daughter think when she was old enough to read these pieces? Would she find the press-cuttings in a drawer somewhere and feel the churn of betrayal? Not for the first time, I could feel the past crashing into the present.

And what is this book, if not the most gigantic theft of all? I can hear you say it. Don't think I haven't thought it, too. Could we write a book together? *Should* we write a book together was probably the more appropriate question. How do you even write a memoir with your mother? This book is an attempt, however flawed, to answer these questions. It's not a manual to stop you or your child from drinking and neither is it a guide to living as the child of an alcoholic. We wanted it to be raw and truthful and ultimately hopeful, but I also suspect we wanted to protect ourselves from each other.

But, one day, when we were arguing over what should go where in the structure, my mother said the most helpful thing of all: 'Shall we just write it down, darling? You know, write down what happened?'

And so, we did.

Julia

Write it Down

I can't remember an exact moment when the idea of drinking was coupled with the idea of writing; it was much more unconscious than that, but somehow unquestionably necessary. Writers drank, didn't they? All the writers I knew drank, and one of them had drunk so much he almost killed himself. He went to AA, but he'd never written another word. That story terrified me – much more than the news of his death by suicide would have done (part and parcel of the myth) – and it also reinforced the idea of alcohol as an essential part of the creative process.

In my early days as a writer, I spent a lot of time in the Chelsea Arts Club, 'the Farts' as we called it, where drinking was, of course, all anyone was doing. The first time I ever had lunch there, an old woman (at least she seemed old to me then, she was probably only about fifty) fell off her chair at the big table, speechlessly drunk, and was carried out by some of the other guests, feet first. It was a laugh – ha ha, look at us and our bohemian life – a great story. I adored it. I felt right at home there. If you got drunk at lunchtime, nobody cared because they were all drunk, too. It was almost mandatory to have too much to drink. There was something about the dappled greenish light in the dining room even in the day that somehow suggested we were all in a parallel dimension where ordinary rules didn't count.

We were the elect, the bohemian elect. Ordinary mortals need not apply. That this was a fatally flawed view was not apparent to me in any way. I was firmly in the grip of the great romance of alcohol as an adjunct to the creative process. Nothing, as I discovered the hard way, could be further from the truth. And yet it was so obvious. The creative life is hard and lonely work: you spend a lot of time alone, a lot of time with yourself, something I found very difficult as I didn't like being with myself – one of the reasons I drank was to shut myself down. Being a writer requires discipline and resilience. I had discipline but very little resilience, and what little I did have was very soon undermined by alcohol. I began to drink in my teens to soothe the appalling fear I felt as my world fell apart, but I had always wanted to be a writer, that desire had been there as long as I could remember, since I was a child. Reading and writing were bedfellows in my mind – you had to practise one in order to succeed at the other – and very soon, booze snuck into the equation. It seemed a natural part of the order of things, the amniotic fluid that fosters the growth of the writer.

I had used books very successfully to change the way I felt as soon as I could read. I didn't know then that I was using books to escape from reality, but I was. Nobody would use the word addict in relation to a small child, but that's what I was. I read all the time. My mother used to say to me of some view or town we had driven through, 'You won't have noticed, you were buried in your book.' And I vividly recollect that when she said that I felt a surge of power, what I would now call a hit. Books were a legal high, a licensed hit. Books were, by definition, good, so nobody could gainsay me.

I can still recall clearly the thrill when I realised I could read, my five-year-old finger going faster and faster under the sentence and the congratulations it elicited from my mother. The crucial link between reading and drinking was created in me, I suspect, because I used both to get a hit right from the beginning. With books I could escape from my situation into other worlds – this is so obvious as to be a cliché – but drink, when I began to really go for it, had the same effect, and it was quicker. I think the fact that I used reading for the purposes of escape and self-soothing meant that the pathways were already there, the road built, signposted and lit. My first hit was from reading and the way I was flooded with good feelings when I did it was then echoed by the faster hit of booze. At that point the road in my brain became an autobahn without a speed limit.

At nineteen, in 1974, I'd hooked up with a crowd of friends who were a decade older than me and had been at Cambridge together. As a group, they were clever and interesting but also witty and fun. They all drank hugely, and I was quickly sucked into their slipstream. Nobody noticed or commented about how much I drank. It was a given. Everyone who was anyone drank, and drank a lot. We met in various favourite London pubs, and of course the Farts. There was much talk of writers: we were all reading Anthony Powell's *A Dance to the Music of Time*, volume by volume, and I was being introduced by my then-boyfriend, a poet, and a member of this group, not only to new books – poets and historians and novelists I'd never heard of – the world of books as an intellectual pursuit – but also, at the same time, to the world of the Renaissance and the Baroque. He was passionate about painting as well as literature and had already lived in Rome off and on by the time I met him.

Here was another world I could escape into. I'll never forget the way Rome in all her glory broke over my head like a great wave: the churches, the monumental buildings, the sculpture, the insane grandeur of it, the history, the paintings, the way it telescoped time, overwhelming me with its majesty and truth. Why had nobody told me about it? I wondered. I was in love with a man who knew this place, who knew where to go for the best of everything on the cheap. We drank wine from the barrel in dark little bars with sawdust on the floor and in restaurants. Local wine, nothing fancy, but when you step out into the Campo dei Fiori after supper, slightly drunk, and walk to Piazza Navona under the stars, drink seems like a pathway to the gods. I was young and in love and drink seemed as necessary and as decorative a component as the putti trailing scented garlands above the heads of the figures in the paintings.

In this way, alcohol subtly insinuated itself into the world of the mind I had created; it was a kind of essential colouration, a little phial of magic essence that drop by drop shaded and shaped your day, even if you were only thinking about it: there was sitting down at your desk and working and then there was what I call the 'vedana' of the idea of booze, that happy and joyful colouration bestowed upon the thought by my mind, fatally insistent, utterly enveloping as an idea.

Later, I will have a drink, I'd tell myself. Without even being entirely aware of it, I'd see in my mind's eye a glass of white wine, the condensation on its outside as soft and alluring as the fuzz on a peach. So beautiful, so true, so necessary. Of course it was necessary. It was non-negotiable that I deserved a drink. The idea would make me feel better, even if I didn't immediately pour that glass of wine. The power lies in the idea of it, or it did in my head, anyway. Later on, I would learn that this is one of the weird hallmarks of addiction: feeling soothed by the *idea* of a drink. It was almost as good as the drink itself, which proves why alcoholism is a disease of mind and body. The mental aspect of it all is so powerful. Sometimes I could go on like that until the evening, safe in the knowledge of the coming of the drink, as if the drink was the grail cup that would, by stilling my fears and my anxiety, make me whole again. Quite a lot to ask of a substance. I put such faith in drink. I asked such a lot of it and believed that as I asked, it would give.

All this thinking around the idea of what a drink would do for me was largely unconscious; these powerful thoughts swam like dark shapes in the great depths of my mind. I was barely aware of them but I liked their steadying presence, when I happened to notice it.

I published my first novel at the age of twenty-eight. My marriage to the father of my child was collapsing and in the picture on the dust jacket of that novel I look forlorn and rather lost. I was much more lost than I realised. The upheaval going on in my personal life and the fact that I had a small child played havoc with my writing, hardly surprisingly. My drinking was escalating as my emotional life collapsed around me.

My first novel, based on the published war diaries of a relation who had been killed in 1918, did OK for a literary debut novel and went into paperback. I was officially a 'writer', but the change I'd expected this new status to bring about inside me never really happened. I had a bad case of imposter syndrome, although I didn't know that's what it was called. I remember going to Waterstones in Kensington High Street on publication day in disguise, sort of, waiting for someone to recognise me. Needless to say, Waterstones didn't even have a copy of my book. Hello, publishing. I'd graduated into a world that didn't even know who I was. The feeling of anti-climax was searing. I'd done this huge thing – the thing I'd been wanting to do all my life – but I was still me. It was so disappointing. I'd given it my all – my entire sense of myself had depended on it – and now this sense of emptiness, the feeling of no matter how hard I tried or how good I was, it didn't make any difference.

There were reviews in newspapers and magazines, there was praise. There was the offer of book reviewing, too, but it wasn't enough. I still felt as if I was waiting for something else. After years in the rooms of Alcoholics Anonymous, I realise that this is very alcoholic behaviour: nothing is ever enough, I'm not enough, I'm not as good as everyone else. What AA calls feeling 'less than' is very common in alcoholics; it has roots in self-pity, too, which is corrosive. *Even when good things happen to me, they aren't good* was the subtext. People would tell me it was amazing to have published a novel, but I couldn't feel it. That part of me was numb but I had no idea why. I was baffled as to why I felt the way I did.

I set to and began to write a second novel, as instructed by my agent and editor, but it wouldn't go right. I couldn't get it to come alive; the prose was unrelentingly wooden, the characters ciphers. Second novel difficulties are common, I was to discover, but my situation didn't help. I was a single mother and an active alcoholic. I couldn't admit to myself that I was dependent on alcohol, it was too shaming. My ex-husband was the alcoholic, the bad guy, the man famous in the City for his liquid lunches, and it was easier to point the finger at him. And he was a man. Men were expected to drink. It was regarded by certain people, always men, as almost heroic.

My editor left the publishing house where she had bought my book and moved elsewhere. She then turned down my second novel, having loved the first, saying, as far as I can remember, that she found it 'disappointing', or words to that effect. This was a crushing blow to my wilting self-esteem, unsurprisingly. I can still recall the cold weirdness of those low feelings, rather like being abandoned at the bottom of the ocean in the dark, all alone. I was a failure, an utter failure, I told myself. More alcoholic behaviour. Catastrophising was second nature to me. For me, as I've already said, thoughts were facts. Powerful ones, too. If I told myself I was an utter failure, it immediately made it true. I had no idea how to manage my thoughts and feelings and the more I allowed myself to think that way the more I drank.

After my personal life settled down in my early thirties, I went on to publish five more novels in the next ten years, quite a good hit rate. I failed to see the connection between emotional stability and a good, solid work record, however. My fifth novel sold well, and the film rights were bought. All hail the conquering hero . . . not quite. Yet again, my relationship was breaking down.

By the time I published novel number six, I was with a new man who would become my third husband. My version of this relationship was of the romance of two writers together – he was a journalist who had also published non-fiction and was trying to be a novelist. We had a plan, which never came to anything, to write a novel together, which shows how insane the whole thing was. By this point, I was drinking in the morning. It was as if an unseen hand had smashed the emergency glass: I was in a perpetual state of almost unbearable anxiety.

My next book deal collapsed, and all the old fears gushed in. I was a useless waste of space. My husband turned away coldly. Shortly, I would be discarded. I'd married a male version of my dark, difficult mother, whose love was always conditional. I was no use to him as an unsuccessful, unpregnant, forty-something-year-old. It was all very transactional and desperate.

From a distance, I didn't look too bad, but close up, I was a wreck. If anyone was nice to me, I cried. I remember talking to my brother at a party in London and bursting into tears apropos of not very much. He was really shocked.

When I went to that AA meeting in Oxford in May 2009, I no longer knew who or what I was. All I wanted to do was to stop drinking, full stop. How that was to happen was a mystery. In the end, it wasn't a mystery at all, just a willingness to do a few simple things; no alchemy or shapeshifting required: start from where you are and do today without having a drink. After all that drama, this was the solution. Who knew? But it was a group thing: you couldn't do it alone – I'd never been able to – but now I was in a gang – that marvellous convocation of misfits that is AA – the gang I should have joined at the age of five after my drunken exploits as a bridesmaid. I could have been a founder member of Junior AA; sadly, I don't think such an organisation exists.

When Arabella followed me in nine months later, she was towards the end of her time in Oxford. She was a linguist – French was her thing – and the subject of her doctorate turned out to be linked very closely to the Great War, a subject I had researched so closely for my first book that I felt at the end of it all that I'd actually fought in that war. A certain symmetry was appearing, unbidden.

I accompanied her on a research trip she was making to Verdun: a mother-and-daughter outing with a difference, powerfully flavoured as it was by the emotions of the past and of the present, a sense of the tectonic plates of the family cleaving together instead of endlessly pulling apart. We went to the family grave on the Somme and wept, as we always did. An ordinary summer's day of great beauty. Someone died here: a grave was dug by some of his men, a priest fetched, prayers said, the words of the priest recorded for posterity: *'This morning I arranged the grave and put some flowers on it, encircled with a little crown, for indeed he has well merited his crown, only a more glorious one.'* Now it is the charged stillness around the grave that you notice. Nature has restored that blasted heath, but the scars remain: the grassed-over craters, the cemeteries full of that same distilled bosky grief that we had felt at the grave of our relation.

The area around Verdun, the fields and groves, are quilted to this day with high explosives: the landscape looks innocently verdant but it is in fact deadly. Together, in more ways than one, we were picking our way backwards through deadly territory, defusing the threat that the past continued to pose to the present: the unexamined things lying underground for years, centuries, but still live. Discussion, honesty, restraint, humility: all were necessary. I annoyed her, she annoyed me, the usual mother-and-daughter stuff, but we were both aware that this was a mission into the past that could liberate the present and set the future free.

This memoir is my first book since 2003, twenty-one years since my last, and it's a testament to AA and to the powers of being a sober alcoholic, which has allowed me to return to my calling as a writer, at long last. It's also a testament to AA that I could even begin to contemplate writing a book about such a subject with my daughter.

Epilogue

Into the Open

Arabella

'Both of you? Really? At the same time?'

It's August 2021 and I'm having a conversation with a friend about an article I want to write. I have written around the topic before, but always in a theoretical, intellectual way to protect myself. This time, I have decided to do away with the cleverness and the thinking and just write down what I think happened. It is, I am told, quite a story. A fellow journalist, whom I met at a magazine party, says she thinks she knows an editor who would be interested. We exchange emails. She loves the idea, she says. Can I write it in one day? If I can't, no problem, she'll find me a ghostwriter who will write it for me overnight. I can't have a ghostwriter, I object, because I am a writer myself (or at least I think I am) and the whole story is bound up in the business of writing. Fine, she replies, but just one more thing, can you get your mother to write it with you?

Will my mother write the article with me? I know without even having to ask that the answer is yes. My mother is a journalist herself, after all. She knows the score. She has also written extremely personal pieces in the past, one so inflammatory that her father didn't speak to her for twenty years afterwards. She stuck to novels after that. I call her in Greece, where she is on a six-week long holiday with her current boyfriend. She agrees straight away; 'Fuck what people think,' she adds before ringing off. But no sooner has she agreed than I am beset by doubts. *Whose story is it anyway? And who gets to tell it?* We have different accounts of what happened, we have different approaches to sobriety; all in all, I can't see how it would work. I call my mother back and she sounds irritated by my objections: 'Just start writing it, you might see a way through,' she says before hurriedly ending the call to attend an AA meeting over Zoom.

Writing the article turns out to be surprisingly easy for both of us. Clearly, it doesn't matter if our accounts and tone differ. 'That's *very* meta,' a writer friend points out, laughing, when I put the matter to him over coffee; 'that's memory itself, all very in vogue, doesn't matter at all if you're saying different things.' I file it on a Friday morning and wait for the editor to reply. Days pass. I think the editor has moved on to other things and prepare for the piece to be spiked; I remember the advice of a fellow journalist friend: 'Stories are like fish; they start to smell after three days.' At least I'll get paid, I reason, while scraping my daughter's pasta off a plate and into the bin.

Two days later, my phone erupts with emails, phone calls and text messages. Can my mother and I come to London and have our picture taken? Can we come the next day? I explain to the editor that my mother is still in Greece and the picture will have to be of me alone. 'Hmmm . . . ' she counters, 'but that's not quite the same thing, we really need the two of you together . . . ' I feel a growing sense of annoyance that I no longer own the story outright. I pitched it, won the commission and wrote it, after all. She only added a few hundred words at the end. But *the* story, according to the editor, now belongs to both of us. I call Mum again in Greece; 'I can't come back, I just can't. Find a photo of the both of us from a while back and give it to them instead.' I want to reply that there are very few photos of us taken together since I was a small child but decide against it. The editor, by now exasperated, tells me we will just have to make do. When I arrive at the studio in London to have the picture taken, I feel unusually nervous, as if I have boarded a train I now can't disembark. *Stop the train, I want to get off.*

'You're a writer, yeah? What's the story about? They never tell us in here . . . ' I look at my face in the mirror as the make-up artist is busy applying thick foundation to my face with a large brush. I think about what it means to 'put on a face' – any face – brave face, sad face, happy face, honest face, serious face. I think about the right face to put on to tell her about the story. Sad face, I decide; it's a sad story. 'It's about alcoholism,' I stammer while she brushes dark eyeshadow onto my lids, 'my mother and I are both sober alcoholics. I guess it's about what alcohol can do to families.' The make-up artist looks up and nods. 'My dad was an alcoholic, too.' I look back at my reflection in the mirror and decide I don't need to put on any face at all.

On the day that the article appears in the paper, I feel like a foreigner in my own life. People I know from school and university but have not seen for years text me to say they have read it, with broken-heart and strong-arm emojis as a sign-off. People I don't know on Twitter retweet it and send me messages. An old boyfriend calls me and leaves a long voicemail telling me that he always suspected that I had a problem. I want to call him back and tell him to fuck off, but I manage not to. When I call my mother, she seems wistful and distant. She tells me that she has managed to buy a copy in the small Greek town she is staying in.

Later, I am informed, through a friend, that certain members of my family find it distasteful and refuse to read it. A week later, when I meet this person, she tells me that I have embarrassed them all beyond measure. We end up having a loud argument in the café we are sitting in while people look on, amazed. I want to share about it in meetings, but I stop myself, wary of accusations of breaking anonymity at the level of press, one of AA's core traditions. Privately, I am exhausted.

***

That article was the spark that lit this book. But the writing of the book was filled with far more joy, humour and, in the end, healing. Over a period of almost two years, my mother and I have sat down and discussed our family and our innermost selves. As members of AA, we're used to discussing our feelings in a group. As writers, it has been far thornier to see these feelings on the page. Sometimes, when we have swapped chapters, we have vehemently disagreed over the portrayal of each other and angry ripostes over email have followed. At other times, being each other's readers has been a uniquely exhilarating experience, one I can only clumsily compare to a cross between reading someone's diary and participating in family therapy. Staying true to the singular mixture of these impressions has been the challenge – and the promise – of what we set out to do.

Frequently, other people have intervened to offer warnings. In these uncomfortable moments, we have been reminded that we are not simply writing our story but a broader, family history, too. *You better not write about her*, or, *He'll never talk to you again if you mention him,* or, worse still, *Do you want your daughters to read this?* Who can make the emotional calculations required of the memoirist? I have never known how to answer these warnings. To agree to them always seemed to be enabling the very process of omertà that has caused alcoholism to take root so strongly in our family in the first place. But to ignore them outright hasn't felt right either. Like any warning, they have woven themselves tacitly into the text: an incident deleted here, a reported conversation edited out there. These cautions have made me think long and hard about the nature of silence and the ways in which families protect themselves. They have also made me think deeply about women and the warnings women issue to themselves, a peculiar form of self-censorship that keeps them silent, glued into patterns of addiction for generations.

I, too, am guilty of this silence. When asked what the book I have been writing is about, I have frequently prevaricated and turned away from the question. Too often, I have said that the book is about motherhood and daughterhood. It is, in part, but it is chiefly a book about how motherhood and daughterhood are warped by generational addiction and there is no getting away from this fact. My partial reluctance to say this openly is wound up in all sorts of codes of female propriety that have been drilled into me all my life. Understanding why these codes are as powerful as they are, is, I believe, hugely important.

So, for now, into the open. And yes, you're right. Both of us, at the same time.

Julia

Into the Open

A couple of years ago, Arabella and I were commissioned to write an article in the *Daily Mail* about what it was like to be a mother and daughter who had both got sober in AA within nine months of one another in 2009/10. In the article we talked about the code of omertà that had kept alcoholism a secret in our family with devastating consequences for both of us.

When the piece was published, friends contacted me to tell me they had no idea it was so bad, that they should have done more to help. People told me how brave I was. How strong my will must be not to drink. Their comments, kindly meant, only served to emphasise the lack of understanding of the illness.

The whole subject of alcoholism in our society remains peculiarly misunderstood, even now, partly because drink is legal and partly because it is a very complex illness. It affects the sufferer's mind in ways that other illnesses do not, not least because it tells the sufferer that they don't *have* an illness.

The editor thinks our story should be a book. We set about writing our separate accounts; it's the first time I've ever written anything in tandem with anyone else, let alone my daughter, and I quickly realise, somewhat to my chagrin, that she's the boss. I've written six novels and countless articles and reviews, but Arabella has a PhD from an Ivy League university and a mind as highly trained and focused as an expensive thoroughbred racehorse. My method is much more meandering, along the lines of 'how do I know what I think until I see what I say?' the only way I've ever been able to write anything, in fact. But she grows impatient with me: 'You're telling your creation story again,' she cries, and I realise to my irritation that she's right.

The to and fro of the book between us has been funny, sad, joyful, annoying and sometimes enraging. Whole chapters have been returned to me saying they need rewriting. *How bloody dare you?* I think. She treats me – as all grown daughters do their mothers – as a bit of a twit, a bit, 'Oh, Mum, for God's sake,' but the whole process has been, in a stop-start way, a kind of healing, a way of understanding and forgiving one another.

But a book about a family illness necessitates the appearance of other members of the family. In our family, traditionally, you appear only three times in the press: when you are born, when you get married and when you die. But that mindset – that family code of omertà – kept the illness hidden, and while I sympathise to a certain extent, our story is too important not to tell. I have burnt my fingers in the past writing about my family, so why would I do it again? Because this is an awful illness that has lurked in the shadows for too long, empowered by silence and shame, and because we are women who suffer from it. Not for women the bravura of a Hemingway or a Fitzgerald, all those Faulkners and Dylan Thomases; we're just lushes, sad sacks who die in public lavatories.

I never wanted to be labelled an alcoholic. I had, like so many alkies, an aversion to the word and its connotations. I couldn't, I just *couldn't* be that, could I? I had seen it in my childhood with my stepmother. Not that, *please* not that.

When people ask me what our new book is about, I invariably hesitate before I tell them. Why? Because to admit in public to being an alcoholic is still a bold move. It shouldn't be but it is. I always want to add, 'I'm really an all-right person, I promise you.' Outing yourself as an alcoholic places you firmly in the witness box as the suspect.

But why should I feel so defensive, so exposed? Alcoholism is a savage mental illness containing a very strong genetic component; it's not my fault I'm an alcoholic, I know that now, but for decades I felt it was a moral failing. There was something wrong with me. I was rotten at my core, defective, just plain bad. This feeling of shame lingers, even after years as a sober alcoholic. But why? Is it the stigma still attached to a greater or lesser degree to all mental illness, or is it, as I suspect, something to do with alcoholism in particular, very possibly female alcoholism specifically?

AA was founded by one desperate, recently sober alcoholic talking frankly to another desperate, recently sober alcoholic. But it was 1935 in Akron, Ohio; Prohibition had ended only two years before, having been in force since 1920; one of these two people was a businessman and one was a doctor, both were men. Women's alcoholism was a bit like Queen Victoria's attitude to lesbianism: it simply didn't exist.

This miraculous meeting – one drunk talking to another – was how AA began, but because of the moral climate in mid-1930s America, everyone who sought help in AA was 'anonymous', known only by their first name. Why was this necessary? It's difficult to understand the climate of another age, but in the highly religious, judgemental society of 1930s America, coloured by the long years of Prohibition, being an alcoholic was to be a social outcast. In my view, the sacred stricture of anonymity has condemned alcoholism to remain in the shadows; to not be considered a 'proper' illness, keeping it shrouded in silence and shame, allowing people who don't understand its complexities to say ignorant things like, *It's merely a question of willpower*. No one says that about schizophrenia or any other mental illness, to my knowledge.

The toxic shame I felt around my own alcoholism kept me silent for many years. I knew but I didn't know. My denial kept me imprisoned. The illness had sunk so deep into my being that I didn't have a clue how I could escape. I didn't actually think it was possible until I got so desperate I would try anything.

Talking about it is key, as the founders discovered. All the secrets and all the years of corroding shame vanish like wraiths when exposed to the light and laughter in an AA meeting. You share some terrible dark secret and people shrug and laugh. I was set free by all this, and I hope that this account will set others free, too.

Acknowledgements

This book is indebted to many people, some of whom shall remain anonymous. We wish to thank our agent Matilda Forbes-Watson for her tireless campaigning for the book and for us. To Marleigh Price, our editor at HarperCollins, we thank you for your careful and sensitive reading of our story and the skill and grace with which you edited it.

I, Arabella, am extremely grateful to the Society of Authors for their work-in-progress grant which afforded me the childcare to write during the school holidays. I am also very thankful to Hilary and Piers Henriques at the National Association for Children of Alcoholics for their support and encouragement of this idea from the very beginning and their insistence upon the importance of its message. To my husband Martin, I thank you, with great love, for your unwavering support for my writing, and to my own daughters, A & C, I lovingly thank you both for giving me so much to write about.

I, Julia, would like to give grateful thanks to the Royal Literary Fund for their very generous help.

Finally, we acknowledge each other, mother and daughter, with enormous pride.